The Harmonious Musick of John Jenkins

Volume One
The Fantasias for Viols

The Harmonious Musick of John Jenkins

Volume One
The Fantasias for Viols

Andrew Ashbee

TOCCATA PRESS

First published in 1992 by Toccata Press.

Music examples drawn by the author.

To my wife Brenda

British Library Cataloguing in Publication Data

Ashbee, Andrew, *1938–*
The harmonious musick of John Jenkins.
Vol.1: The fantasias for viols.
I. Title
780.92

ISBN 0-907–689–34–5
ISBN 0-907–689–35–3 (pbk)

Typeset in 11/12½ pt Baskerville
by York House Typographic Ltd, London.

Printed and bound by Short Run Press Ltd, Exeter.

Contents

List of Illustrations

Preface

When George Vertue visited the Music School at Oxford in March 1732/3 to catalogue the pictures there, he was moved to query 'if these following professors of Music are in Print' – the list includes John Jenkins. It is both sad and curious that no portrait is known of one whom the celebrated seventeenth-century composer Christopher Simpson described as 'the ever Famous and most Excellent Composer, in all sorts of Modern Musick'. Yet in one respect scholars are singularly lucky: as a youth Roger North was taught by the aged Jenkins and North's reminiscences, revised and refined over many years, give a unique character study of the composer. From them a biography can be constructed which, though woefully inadequate at times, gives the bare bones of his long and varied life. Nevertheless, with few exceptions, links cannot be made between life and works and any proposed chronology of the latter remains tentative. Yet Jenkins was the most important and successful mainstream composer of instrumental music in England in the fifty years between the death of Gibbons and the emergence of Purcell; a full study of his work is long overdue.

Scholars of Jenkins have always faced something of a dilemma. On the one hand, they are presented with more than a thousand compositions, hundreds of which are of very high quality and acknowledged as among the best of their kind. To discuss this prodigious output in a single volume could only result in many important works, like the viol fantasias and the fantasia-suites, receiving superficial and inadequate attention. On the other hand, a constant stream of new information and manuscripts has added to the picture of the man and his music; the temptation has always been to delay discussion in the hope that new light might soon be shed on particular problems. So, after thirty years' work, Helen Sleeper, the first Jenkins scholar, left no major study of the composer, although she published an important collection of his work. Later scholars, such as Robert Warner, Carolyn Coxon and myself, have tended to focus on particular aspects of Jenkins' work. In limiting discussion to Jenkins' fantasias for viols, this book continues the latter trend. There are two reasons. One is the aim to treat this important series of pieces in some depth – which their quality demands; the other is that for a spare-time scholar the project assumes manageable size. A second volume, to deal with the fantasia-suites and with the remaining works, is in preparation.

There are very many fine works by Jenkins awaiting publication, but fortunately the bulk of the music with which this study is concerned has been printed, thanks to the Viola da Gamba Society of Great Britain – and to the particular energies of Marco Pallis and Richard Nicholson – who initiated a project to publish the complete four-, five- and six-part fantasias by Jenkins. A generous grant from the Gulbenkian Foundation supported publication of scores and parts of all three series by Faber Music. In addition, scores of the six-part music, edited by Donald Peart, form *Musica Britannica*, Vol. XXXIX. Currently the two three-part series have fared less well, although some of the fantasias for treble, two basses and organ appear among the Supplementary Publications of the Viola da Gamba Society and a number of those for two trebles and bass appear in Helen Sleeper's *Wellesley Edition No. 1* (1950) and in Bärenreiter's *Hortus Musicus* series. Both series are being edited by myself for publication in *Musica Britannica*. Details of all these editions are listed on pp. 338–9.

In spite of Ernst Hermann Meyer's invaluable pioneering studies, much work remains to be done in tracing the origins and trends of English seventeenth-century consort music. The Jacobean era in particular is of crucial importance here and the contributions of composers like Ferrabosco II, Lupo, Ward and Coprario require separate appraisal, as does the interaction of vocal and instrumental music. Chapter Two here attempts to do no more than give the broad outlines from which such studies might develop, but it is vital in attempting to set Jenkins' viol consorts in some sort of context. Since so little of the music can be properly linked to biographical information, its dating and chronology lean very heavily on what is known of the manuscripts and their history. I hope that Chapter Three – 'Music and Manuscripts in Seventeenth-Century Oxford' – is a relatively painless way of tackling the bulk of a subject which some find tedious, but which contributes substantially to knowledge of Jenkins' work. In the four-, five- and six-part chapters, bar-numbers refer to the Faber edition. (Cross-references with bar-numbers from *Musica Britannica*, Vol. XXXIX, are given in Appendix II on pp. 323.) In the fantasias for two trebles and bass, bar-numbers are for standard $^{4}_{4}$ bars, or $^{6}_{4}$ bars in the triple-time sections. No standard form has been adopted for the other three-part series, but it should be evident from the musical examples which is used.

In Jenkins' time the calendar year changed on 25 March. For dates between 1 January and 24 March, inclusive the convention of showing both years is used. Thus '8 February 1593' would today be expressed as 8 February 1593/4.

Acknowledgements

Study of Jenkins and his work has been a part of my life for some thirty years. In that time I have had cause to be grateful to hundreds of people for much help and many kindnesses. A few of them are mentioned in footnotes, but inevitably a larger number go unrecorded. Early on it was my good fortune to come under the watchful eye of two scholars whose work it has been a challenge to emulate in some small measure: Professor R. Thurston Dart was a most stimulating and fastidious adviser for my dissertation and always gave very generously of his time in setting me on the right path; his sharp mind was a revelation. Professor Robert Warner warmly welcomed a young researcher treading in his own footsteps. The Atlantic divide notwithstanding, friendship with Bob and Maretta Warner has blossomed as the years have passed. Opportunities for globe-trotting have been very few, but information and microfilm have been readily forthcoming from libraries throughout the world – I am most grateful to them all. My special thanks must go to the staff at the three centres who hold the largest collections of Jenkins' music, especially Pamela Willetts, formerly at the British Library, the late Margaret Crum at the Bodleian Library, and John Wing at Christ Church, Oxford. Warmest thanks, too, to my many friends in the Viola da Gamba Society, who in conversation, correspondence and musical performance have shared delight in Jenkins' music for twenty years. Commander Gordon Dodd, custodian of the Society's *Thematic Index of Music for Viols*, has been of immense help in the major task of cataloguing and indexing Jenkins' music.

Above all, I must single out Richard Nicholson, the late Marco Pallis and David Pinto, whose superior knowledge of the whole English consort repertory has been of enormous help while I have been writing this book. They have read most of it and I am immensely grateful to them for the criticisms and comments which have improved and enlightened many dark corners. I hope they will feel that their efforts have not been in vain, though I bear responsibility for what is set down. From a lifetime's devotion to the cause of viols and their music, Richard and Marco have been a constant inspiration, not only in their championship of Jenkins' music with the English Consort of Viols, but also in our happy collaboration in producing the Faber edition and in many equally happy hours of shared discussion and reminiscence.

chapter one
A Biographical Introduction

Much of the life of John Jenkins is clouded in obscurity, and any attempt to piece together the fragmented information into a convincing framework must rely heavily on conjecture. According to the Oxford chronicler Anthony Wood (1632–95), Jenkins was born in Maidstone, Kent. Wood gives as his sources a Mr Fisher and Dr John Wilson, Heather Professor of Music at Oxford between 1656 and 1661, who

> used to say that, for the honour of his country [Kent] Alphonso Farabosco born of Italian parents at Greenwich, and John Jenkyns at Maidstone were admired not only in England but beyond the sea for their excellent compositions.[1]

Wilson was personally known to Wood through the weekly music meetings which both frequented in Oxford in the 1650s and had met Jenkins in London during the rehearsals and performances of the extravagant masque *The Triumph of Peace* in 1633–4 and again in the early 1660s at the Restoration court.[2] The year of Jenkins'

[1] Wood's MSS. Mus. Ashmole 8568.106. W and H., quoted in Philip Bliss (ed.), *Athenae Oxoniensis*, 5 vols., 3rd edn., London 1813–20, I, p. xxvi. *The Life and Times of Anthony à Wood* [...], ed. Andrew Clark, Oxford Historical Society, Oxford, 1891–1900, I, p. 233, has:

> Musicians borne in Kent: Alphonso at Greenwich: J. Jenkins at Maidston: J. Wilson, D:Mus., at Feversham.

Clark adds: '"Maidston" is substituted for "Sandwich"; and a note added: "Mr. Fisher told me that Jenkins was born at Maidston"'.

[2] *Cf.* p. 33 and pp. 76–80.

birth, 1592, is deduced from the closing lines of his epitaph, carved on the memorial slab above his grave in the chancel of Kimberley Church, Norfolk:

> Aged eighty six October twenty sev'n
> In Anno sev'nty eight he went to Heaven.

The parish church of All Saints was the only Maidstone church in general use at the end of the sixteenth century. The registers are generally well kept, but there is an unfortunate gap in the register of christenings from March 1588 to 3 November 1593, apparently depriving posterity of any entry for Jenkins.[3] Luckily, surviving Corporation and Probate records go some way towards alleviating this deficiency. Maidstone had an estimated population of about 2000 people at this time,[4] with perhaps more than one family called Jenkins, although the precise relationships are difficult to establish. The couple who seem to have been the composer's parents were Henry Jenkins, a carpenter, who married Ann Jordaine in All Saints Church on 28 June 1591.[5] They apparently set up home in East Lane (now called King Street), the principal road extending from the town centre out towards Ashford. Their large and comfortably furnished house of eight rooms (including the 'Shoppe') was probably rented since no mention of the property is made in the will of either Henry or Ann. On 9 May 1592, Henry was made a Freeman of the town:[6]

[3] Contemporary (Bishop's) transcripts of the register preserved at the Chapter Library, Canterbury Cathedral, are also incomplete for this period. *Cf.* Andrew Ashbee, 'Genealogy and John Jenkins', *Music & Letters*, 46, July 1965, pp. 225–30.

[4] C. W. Chalklin, *Seventeenth Century Kent: A Social and Economic History*, Longmans, London, 1965, p. 31.

[5] *Cf.* Rev. J. Cave-Browne, *The Marriage Registers of the Parish Church of All Saints, Maidstone*, London, 1901.

[6] At the time of writing the Maidstone Corporation Archives are awaiting re-cataloguing at the Kent Archives Office, having been transferred from Maidstone Museum (where I saw them). Former

> The nineth daie of Maye in the four and thirteth yeare of the Raigne of or most gra[cious] sovraigne lady Elizabeth [...] Md. that the daie and yeare above written Henry Jenkyns Carpenter was by gen[er]all consent admitted o[ne] of the Corporacon and body politique of Maidestan aforesaid from thenceforth to enjoy the lib[er]ties, Frannchises and fredomes theof as other freemen of the same do & he was then sworne & his contribucon set downe to [amount not entered].

The fee for freedom by purchase was one pound, but it seems Maidstone Corporation allowed this sum to be paid in instalments. The Chamberlains' Accounts show that Henry paid only ten shillings at the time of his admission:

> [1591/2] The payts of ye ffredomes [...] Received of henrey Jynkyns [...] xs

and then list him each year among the 'detters to the towne' until the remainder was eventually paid in 1608–9:[7]

> Receipts of ffredomes viz t [...] Of Henry Jenkyn in ffree paymt [...] xs

Curiously, Henry's name is not included in the official lists of Freemen.

Four children were born of the marriage: Henry, John, William and Mary – but the baptisms of only two of these occur in the register:

> [8 February 1593/4] Mary dau. of henrie Ginken
> [4 May 1595] Henry s. of Henry ginken

Yet Ann's will specifically states that her eldest son was Henry, implying that John and William were born after 1595. Without this statement one would assume that John, at least, was born before Mary and his baptism duly entered in that part of the register now lost. Is the

---

reference: Maidstone Corporation Archives: IV.1.116v. Burgmote Book AA.

[7] *Ibid.*: Chamberlains' Accounts for 1591/2 and 1608/9.

memorial at Kimberley wrong? If so, why is there no entry for John in the register? The mystery may never be solved, although it is worth noting that a gap of nearly two years exists between Ann's verbal will and her death. Perhaps Thomas Moore and John Howtinge knew nothing of the youthful John Jenkins, who almost certainly had left the town years before.

Henry Jenkins senior made his nuncupative (or verbal) will on 20 December 1617,[8] and must have died soon after, for the burial of 'Henry Ginckings carpenter' was recorded in the All Saints register on 22 December.

> Memorand. That the Twentith day of December Anno dni 1617 And in the yeare of the reigne of our most gracious soveigne Lord James by the grace of god of England France & Ireland kinge defender of the fayth & the Fyftenth & of Scotland the One & Fyftieth Henrie Jenkins of Maydestone in the County of Kent Carpenter. Did make A Nuncupative will in forme followinge First hee gave to his son Henry A Trebble Viall to his son John A Bandore & to his son William A Trebble Viall & to his daughter Mary hee gave nothing then because hee had given her certeyne goodes & mooveables at her marriage before that tyme And the residue of all his goodes mooveables & houshold stuffe Plate & readie money hee gave unto Anne his wife & made her sole Execatrix of his testament & last will. Hee beinge then sicke in body butt of good & perfect memorie. In the prsence of
>
> Wa: Fisher
> Thomas Reve

It is a remarkable coincidence that the Walter Fisher who here witnesses Henry's will proves to be the father of the 'Mr. Fisher' who told Anthony Wood that Jenkins was born in Maidstone. 'Mr. Fisher' can safely be identified as Alexander Fisher, senior fellow of Merton College,

[8] Kent Archives Office: Canterbury Consistory Court Wills, vol. 44. f. 260. A nuncupative will was made verbally before witnesses, who later testified to the authorities what had been declared.

Oxford, at whose death, on 23 October 1671, the chronicler noted that he was 'a fatherly acquaintance of A. W.'. Elsewhere he wrote:

> He [Alexander] was born at Maidstone in Kent, where his father Walter Fisher, who was mayor of Maidstone, was a trader and sold drapery and mercery wares [...].[9]

Alexander was three years younger than John Jenkins and it is just possible that the two were boyhood friends. The Fisher family may even have been the Jenkins' landlords since they certainly owned a house and garden in East Lane; the tenants have not been identified.[10]

The prominence given to musical instruments in Henry's will is remarkable: they seem to have been bequeathed as keepsakes for a remembrance of the deceased in place of the more customary ring, suggesting that the family held music-making in affection and esteem. The inventory of Henry's estate, taken on 11 March 1617/18, shows that there were no less than nine instruments in the house:

> In the Hall: [...] Item. Seven Vialls and Violyns, One Bandora and Cytherne iii li

– an extraordinary collection to be found in the household of an ordinary craftsman, ostensibly not a professional musician. Quite possibly some, if not all, of these instruments were made by Henry himself. It is unlikely that a provincial town the size of Maidstone could have supported a full-time instrument maker, but this activity might well have formed one aspect of his trade alongside

[9] *The Life and Times of Anthony Wood*, II, pp. 233–4.

[10] The position of the house is shown on a reconstructed map of 'Maidstone in 1650', Allen Grove and Robert Spain, Maidstone, 1975, and three early twentieth-century photographs showing the front of it are in H. R. Pratt Boorman, *Pictures of Maidstone*, Kent Messenger, Maidstone, 1965, pp. 84–5. The house was demolished some years ago.

more traditional work.[11] Evidently Henry was a good carpenter: his estate was valued at £50. 10s., an amount well above average for such a craftsman.[12] His house was well-furnished for the time and included a considerable amount of the better quality 'joined' furniture – perhaps more of his handiwork – and he also owned small but treasured collections of glass, pewter and brass.[13] Nevertheless, one suspects that there was little ready money to hand: two years later 'Widow Jenkins', along with other less wealthy residents of East Lane, spent four days helping to repair the road; richer residents paid others to do the work for them.[14]

Ann Jenkins made her nuncupative will in July 1621, though she lived on for nearly two more years. She was buried at All Saints on 22 June 1623. Her will disposes of two more of the instruments:

> The last will & testament nuncupative of Ann Jenkins Widow late of the Towne of Maydstone in the County of Kent and dioces of Canterbury deceased; By her uttered and declared in the moneth of July Anno dni 1621 shee beinge then sick and weake in body but of good and per-

[11] Another musician, Peter Maylim, also lived in East Lane at this time: *cf.* Richard Marlow, 'Giles & Richard Farnaby: Keyboard Music', *Musica Britannica*, Vol. XXIV, Stainer & Bell, London, 1965, p. xix, for comments that the making of at least some keyboard instruments came within the scope of the London Joiners' Company.

[12] *Cf.* Chalklin, *op. cit.*, p. 261, who includes carpenters among 'the largest and least wealthy group in the town, living near or a little above subsistence level.'

[13] The complete inventory (Kent Archives Office: Inventories, PRC 28/9, f. 294) is transcribed on pp. 317–9. *Cf.* Elizabeth Melling (ed.), *Some Kentish Houses*, Kent County Council, Maidstone, 1965, for a comparative study of Kentish houses and their contents.

[14] Kent Archives Office, Maidstone Corporation Archives: 'An Accompt for the repairinge of the high waies Anno Do 1619: made by Tho: Henman & Tho: Highwood Surveiors'. Charges levied range between 2s. and 6s. Marks such as the '0000:/' against 'Widow Jenkins' appear to indicate time spent helping with the repairs and in these cases no charge was made – or at most a token of a few pence only.

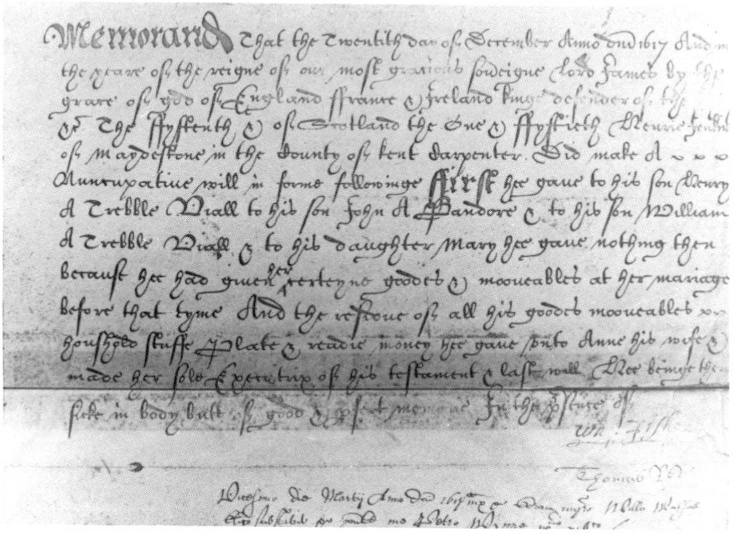

Memorand That the twentith day of December Anno dni 1617 And in the yeare of the reigne of our most gracious soveigne lord James by the grace of god of England ffrance & Ireland king defender of the &c The ffyfteenth & of Scotland the one & ffyftieth Henrie Jenkins of Maydestone in the County of kent Carpenter did make a Nuncupative will in forme followinge ffirst hee gave to his son Henry A Trebble Viall to his son John A Pandore & to his son William A Trebble Viall & to his daughter Mary hee gave nothing then because hee had given certeyne goods & moueables at her mariage before that tyme And the residue of all his goods moueables household stuffe plate & readie money hee gave unto Anne his wife & made her sole Executrix of his testament & last will Hee beinge then sicke in body but of good & perfect memorie In the presence of

The will of Henry Jenkins, 20 December 1617
(courtesy of Kent Archives Office)

fect memory with an intent and purpose to make her will and to dispose of her estate in theise words followinge or the like in effect vizt. First she gave unto Henery her eldest sonne one trebble Violin and ten shillings in mony – Item to her sonne John five shillings in mony – Item to her sonne William twenty shillings of lawful English mony and one treble Violin togeather with a flockbed. The residue of all and singuler her goods, Cattels, Chattels and debts Whatsoever she gave absolutely unto Thomas Viny hir sonne in lawe conditionally that he should pay hir debts and legacyes. And lastly she made, and constituted the said Thomas Viny full and Wholl Executor of hir said last will and testament. In the prsence and heeringe of Thomas Moore and John Howtinge.[15]

What of John Jenkins at this time? It is immediately apparent that he received less than the others. A likely

[15] Kent Archives Office: Canterbury Consistory Court Wills, vol. 45, f. 329. The associated inventory (PRC 28/11, f. 345) is transcribed on p. 319.

reason is that he had previously left the district and was by this time earning his livelihood elsewhere. He would have been aged about 25 at the time of Henry's death. The choice of a bandora for him in Henry's will seems particularly apt in the light of his later fame as a performer on the lyra viol and lute. Furthermore, the presence of both viols and violins in the household suggests that the latter instrument was well established in England, even outside the Court, early in the century and also indicates that its characteristics and tone qualities were known to Jenkins throughout his life, even though he seems not to have taken up the instrument himself until very late.[16] Nothing at present is known of the two brothers William and Henry. One wonders whether they were amateur musicians or whether they ever played in a professional capacity, either as waits or in private households. That Ann gave the residue of her estate to her son-in-law Thomas Viney might mean that they too were no longer at hand, though Viney, who was a gaoler at Maidstone Prison, lived close by in East Lane and the relatively impoverished state revealed by his inventory suggests that he would have been very grateful for the bequest.[17]

Precisely when Jenkins left Maidstone or what sort of education he received is not known. But it is clear, both from the written appreciations of him by his contemporaries and from those of his own poems that have come down to us that he was well taught. It seems unlikely that his family were in a position to have sent him to the town grammar school, founded in 1549; more probably he was fortunate enough to have been apprenticed to a professional musician in the household of a gentleman. Such apprentices, though perhaps few in number, were among

[16] *Cf.* p. 82.

[17] He, unfortunately, died only a month after Ann and was buried on 30 July 1623. Letters of Administration were granted to his widow Mary (Kent Archives Office: PRC 22/16, f. 23) and she also took charge of Ann's estate (PRC 22/16, ff. 23v and 20). Thomas Viney's inventory is PRC 28/11, f. 658.

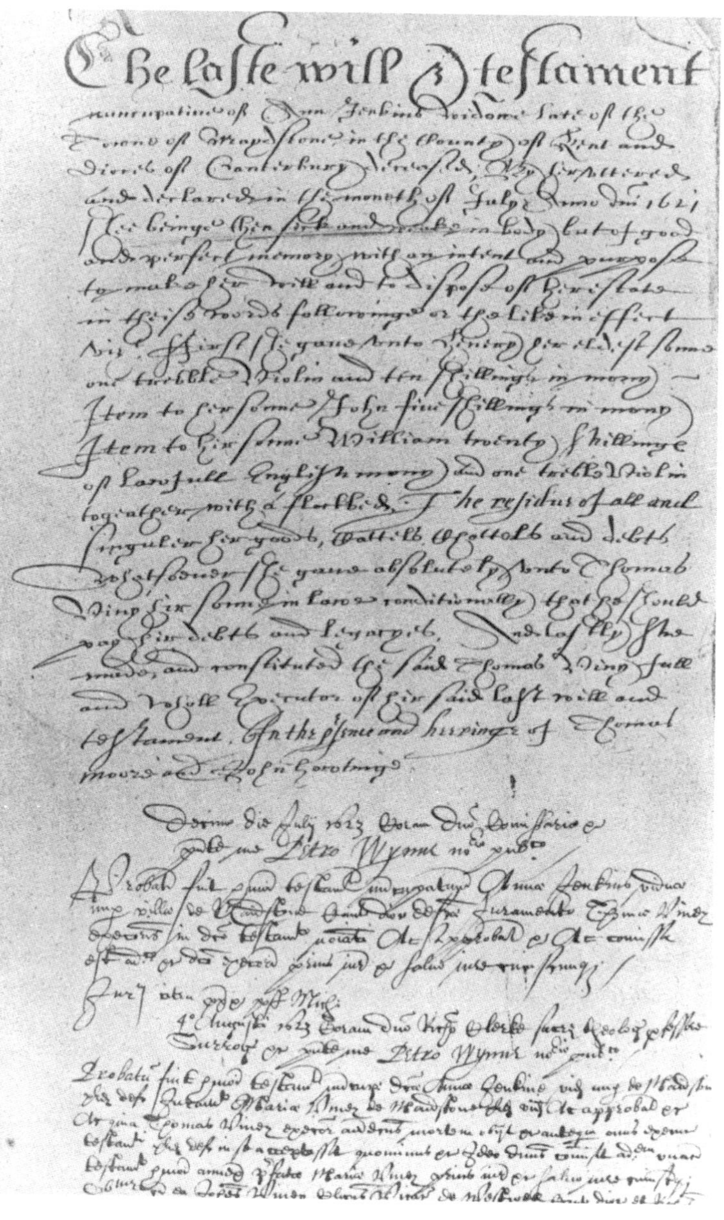

The laste will & testament nuncupative of Ann Jenkins widowe late of the Towne of Maydstone in the County of Kent and dioces of Canterbury deceased, by her uttered and declared in the month of July Anno dni 1621 She beinge then sicke and weake in body but of good and perfect memory with an intent and purpose to make her will and to dispose of her estate in theis words followinge or the like in effect viz. ffirst she gave unto Henry her eldest sonne one trebble violin and ten shillinge in money Item to her sonne John five shillinge in money Item to her sonne William twenty shillinge of lawfull English money and one trebble violin togeather with a flask [illegible]. The residue of all and singuler her goods, cattells chattells and debts whatsoever she gave absolutely unto Thomas Winn her sonne in lawe conditionally that he should pay her debts and legacyes, And lastly she made and constituted the said Thomas Winn full and whole executor of her said last will and testament. In the presence and hearinge of Thomas Moore and John Harding

The will of Ann Jenkins, July 1621 (courtesy of Kent Archives Office)

the luckiest of their kind.[18] The aura of their surroundings and its accompanying security were undoubtedly prized, but, more important, it is likely that the training they received was better than most. On occasion they may have served as substitutes for adult professional musicians. Perhaps a fortunate few even benefitted from personal friendship with aristocratic children (notwithstanding their difference in station) and may even have had some instruction from the same tutor. Something of such a friendship might be read into a remark made by Lady Anne Clifford, who in 1603, aged thirteen, wrote in her diary:

> I used to wear my hair coloured velvet every day and learned to sing and play on the bass viol of Jack Jenkins, my aunt's boy.[19]

If the reference is to the composer he would then be eleven years old and resident at Northall, Hertfordshire, at the country house of Anne Russell, Lady Warwick, the widow of Sir Ambrose Dudley, or at her house 'in or neere Broadstreet' in London. If Jenkins had shown early promise as a boy musician – and it would seem that his home environment gave this talent every encouragement – there were in Maidstone a number of people associated with London and the Court who could have helped find him a suitable position. Most prominent of these was Sir John Astley (1572–1640), Master of the Revels to James I.

In her will, dated 11 October 1603,[20] the Countess bequeathed to her brother Lord William Russell of Thornehaugh a lease of the parsonage of Hitchen with the following proviso:

[18] *Cf.* Walter L. Woodfill, *Musicians in English Society from Elizabeth to Charles I*, Princeton University Press, Princeton, 1953, pp. 68 *et seq.*

[19] Victoria Sackville-West, *The Diary of Lady Anne Clifford*, William Heinemann, London, 1924, p. 16.

[20] Public Record Office, London: PROB 11/103, f. 13.

> I will that my severall servaunts hereafter following (during soe manie yeres of my lease and terme of the parsonage of Hitchen in the Countie of Hertforde as they shall severally live) shall seaverallie have and enjoy the seaverall rents, chargs under mencioned and to them seaverallie limitted, payable at the feaste of saint michaell th'archangell, and thannunciation of the Virgin Marie by even porcons, to be yssuing out of the saide Parsonage. That is to saie:
>
> | | |
> |---|---|
> | William Dennys | thirty poundes |
> | Richard Danford | one hundred marks |
> | George Hackwell | twentie poundes |
> | Symon Chamber | twentie marks |
> | John Jenkins | tenn poundes |
> | John Morgan | twentie nobles |

He in turn, in his will dated 16 October 1612,[21] passed the lease to his son Sir Francis Russell asking

> that he shall trulye paye all payments, Annuyties and somes of money heretofore appointed to be paid forth of the same to any by the last will and Testament of the late Right honorable my lovinge Sister the Countess of Warwicke deceased.

On 1 November 1612 this will was witnessed by Thomas Derham, whom Anthony Wood records as being an early patron of Jenkins. Again, this pairing of names may be coincidence. As a lawyer, Thomas Derham may have witnessed the will in a professional capacity rather than as a friend of Lord Russell, but the connection adds significance to what might otherwise seem too loose an identification. Nevertheless, even if it is accepted that Jenkins was the Countess of Warwick's 'boy', many questions remain unanswered. Who was his master? Where did he go after the Countess had died in 1604? Did he, perhaps, transfer to the household of her brother, or even to that of Thomas Derham? It can only be guessed. In that year he was still too young to have completed his apprentice-

[21] Public Record Office: PROB 11/122, f. 86.

ship, and so could hardly have obtained a musician's post immediately. When Lord Russell died on 9 August 1613, on the other hand, he would have been about 20 and ready to seek his fortune. The fact that Thomas Derham had inherited substantial estates in Norfolk a few months earlier may have led him to cast around for a music master for his new home, perhaps providing the very opening Jenkins required.

Such an interpretation is feasible. But an equally plausible route should not be overlooked whereby Jenkins met up with the Derham family in London, in which contact came rather through Maidstone's flourishing (and somewhat specialised) textile manufactures.[22] Together with Canterbury and Sandwich, the town absorbed a considerable number of Dutch and Walloon refugees in the 1560s, many of whom settled in East Lane. At the time of Jenkins' childhood the street could boast at least one silk-weaver, fustian weaver, mercer, threadtwister, lace weaver, clothier and tailor, to the virtual exclusion of the non-textile trades. Could it be that, when the decision was made that Jenkins should go to London, the established links with the London mercers were used to find him a position? Mercers were among the wealthiest of tradespeople; the Maidstone mercer Walter Fisher who witnessed Henry Jenkins' will was three times mayor of the town in 1601, 1609 and 1618. In London, Baldwin Derham of Milk Street, the father of Thomas mentioned above, was Master of the Mercers' Company in 1596.

The Derham family, though prosperous, belonged among the minor gentry of their day. It is unfortunate that very few personal papers of the family appear to have survived, for possibly they were Jenkins' principal patrons until about 1644, after which he seems to have settled for a time with the L'Estranges at Hunstanton in Norfolk. According to an impressive pedigree drawn up

[22] *Cf.* Valerie Morant, 'The Settlement of Protestant Refugees in Maidstone during the Sixteenth Century', *The Economic History Review*, 1951, pp. 210–4.

for Sir Thomas Derham in 1631,[23] the family could be traced back to the time of the Norman Conquest, though Walter Frye, the Norfolk historian, is rightly sceptical about the earlier part of this family tree. Nevertheless, there is no doubt that by the fifteenth century the family were settled in and around Crimplesham and West Dereham in the south-west corner of Norfolk.[24] One member, Francis was soon to achieve notoriety as the lover of Catherine Howard; Henry VIII had him beheaded in 1541. With the Dissolution of the Monasteries the Abbey of West Dereham and its lands were granted to Thomas Derham (1503–54), an elder brother of Francis, on 3 December 1541.[25] The Abbey became the principal home of the family, but other members lived at Dereham Grange (a farm-house about two miles to the north-east) and at Crimplesham. The already large acreage in their control was further increased during the later sixteenth century by purchases from other sources. With the death of Thomas Derham in 1554 the estates passed to his son Thomas (1531–77), then to the next eldest brother, Robert (1532–1612), neither of whom had children. This deficiency was remedied by their brother Baldwin (1535–1610), of whose nineteen children the eldest, Thomas (1568–1645), inherited not only the estates from his uncle Robert, but also others from his father and father-in-law. He evidently took up residence in the Abbey around 1613 and, like many in his position, joined in the scramble for prestige, acquiring (by purchase) a knighthood in 1617,[26] and compiling that suspect pedigree to proclaim his ancient and honourable ancestry. Against such a background it seems probable

[23] British Library, Stowe MS 638.

[24] British Library, Harleian MS 1688 is a fifteenth-century Psalter, with entries of births, marriages and deaths of the Derham family up to 1529.

[25] Public Record Office: E318/8/372.

[26] Knighted at Newmarket on 1 December 1617 by James I.

Eighteenth-century engraving of the front of West Dereham Abbey (courtesy of the British Library)

that he would include some form of musical establishment as part of the accoutrements of his position, but, if so, no record of one has yet come to light. Indeed, a nagging doubt persists that Jenkins had little, if any connection with the Derhams, at least in Norfolk, until the outbreak of the Civil War in 1642. The evidence, vague though it is, suggests rather that he was based in London until then.

With so many London records devastated by the Great Fire, all attempts to trace Jenkins in the city have so far failed. Yet there are reasons for continuing the search. When, for instance, did he write that 'peice called the *Cryes of Newgate*, which was all humour, and very *bizarre*'?[27] This work sounds like an emulation of the 'Cries' by Gibbons, Dering, Weelkes, and others. Did it record life in that part of the city in which he lived? Are the six bells in the 'Bell Pavan' and in the 'Six Bells' lyra

[27] Roger North, *Roger North on Music*, ed. John Wilson, Novello, London, 1959, p. 345. The piece is lost.

Eighteenth-century engraving of the front of West Dereham Abbey (courtesy of the British Library)

consort a memory of the clock of St Mary le Bow[28] (near the south end of Milk Street), or of the six bells of St Sepulchre-without-Newgate?

A related problem is the relative paucity of Jacobean manuscripts containing viol consorts, so limiting the present view of the development and chronology of the genre. North remarks that Jenkins 'lived in King James time, and flourished in King Charles the First's',[29] a view which accords well with current knowledge of manuscripts containing his music. Nothing by Jenkins found its way into Francis Tregian's three large

[28] Tradition connects the six-bell theme with Bow church and the ancient tune 'Turn again, Whittington', but if the chime was played by the clock, it was destroyed in the Great Fire of 1666. Doubt has also been cast on how 'ancient' the Whittington tune is. I am indebted to David Pinto for a reference to it in Shirley's *Constant Maid* (1640): '[...] six bells in every steeple, / And let them all go to the city tune, /Turn again, Whittington [...]'. I do not know of an earlier reference.

[29] *Op. cit.*, p. 343.

collections,[30] for instance, and the earliest extant copies of the composer's pieces seem to belong to the 1620s. The latter manuscripts hint both at a London connection and at Jenkins' association with music-making in and around the inns of court.

Although the royal court was the power-house energising England's musical life, a centre from which the latest ideas and fashions were filtered to the estates of the nobility, the inns of court are likely to have played a larger part in the dissemination of the arts than has been so far acknowledged. Both court and inns were in London and gave their members access to the latest artistic developments and to the finest musicians and composers; indeed, Lord Clarendon, Edward Hyde, characterised the law societies as 'suburbs of the court itself'[31] and the inns were often a stepping stone for those seeking preferment at court. To them would come young men from the upper and mercantile classes, not only to study law, but also to acquire some of the social graces. Lessons in dancing, fencing, and music were readily available to all who required them, and the London playhouses were nearby. Some would call upon the house musicians for instruction, while others would get their tuition from professional musicians outside. Jenkins might have fitted any of these categories. Since Sir Thomas Derham (1568–1645) was a barrister and his son Thomas was admitted to the Inner Temple in 1618, the Derham link

[30] Francis Tregian (d. 1619) compiled 'The Fitzwilliam Virginal Book', now at the Fitzwilliam Museum, Cambridge; British Library, Egerton MS 3665; New York Public Library, Drexel MS 4302. These enormous manuscripts appear to have been compiled between 1609 and 1619, when Tregian was imprisoned for recusancy in the Fleet prison. In spite of his confinement there, he seems to have been allowed both books and visitors.

[31] Quoted in Wilfred R. Prest, *The Inns of Court under Elizabeth I and the Early Stuarts: 1590–1640*, Longman, London, 1972, p. 223, where connections between court and inns are fully discussed.

is not invalidated by this hypothesis. Both inns and court cultivated that extravagant form of entertainment, the masque, and dancing played an important part in the Revels held at the inns every Saturday night between All Saints and Candlemas. A later patron of Jenkins, Sir Nicholas L'Estrange (1604–55), compiled a book of masque dances during his time at Lincoln's Inn,[32] yet no music by the composer is included. But a tablature book belonging to a Middle Templar, John Browne (1608–91), apparently begun in the late 1620s, has ten airs for lyra viol by Jenkins.[33] Browne went on to become Clerk of the Parliaments and amassed a large collection of music by pre-Commonwealth composers, among whom are several quite obscure London-based musicians like John Milton (father of the poet), Maurice Webster, and George Gill. Jenkins is represented in Browne's books by 91 pieces – nearly twice as many as any other composer – and several of these are unknown elsewhere. In truth, that picture is a little misleading, since Jenkins' pieces are predominantly masque-type dances – surely significant in itself – rather than the weightier but less numerous consorts by Ferrabosco II, Coprario, Lupo and Ward, but even so his contribution would hardly be so large if he were away in Norfolk. Surprisingly, there is no indication yet that his outstanding series of fantasias for viols were in general circulation before 1630, although surely many of them must have been composed by then.

Towards the end of 1633 Jenkins was caught up in one of the most lavish entertainments of the age: James Shirley's masque *The Triumph of Peace*, designed by Inigo Jones and with music by Simon Ives, William Lawes, and

[32] British Library, Add. MS 10444. *Cf.* Pamela J. Willetts, 'Sir Nicholas Le Strange's Collection of Masque Music', *British Museum Quarterly*, Vol. XXIX, 1965, pp. 79–81.

[33] Owned by Robert Spencer. *Cf.* Andrew Ashbee, 'Instrumental Music from the Library of John Browne (1608–1691), Clerk of the Parliaments', *Music & Letters*, 58, 1977, pp. 43–59.

Davis Mell.[34] It may have been the birth of the Duke of York, later James II, in October of that year, or perhaps, as Bulstrode Whitelocke states, a repudiation of William Prynne's puritanical attack on plays and actors in *Histrio-Mastix* – an attack which some maliciously pointed out reflected upon Queen Henrietta Maria herself since she had acted in a court Pastoral – which gave the origin to this project. Whatever the reason, Whitelocke wrote that

> About *Allholantide*, several of the principal Members of the societies of the four Inns of Court, amongst whom some were Servants to the King, had a design that the Inns of Court should present their service to them, by the outward and splendid visible testimony of a Royal Masque of all the four Societies joyning together, to be by them brought to the Court as an expression of their love, and duty to their Majesties.[35]

Response from the court was swift:

> 1633, 17 Oct. No law studied in the Inns of Court; now all turned dancing schools. There came a desire from the King about a fortnight ago to the Inns of Court by my Lord Keeper that the gentlemen of the several Inns would show themselves at Court by the presentation of a mask, which desire was suddenly accepted, and speedily concluded upon. There are four maskers of every Inn of Court appointed, and 25 gentlemen of every house, in all

[34] *Cf.* Murray Lefkowitz, *Trois Masques à la Cour de Charles Ier d'Angleterre*, Centre National de la Recherche Scientifique, Paris, 1970; Murray Lefkowitz, 'The Longleat Papers of Bulstrode Whitelocke: New Light on Shirley's Triumph of Peace', *Journal of the American Musicological Society*, xviii, 1965, pp. 42–60; Andrew Sabol, 'New Documents on Shirley's Masque The Triumph of Peace', *Music & Letters*, 47, 1966, pp. 10–26; Peter Walls, 'New Light on Songs by William Lawes and John Wilson', *Music & Letters*, 57, 1976, pp. 55–64; Peter Holman, 'The Symphony', *Chelys*, 6, 1975–6, pp. 10–24; Andrew Ashbee, 'A Not Unapt Scholar: Bulstrode Whitelocke (1605–1675)', *Chelys*, II, 1982, pp. 24–31.

[35] Bulstrode Whitelocke, *Memorials of English Affairs*, London, 1682, p.18.

Sir Nicholas L'Estrange (1604–55) (courtesy of Norfolk and Norwich Record Office)

> 100, to attend the maskers to the Court upon light horse out of the King's stable, all in trappings as gallantly accoutred as can be imagined [...].[36]

Organisation was undertaken by two representatives from each of the four Inns, with sub-committees responsible for different aspects of the production: Grand Masque, Antimasques, Musique, and Procession. It fell to Whitelocke, appointed by the Middle Temple, 'to take care for all the Musique & all things belonging to them and for any alteration [that] shall be fitt'. No expense was spared; the inns raised more than £6,000 by levies on their members and Whitelocke recorded that 'the charge of the whole *Masque*, which was born by the Societies, and by the particular Members of it, was accounted to be above one and twenty thousand pounds'. His appointment as Master of the Revels at the Middle Temple in the autumn of 1628 was evidently useful preparation for the prominent role he was to play in this important venture, a role he undertook with both enthusiasm and pride. He chose William Lawes and Simon Ives to compose the music, four French musicians from the Queen's chapel and other foreign musicians,

> not in the least neglecting any of my owne Country-men, whose knowledge in Musick rendered them usefull in this Action to bear their parts in the Musick, which I resolved if I could, to have so performed, as might excell any musicke that ever before this time had bin in England. Herein I kept my purpose, and for the better preparation and practice of the Musick, and that I myselfe might take the better care, and be present with them, I caused the meetings of all the Musitians to be frequent att my house in Salisbury Court, and where I have had togither att one time, of English, French, Italian, German, and other Masters of Musicke [...].[37]

Final preparations were conducted at the Banquetting

[36] Letter of Thomas Coke to Sir John Coke, quoted in Lefkowitz, *Trois Masques*, p. 38.

[37] British Library, Add. MS 53726, f. 90r.

House in the palace of Whitehall where the masque was eventually staged on Candlemas Day, 3 February 1634. A glittering torchlight procession paraded from Ely House in Holborn, down Chancery Lane, through Temple Bar and via Charing Cross to Whitehall Palace.

> The Torches and Flaming huge Flamboys born by the sides of each Chariot, made it seem lightsom as at Noon-day, but more glittering, and gave a full and clear light to all the streets and windows as they passed by. The march was slow, in regard of their great number, but more interrupted by the multitude of the Spectators in the Streets, besides the windows, and they all seemed loth to part with so glorious a Spectacle.[38]

One of the participants, Justinian Paget, wrote to his cousin Tremyll:

> The K and Q supt that night at Salisbury House, and there saw us ride in the streets, after which they presently went by water to Whitehall, and there saw us again from the long gallery at the upper end of the tilting yard.[39]

Whitelocke adds that

> being delighted with the noble bravery of it, they sent to the Marshall to desire that the whole show might fetch a turn about the Tilt-yard, that their Majesties might have a double view of them; which was done accordingly, and then they all alighted at Whitehall-Gate, and were conducted to several Rooms and places prepared for them.[40]

Whitelocke's papers show Jenkins to have been in the 'second Musique Charriott' with seven other lutenists and violists.[41] But it seems that their music was swamped by the general noise and bustle of the occasion and at the

[38] *Ibid.*, f. 94r.

[39] Quoted in Lefkowitz, *Trois Masques*, p. 39.

[40] *Memorials*, p. 36.

[41] Longleat House, Whitelocke Papers, Parcel II, No. 9, Item 13, f. 2. The others were 'Mr. Jo: Lawrence, Mr. Coleman, Mr. Wilson, Mr. Webb, Mr. W. Tomkins, Mr. Kelley, Mr. Woodington.'

repeat performance on 13 February this chariot was filled by members of the 'King's loud musique'. Jenkins then became one of six musicians 'on horseback, with Foot-clothes habited, and attended with torches' in front of the silver and blue chariot of the Middle Temple Grand Masquers.[42]

In the performances of the masque itself Jenkins was given a position of prominence and responsibility. Various surviving lists and diagrams for the production show that at different times he played treble and bass viols, mean lute, and theorbo. The masque dances proper were accompanied by 'ye Kinges Musitions of ye violines', but the nine set-piece songs employed a huge battery of lutes supported by a group labelled 'Symphony'. It has been suggested that the latter 'played instrumental music, as in the Jacobean masques, to cover the gap needed by the musicians to come forward to their singing positions'.[43] The 'symphony' comprised:

Mr. Jenkins	Base Viole
Mr. Lawrence	Lute
Mr. Kelley	Lute
Mr. Kithe	Lute
Mr. Page	base Lute
Mr. Miller	Lute
Mr. Bedowes	harpe
Mr. Will Tomkins	Viole
Mr. Steffkin	Viole
Mr. Gotiere	Lute
Mr. Jacob	Lute
Mr. Woodington	violin[44]

Jenkins also belonged to an even more selective ensemble whose function is unclear:

[42] Sabol, *loc. cit.*, p. 25, states that a third list in which 'Mr. Jenkins & Mr. Tomkins' are included among musicians going 'Before ye Orange & Silver Charriott' is an earlier scheme for the second procession.

[43] Holman, *loc. cit.*, p. 13.

[44] Longleat House, Whitelocke Papers, Parcel II, No. 9, Item 8, f. 1.

Mr.	
Bedoes	Harpe
Coleman	Treble violl
Jinkins	Treble violl
Page	bass violl
Will: Tomkins	bass violl
Willson	Theorbo
Caesar	Theorbo
Lawrence	
Kelley	
Kithe[45]	

Possibly this group played prior to the performance, drawing on music such as William Lawes' 'Harp Consorts'.

> *The Triumph of Peace* was a resounding success; indeed The Queen who was much delighted with these Solemnities, was so taken with this Show and Masque, that she desired to see it acted over again: whereupon an intimation being given to the Lord Mayor of *London*, he invited the *King and Queen* and the *Inns of Court Masquers* to the City, and entertained them with all state and magnificence, at *Merchant Taylor's Hall*. Thither marched through the *City* the same show, that went before to Whitehall, and the same *Masque* was again presented to them in the *City*: the same Horsemen, Lacquies, Liveries, Torches, Habits, Chariots, Musick, and all other parts of the former Solemnity, and in the same state and equippage, as it was before presented.

This second performance, that of 13 February,

> also gave great contentment to their Majesties, and no less to the citizens, especially to those of the younger sort, and of the female sex: and it was to the great honour, and no less charge of the Lord Mayor *Freeman*.

Yet, as Whitelocke was quick to add,

> Thus was this earthly pomp and Glory, if not Vanity, soon past over and gone, as if it had never been.[46]

[45] *Ibid.*, Item 12.

[46] *Memorials*, p. 36.

All the performers were paid generously. Jenkins received ten pounds, and his signature on the receipt, which Whitelocke carefully preserved, has led to the identification of a number of his holograph music manuscripts.[47]

The rehearsals and performances of this masque enabled Jenkins, if opportunities had not arisen before, to meet and make friends with many of the principal English musicians of his day: the brothers Lawes, Wilson, Coleman, Ives, Woodington, Mell, Gaultier, and others of the King's Musick. Opportunities for gossip and *camaraderie* perhaps presented him with three stories concerning the court which he later passed on to Sir Nicholas L'Estrange for inclusion in his collection of 'jests':[48]

> The Earle of Pembroke, Lord Chamberlaine, Received a disgraceful Switch over the Face by a Scott, (by occasion of the Lye) at King James his first comming into England: The Impression of which Affront, so patiently put up, remained in the Memorie of many, a fowle staine to his Honour: And being at Boules in the Spring garden afterward, there grew an hott context betwixt this Lord and Sir

[47] Longleat House, Whitelocke Papers, Parcell II, No. 6, f. 5: '4 Martii 1633 [1634], Received of Bulstrode Whitelocke Esqr the summe of tenn pounds for service performed in the Musique of the Inns of Courte Masque, by me Jo: Jenkins [signature]'.

Holograph copies of music by Jenkins with a similar signature are in British Library, Add. MS 29290; Bodleian Library, Mus. Sch. MS C.88; Bodleian Library, Mus MS 184.c.8; Bodleian Library, North MS e.37.

[48] British Library, Harleian MS 6395, stories Nos. 535, 536 and 599. A modern transcription and edition of this manuscript is H. F. Lippincott, *'Merry Passages and Jeastss', A Manuscript Jestbook of Sir Nicholas Le Strange (1603–1655)*, Institut für Englische Sprache und Literatur, Salzburg University, Salzburg, 1974. Lippincott traces the first story to an incident in March 1611/12. Thomas Holmes sang in *The Triumph of Peace* and had been sworn as Gentleman of the Chapel Royal on 17 September 1633. Sir Nicholas had previously received the story about Wilson, in more detail, from his servant Thomas Brewer (story No. 361).

Tentandi Gratia: 'by the grace of knowing'.

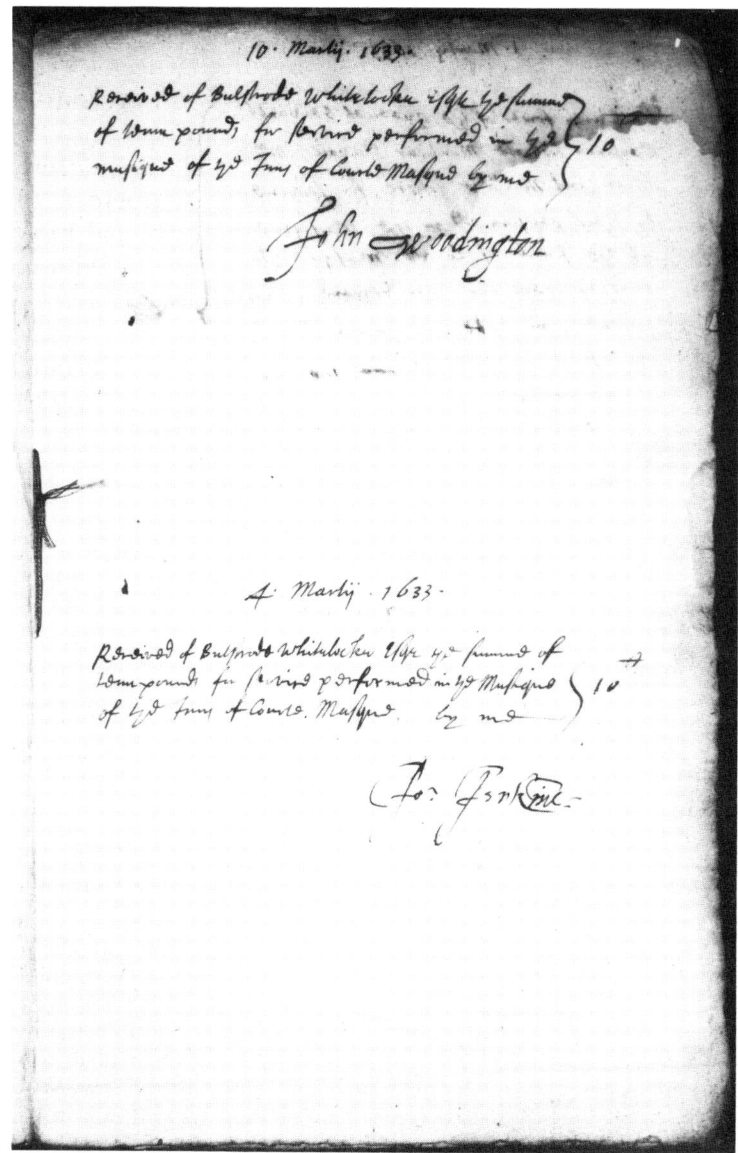

10 Martij 1633

Received of Bulstrode Whitelocke Esqr the summe of tenne pounds for service performed in the musique of the Inns of Courte Masque by me } 10

John Woodington

4 Martij 1633

Received of Bulstrode Whitelocke Esqr the summe of tenne pounds for service performed in the Musique of the Inns of Courte Masque by me } 10

Jo: Jenkins

Signature of Jenkins for his £10 fee for performing in The Triumph of Peace *(courtesy of the Marquess of Bath)*

> Rob: Bell about the Distance of 2 Boules; and so far, that the Lord gave the Knight the Lye: Sir Rob: startles and stormes about, and in a well Dissembled Rage, (knowing how to wound him deepe without a stroake) cryes out, Give me a Switch: The Company smiled, and the conscious Lord scornfully Replyes; And what dare you and That Doe? Measure the Cast, and beate you my Lord Ile warrant you sayes He.
>
> One Mr Homes of the Chappell, who sang very bravely, but had one false Eye of Glasse; at a meeting for voyces, He standing off from the Table, one in favour to his Infirmitie, was Removing the Desk closer to Him; I pray hold your Hand Sir sayes he, that needs not, I see well, and have the advantage of all the company, for if need be (withall pulling out his eye, and holding it to) I can bring my Eye as neere as I will to the Booke.
>
> Jack: Wilson the Musitian, stumbling out of a Taverne, and Rubbing against a sober grave Gentleman that passed By; What art Thou, sayes Wilson, a Papist? Yes sayes He, (Tentandi Gratia) whats that to you? Why then Th'art a Knave sayes Wilson: I scorne your words sayes the Gentleman, I am no Papist; Nay that's worse, (sayes Bold Jacke) for Then Th'art a Lying Knave: and so gett Thee Gone and be Hangd.

There had been a lack of royal pageantry throughout Charles I's reign and the grand procession through the streets before the performances of *The Triumph of Peace* clearly delighted the populace at large. London citizens had earlier been disappointed by Charles' refusal to make a 'royal entry' at the time of his coronation – as had the Corporation who had spent £4,300 in anticipation of the event – so that this tremendous show must have been some consolation. There was to be one more royal pageant in the city, only weeks before the final break with Parliament. On 25 November 1641 the King was welcomed by the Lord Mayor and Corporation, and

> As their *Majesties* passed along, the Trumpets and Citie *Musique* were placed in severall parts, sounding and play-

> ing, which together with the severall, continuall, and joyfull acclamations of the people, gave great content to both their *Majesties* [...].[49]

The choir of St Paul's sang an anthem, and during the nocturnal journey from Guildhall to the palace of Whitehall there was the sound of fourteen trumpets and

> all instruments of musick usuall, with Bells ringing at 121 parish Churches

But if the King had generally spurned such public spectacle throughout his reign, this pageantry had rather transferred to the Lord Mayor's Show. Ceremonial and celebration surrounding the annual inauguration of the Lord Mayor developed into a considerable event, generously funded by the Corporation and guilds and involving artists of all kinds as well as the civic dignitaries and guilds. Writers like John Webster, Thomas Middleton and Thomas Heywood all contributed sophisticated street dramas as part of the spectacle, and music played its part on and around the huge triumphal arches and other sets erected for the occasion. Prophetically, Heywood's last show of 1639, *Londini Status Pacatus*, is primarily concerned with contrasting the 'calamities of War, and the blessedness of Peace', but his vision of 'this sole-happy Isle' enjoying 'calme Peace, Prosperity, and Plenty with increase of all concatinated Blessings' was shortly to be disappointed. A year later the citizens lamented that 'their is noe publike show eyther with Pageats or uppon the water'. And so it was to remain until the Restoration. Unfortunately descriptions of these pageants mention music only in general terms and one would like to know who the musicians actually were. Could Jenkins have been one of them? It seems very likely, for he composed hundreds of masque-type dances during the earlier part

[49] *Ovatio Carolina*, London, 1641, quoted in David M. Bergeron, *English Civic Pageantry, 1558–1642*, Arnold, London, 1971, p. 119, to which my account is heavily indebted.

of his career, none of which has been linked to a particular production.

> On one occasion
> he was once carryed to play on the viol afore King Charles I, which he did in his voluntary way, with wonderful agility, and odd humours, as (for instance) touching the great strings with his thumb, while the rest were held imployed in another way. And when he had done the King sayd he did wonders upon an inconsiderable instrument.[50]

Presumably Jenkins told North about this audience in later years, and one wonders whether it was a kind of audition: an attempt to secure for the composer a court post by outflanking the nepotism rife in the King's Musick.[51] If so, it seems to have come to nothing, but then there is no reason to suppose that Jenkins was other than contented with his lot:

> Mr Jenkins was a very gentile and well bred gentleman, and was allways not onely welcome, but greatly valued by the familys wherever he had taught and convers't. He was constantly complaisant in every thing desired of him, and wherever he went Mirth and Solace (as the song hath it) attended him.[52]

Elsewhere North says

> He [Jenkins] was a lutenist profes't, and used the lyra way upon the violl, which followed the manner of the lute, and he had a very great hand upon the consort viol [...].[53]

Yet his appearances at *The Triumph of Peace* remain the only conclusive sightings of him during his first fifty

[50] North, *op. cit.*, p. 295; elsewhere he notes the instrument as a lyra viol.

[51] For a discussion of this nepotism, *cf.* G. A. Philipps, 'Crown Musical Patronage from Elizabeth I to Charles I', *Music & Letters*, 58, 1977, pp. 29–42.

[52] North, *op. cit.*, p. 297.

[53] *Ibid.*, p. 295.

years, though North implies that he remained in the capital until the outbreak of hostilities.

When Charles I left London for Hampton Court on 10 January 1642, he was not to know that he would only enter the capital again briefly years later as a prisoner, but from that date he was effectively removed from the seat of government; henceforth there were to be two rulers in the land. It cannot have been long before the population at large realised that open conflict would soon break out. The King spent some months stumping the country trying to raise support for his cause, hoping all the time that the trappings of court life could be retained. His musicians were summoned to attend him at York, but without financial guarantees they wisely declined, deciding rather to go their separate ways. Only when the King established a more permanent base at Oxford late in the year did a few musicians rally to him. London, meanwhile, was firmly controlled by Parliament, and some of the ordinances which it began issuing on 5 March 1642 were hardly encouraging for musicians and their like. On 2 September, for instance, stage plays were banned because they 'do not well agree with Public Calamities, nor [...] with the seasons of Humiliation, this being an exercise of sad and pious solemnity'. A further casualty of this ordinance was the Lord Mayor's Show. The inns of court, if located elsewhere, might have rallied to the King. As it was, they adopted a neutral, passive stance, while

> admissions shrank to a handful, learning exercises ceased altogether and the houses were virtually deserted between the summers of 1642 and 1646.[54]

For a composer with Royalist sympathies like Jenkins, the omens were not good. Musical life in London lost the focus of the royal court, the support of civic pageantry and of the work generated by the inns; opportunities for

[54] Prest, *op. cit.*, pp. 236–7.

playing and teaching were clearly ebbing away. Though musicians were treated magnanimously by Parliament, that could not be depended upon as the Civil War erupted, and many obviously felt it safer to move out of the capital. Some joined the armies, mostly, though not entirely, on the Royalist side, while others sought refuge in the country homes of the nobility. Jenkins was among the latter:

> After the Court was disbanded he left the towne, and past his time at gentlemen's houses in the country where musick was of the family, and he was ever courted and never slighted, but at home wherever he went; and in most of his freinds houses there was a chamber called by his name. For besides his musicall excellences, he was an accomplisht ingenious person, and so well behaved, as never to give offence, and wherever he went was always welcome and courted to stay. [...] I never heard that he articled with any gentleman where he resided, but accepted what they gave him.[55]

Fortunately Anthony Wood names the gentlemen concerned:

> in his manly years [Jenkins] was patronised by [...] Deerham of Norfolk, Esq and though a little man, yet he had a great soul. [He] (lived mostly in the family of Ham. Lestrange of Norfolk Esq., so [says] Dr B[enjamin] Rogers, and taught privately.)[56]

[55] North, *op. cit.*, p. 344. On music and musicians in the Commonwealth period generally, *cf.* Percy A. Scholes, *The Puritans and Music in England and New England*, Oxford University Press, London, 1934. Fragmentary accounts survive which show that the court musicians received occasional payments from the Committee of the Revenue in partial settlement of their arrears of wages. These are published in Andrew Ashbee, *Records of English Court Music*, Vol. III, Ashbee, Snodland, 1988, and Vol. V, Scolar Press, Aldershot, 1991.

[56] Bodleian Library, MS Wood D 19(4), f. 73. For a full transcription and commentary *cf.* John Derek Shute, *Anthony a Wood and his Manuscript Wood D 19(4) at the Bodleian Library, Oxford: an annotated transcription,* unpublished Ph. D. dissertation, International Institute for Advanced Studies, Clayton, Missouri, 1979.

Little trace of the Abbey of West Dereham can be seen today, apart from fragments of the gateway. Founded in 1188, it was bought by Thomas Derham in 1541 at the Dissolution of the Monasteries, remaining with the family until the end of the seventeenth century. Elizabeth, the last daughter of the line, married Sir Simeon Stuart of Hartley, Southampton, at the Abbey on 14 June 1701,[57] but after his death in 1761 it passed to others and appears to have been pulled down around 1810.[58] Two eighteenth-century engravings, reproduced,[59] show it in its final state 'built [...] anew at his own cost' by Sir Thomas Derham (d. 1697), who 'erected a wing on each side of the gateway, with a cloister on the south'.[60] The forbidding 'Fore Front' which resulted would not have disgraced a prison, but older wings tucked away behind, like the fifteenth-century tower, seem to have been left untouched, and suggest that the building known to Jenkins was similar to the lovely Oxburgh Hall a mere five miles to the east.[61]

[57] *Cf. Notes and Queries*, No. 278 (Ninth Series), p. 326.

[58] *Cf.* Samuel Lewis, *A Topographical Dictionary of England*, 7th edn., London, 1849, II, p. 42.

[59] Original copies in British Library, Dept. of Prints and Drawing, MS K TOP XXXI, ff. 41, 5a and 5b. These are also reproduced in Add. MS 23028 (Dept. of MSS), Nos. 187–8, together with copies of two frescoes from the walls of the Abbey and other *memorabilia*, Nos. 189–198.

[60] The original captions to the engravings on pp. 26–7 state that the Abbey was 'part of it Rebuilt by Sr. Richard Dereham, whose Heirs now Enjoy it', but a tablet in West Dereham church, dated 1722, erected by the last Sir Thomas Derham (1678–1739) states that it was 'Thomas Dereham, Knight, formerly Envoy of James II, King of England, at [the court of] Cosimo III, Grand Duke of Tuscany, eldest son of Richard Dereham, Knight and Baronet [who] returned to the manor of Dereham [and] built the Palace anew at his own cost.'

[61] One description notes: 'In a wainscotted parlour are the arms of Dereham, Vere, Goddard, Denver, Anderton, Fincham, Audley, Lovell, Catlyn, Repps, Guybon, Carvile, Hamersley, Montford, Gawsel, Pratt, Heath, Penniston, Painell, Scott, Booth, Haltoft, and

It is not known whether Jenkins came to Dereham Abbey, or whether he went instead to Dereham Grange, the farmhouse home of Thomas Derham the younger a mile and a half to the north-east.[62] Possibly he did neither, but travelled further north to Hunstanton where lived the L'Estranges, the most ancient and eminent of families in that corner of England. For a year or so references to Derham, L'Estrange and Jenkins are inexorably intertwined and it is probable that the composer moved between the two families as circumstances dictated at a time when both were caught up in the civil strife.

Throughout 1642 preparations were made for war. Orders issued by Parliament in London were quickly countermanded by the King at York – and vice versa – while the sympathies of the nobility towards one or other side were gradually made manifest. Parliamentarian leaders in Norfolk were efficient and systematic in acquiring control of the militia and administration in the county.[63] Soon they proposed that 'such persons as shall appear by speech or action to have encouraged and practised any opposition to the proceedings of Parliament and disturbance of the public peace shall be disarmed for the service of the county'. The L'Estranges were among peacetime commanders of the trained bands, but they refrained from signing any undertaking to abide by orders from Parliament in any forthcoming unrest. They, and others whose loyalty to Parliament was questionable, were therefore replaced, and on 18 October 1642 Parliament issued orders naming Sir Hamon L'Estrange among those to be disarmed 'for not contributing with the good

---

Bennet'. All these families were linked to the Derhams by marriage before 1640.

[62] A modern building, 'Grange Farm', now occupies the site; the Ordnance Survey ref. is TF 671033.

[63] The ensuing paragraphs are heavily indebted to R. W. Ketton-Cremer, *Norfolk in the Civil War*, Faber & Faber, London, 1969. *Cf.* also Clive Holmes, *The Eastern Association in the English Civil War,* Cambridge University Press, Cambridge, 1974.

subjects to the common charge in this time of imminent danger'.[64] Two months passed before the arms, horse-furniture and ammunition were moved from Hunstanton Hall to the magazine at Lynn, leaving only enough 'fit weapons for the defence of Sir Hamon L'Estrange his house against any rude or pilfering people'. December also saw the formation of the Eastern Association, in which initially Norfolk, Norwich, Suffolk, Essex, Cambridgeshire, Hertfordshire and the Isle of Ely agreed to mutual aid and defence; it was to prove an impenetrable barrier capable of withstanding all Royalist assaults. Until now the L'Estranges had not flaunted their Royalist sympathies (though they had not hidden them either); with friends in both camps, no doubt they were anxious not to stir up unnecessary conflicts. But at a December meeting in Norwich to consider how best to prevent an invasion of Royalist forces from the continent, 'Master Hamon L'Estrange and others were commanded to depart the meeting' for 'affirming that if the Cavaliers were in the county, they should account them their friends'. Shortly afterwards orders were issued that they were 'to be sent for as delinquents, for affronting the Committees when they were met upon the service of the public; and thereby, as much as in them lay, obstructing and prejudicing the service of the Commonwealth'.[65] All then remained quiet until March when several abortive moves by Royalists failed to upset the established forces of the Association. Parliamentary pressure increased with two further ordinances, one imposing a weekly levy on every county and city to support the war effort and, more ominously for the nobility, another 'for Sequestering the Estates of notorious Delinquents', which empowered local committees to impound rents and revenues from Royalist estates and use them to maintain Parliament's forces. On 1 March Lord Grey of Werke, commander of the forces of

[64] Bodleian Library, MS Tanner 64, f. 70.

[65] See Ketton-Cremer, *op. cit.*, p. 166.

the Eastern Association, ordered the arrest of a number of Royalists and the seizure of their arms and houses.[66] Sir Hamon L'Estrange was one of them; he escaped arrest, although he appears to have been on the run for some time. In later years the Rev. Thomas Thorowgood, rector of Grimston and Little Massingham, claimed to have sheltered him in his house:

> Sir Hamon L'Estrange came after midnight to my house, hardly scaping the troopers; all the long day before he had wandered without food. The next morning I found him very ill in bed; I rode to Dr. Baron for his advice. Sir Charles Morduant lay in the same chamber the night before; he was then gone, but came again often in that squirrel-hunting season as it was then called.[67]

On 5 July 1643, Sir Hamon's wife entered in the Hunstanton account book:

> Laid out as appeareth by a bill of Mr. Strange's when he travelled to avoid the troopers £5. 5s. 0d.[68]

Five days later he was at West Dereham:

> [10 July] Layd out in the house of Sr Thomas Dearhams and at Fakenham £0. 15s. 0d.
> [11 July] To Sr Thomas Deerham which Roger [L'Estrange] borrowed of him £10. 0s. 0d.

Succeeding events suggest that Sir Hamon was more than a mere fugitive, for it was the Morduants of Little Massingham and Thomas Derham the younger who were among the few 'gentlemen strangers' involved with him in a dramatic declaration of support for the King by the town of Lynn on 13 August. Sir Hamon was appointed as its Governor, and his visits to Little Massingham and West Dereham must surely have been connected with the planning of the *coup*. It was a brave gesture; that it ulti-

66 British Library, Add. MS 22619, f. 29.

67 Quoted in Ketton-Cremer, *op. cit.*, pp. 189–90.

68 Norfolk and Norwich Record Office, L'Estrange MS P.7.

mately failed was due in large measure to the decision of the Royalist commander Lord Liverpool not to march to relieve the town – a reversal of his earlier promise (and caused by his preoccupation with continued resistance at Hull) – and also to Parliament's blockade of land and sea, preventing supplies getting through. Parliament, to be sure, had many problems on its side, particularly lack of reinforcements, so though some skirmishing and bombardment took place, a siege was inevitable for a time. Eventually the Earl of Manchester sent word that the town would be attacked on 16 September unless he received notice of a surrender before nine o'clock that morning. The defenders complied a day earlier 'not as fearing the taking of the town, but to avoid the effusion of blood'. Eight commissioners were appointed by each side to negotiate the terms of surrender; among those acting for the town were Sir Hamon L'Estrange and 'Master Dearham'. Various conditions were agreed after prolonged debate, including one

> that neither the person nor estates of any inhabitants, gentry, or strangers, now residing in Lynn, shall be hereafter molested for any thing past, or done by them, since the Earl of Manchester's first coming into these parts.[69]

In the meantime a number of the Royalists, again including Sir Hamon and 'Master Dearing' (*sic*) were to be kept as hostages until these conditions had been met. If they thought that the agreement would be sufficient to keep them from later persecution they were wrong, for on 9 December Parliament ordered

> that such persons as did take any of the goods of the well affected by themselves, or such as they appointed, or did any damage to their houses, or mills, or any other ways, shall make restitution to all such well affected persons as has been damnified, according to the greatness of their losses, [...] and if any of them shall refuse to make such

69 Anon., *A brief and true Relation of the Siege and Surrendering of King's Lynn to the Earl of Manchester* (1643).

> reparation, that the [...] Governor, Mr. Percival and Mr. Toll [MPs] shall have power to sequester so much of the estates of such malignants, as will make them reparation, and assign it to those that have been damnified.[70]

Blame for damage naturally fell on Sir Hamon as Governor during the siege, and for years afterwards he was subject to claims arising from it. Thomas Derham, too, was to complain of the treatment he later received, although one suspects that his given reason for going to Lynn was no more that a half-truth at best:

> [...] your Peticioner about [16]43 haveing an extraordinary occasion by reason of the sickness of his Childe to goe to Linne in Norfolke, where your Petitioner was detained and his horse taken from him by Command from the then Mayor of the Towne, whoe immediately afterward declared his disaffection to the Parliament for the King, which was afterwards surrendered upon Articles to the Earle of Manchester, then Major Generall of the association, by which aforesaid Articles your petitioner's Estate both reall and Personall was to be preserved from molestation for any Act or thing done in that place, and notwithstanding your Peticioner had the major Generall's warrant for his protection and safe returning home, your Peticioner for Eight yeares space not haveing Acted or done anything predudiciall to the State, his Estate is by the Commissioners in the Country seized and secured to his very greate damage.[71]

With the Hunstanton estate suffering much in the aftermath of the siege, it is the more remarkable that in the autumn of 1644 Roger L'Estrange could persuade the King that the town was still sympathetic to his cause, receive a royal commission for it to be 'reduced unto our obedience' and return from Oxford to put the scheme into action. But he was betrayed, arrested, tried, and sen-

[70] Ed. Edward Husband, *A Collection of all the public Orders, Ordinances and Declarations of both Houses of Parliament*, London, 1646, p. 396.

[71] *Proceedings of the Committee for Compounding*, first series, xx, p. 207 – one of several related documents dated 1651–2.

Hunstanton Hall, from a drawing by J. S. Cotman

tenced to death. Only a petition on his behalf from Prince Rupert saved him, and after spending three years in Newgate prison he escaped, joining the abortive rising in Kent before finally fleeing to the continent. None of this activity was helpful to Sir Hamon, of course, who 'was taken and carried to Lynn and there retained ten days about receiving of his son Roger, and divers days at Lynn attending that before he was descharged'.[72]

Yet there was to be one more remarkable incursion into this corner of Norfolk before the struggle was concluded. On 22 April 1646 the King wrote to Henrietta Maria:

> To eschew all kind of captivity, which, if I stay here, I must undergo, I intend (by the grace of God) to get privately to Lynn, where I will yet try if it be possible to make such a strength, as to procure honourable and safe conduct from the rebels; if not, then I resolve to go by sea to

[72] Norfolk and Norwich Record Office, L'Estrange MS P.10.

> Scotland, in case I shall understand that Montrose be in condition fit to receive me, otherwise I mean to make for Ireland, France or Denmark, but to which of these I am not yet resolved [...].[73]

Four days later he left Oxford secretly at night, disguised as a servant to two of his attendants, John Ashburnham and Dr Michael Hudson. The ploy worked: the group survived all challenges by Parliament's forces. Hudson went separately to meet the French envoy Montreuil and agree terms with the Scots at Southwell, while the others pushed on to Norfolk, arriving at the White Swan, Downham Market, on Wednesday, 29 April. There they made contact with Ralph Skipwith of Snore Hall, Fordham, and one wonders whether his neighbours, the Derhams, were alerted to the King's presence. Soon after, afraid that Charles might have been recognised by a barber who trimmed his beard, they travelled further south-east to Mundford, where Hudson rejoined them. News of the King's escape from Oxford was now common knowledge and the ports were carefully watched. Charles decided that the only course remaining to him was to appeal to the Scots, if he could reach them safely. On Saturday morning, 2 May, the fugitives arrived at an ale-house at Crimplesham, changed disguises, and eventually set out for Southwell. Their journey brought the King one last time to the religious community at Little Gidding where the three spent the night. Charles reached Southwell on 5 May. The Scots made demands which he could not accept; they kept him for a time, but handed him over to Parliament early in 1647, his freedom and his power finally taken from him.

Such is the background against which Jenkins' work in the 1640s must be viewed. Dereham Abbey may have been something of an oasis in the midst of these storms: Sir Thomas Derham was in his mid-seventies and too old

[73] John Bruce (ed.), *Charles I in 1646*, Camden Society, London, 1856, p. 38.

to play an active part in the strife himself, although he may, of course, have given shelter and support to beleaguered Royalists in the area. His son, as has been seen, struck at least one determined blow for the cause, a blow which apparently cemented a friendship with the L'Estranges after 1643, as the latters' accounts show. Some contacts were official, as in March 1645/6, when 2s. 4d. was 'layd out at Geywood when Mr. Strange went to Meete Mr. Deerham, Mr. Parlett and others Concerning Mr. Toll & Mr. Persivall's demand for their pretended imprisonment', but others were merely neighbourly:

> [February–March 1652/3]
> To Mr. Deerham's Brewer sent by Nicholas Markant 2s.
> To Nicholas Markant for bringing of water from Mr. Deerham's 1s.
> To Springhall for digging of Erringe Rootes for Mr Dearham 1s.[74]

Indeed, there is an obvious determination in these accounts and elsewhere that life should be presented as going on normally. The civic books at Lynn, for instance, make no mention of the siege or bombardment, and Lady Alice maintains the L'Estrange accounts meticulously throughout the troubles, although not without the occasional tirade against 'the unjust tyrannical oppression of Mr. Toll and others of his faction':

> Wee were plundered by the Rebells of 1660 sheep, all our Corne & divers Horses

– perhaps the latter were the same to have run up expenditure of £3. 6s. 8d. for 'horsemeat at Lynn for 6 horses, 3 weeks & 5 days' during the siege.

Of Jenkins the surviving accounts say nothing,[75] though more are lost – including any kept personally by

[74] Norfolk and Norwich Record Office, L'Estrange MS P.10.

[75] Unless the entry on 25 April 1651 concerns him: 'Received of Mr Jenkin [*sic*] for a horse that was bought of John Johns: £8': Norfolk and Norwich Record Office, L'Estrange MS P.11.

Sir Nicholas. Lady Alice implies that he managed (or mismanaged) his own affairs when in 1641 she wrote: 'Payd to my sonne Nicholas Le Strange to pay his debts: £400'. Fortunately others of his books are extant which provide convincing evidence of Jenkins' association with both L'Estranges and Derhams at this time.

Like his brothers, Sir Nicholas had received musical instruction as part of his education, and in the early 1620s 'Nicholas his voyall' features among a wealth of references to 'violl stringes' and 'violl bookes' in the accounts. Nicholas evidently took his viol to Eton and on to Cambridge and the inns of court,[76] while a good deal of purchasing and refurbishing of musical instruments at Hunstanton in 1629–30 seems connected with his setting up house there:[77]

[76] The accounts record 'Nick and Ham. placed att Eaton' on 18 May 1620 and that Nicholas left Eton on 1 June 1622, but the College has no record of his having been there (letter from Patrick Strong to me, dated 15 September 1967). He was at Trinity College, Cambridge, between Michaelmas 1622 and July 1624, transferring to Lincoln's Inn in October of that year.

[77] Norfolk and Norwich Record Office, L'Estrange MS P.7. His father purchased a Baronetcy for him on 1 June 1629 and he was married to Ann Lewkenor at St Stephen's, Norwich, on 26 August 1630. Michael Wilson, *The English Chamber Organ – History and Development 1650–1850*, Cassirer, Oxford, 1968, p. 100, has the following:

> In 1949, at a sale of effects from Hunstanton Hall, Norfolk, Capt. J. Lane of Snarebrook, Essex, purchased a positive organ and stand. The organ, apparently anonymous, was in a panelled oak case with two painted wings, one showing David and Saul, the other Jeptha's daughter. The display pipes were placed in an architectural setting very similar to [an organ by Christian Smith described earlier in Wilson's book] although this second organ would appear to have been an even earlier instrument. Its compass was from CC to c3. CC# sounding AA. The specification was as follows:
>
> Fifteenth Bass Fifteenth Treble [middle c]
> Principal Bass Principal Treble [middle c]
> Open Diapason
> Flute [tenor c]
> Flute Bass
> All the pipes were of wood

[20 November 1629]	for mending of a voyall	£0. 2. 6.
	for mending of another voyall	£0. 1. 6.
[1629]	'NLS': for voyall stringes	£0. 7. 0.
	for a voyall and a Case	£1. 0. 0.
[1630]	'N': for a payer of Organs	£11. 0. 0.

Two fine collections of viol consorts[78] were compiled in succeeding years, which incorporated all Jenkins' five-part fantasias and a pavan. It seems likely that one of the copyists was the composer Thomas Brewer, who is noted as teaching Roger L'Estrange on the viol in the accounts for 1636[79] and who was the subject of a 'jest' told to Sir Nicholas by Jenkins:

> Thom: Brewer, my Mus: servant, through his Pronenesse to good-Fellowshippe, having attaind to a very Rich and Rubicund Nose; being reprooved by a Friend for his too frequent use of strong Drinkes and Sacke; as very Pernicious to that Distemper and Inflammation in his Nose.

The instrument is now in the United States. It seems to me quite probable that this is the organ mentioned by Lady Alice L'Estrange in the account book.

[78] British Library, Add. MSS 39550–4 and Royal College of Music MS 1145. There are detailed commentaries in Pamel J. Willetts, 'Sir Nicholas Le Strange and John Jenkins', *Music & Letters*, 42, 1961, pp. 30–43, and Andrew Ashbee, 'A Further Look at Some of the Le Strange Manuscripts', *Chelys*, 5, 1973–4, pp. 24–41.

[79] Norfolk and Norwich Record office, L'Estrange MS P.7: 'to Thomas Brewer for teaching of Roger on the voyall: £2. 0. 0.' (third quarter of 1636). Brewer, aged three, was admitted as a pupil at Christ's Hospital on 9 December 1614. He was discharged on 20 June 1626 when Thomas Warner took him to be his apprentice. I am indebted to Timothy Cooper for the information that Brewer became songschoolmaster at Christ's Hospital. He was appointed in 1638 (his predeccessor having been dismissed 'for his ill Carriage and Misdemeanor towards the Children'), but was himself dismissed at Christmas 1641 since he had married, this being contrary to the regulations governing the post. *Cf.* Guildhall Library, London, Christ's Hospital, Court Minutes: MS 12.806/4, pp. 241 and 343 *passim.*

> nay-Faith sayes he, if it will not endure Sack, it's no Nose for me.[80]

But there is no indication that Jenkins was at Hunstanton when these manuscripts were being written, nor that he had any hand in copying or checking his own compositions in them. The jest book, evidently compiled over many years, supports the view that he did not take up residence at the Hall until the mid-1640s. Although dating of the stories cannot entirely be relied upon, some have value in establishing a rough chronology: No. 407 begins 'When the Scotts invaded the Northern parts, 1640', Nos. 455–6 concern conflicts between Parliament and the King and No. 503 is 'Upon the first Breach betwixt the King and Parliament 1642'. The five stories attributed to Jenkins are Nos. 535, 536, 543, 578 and 599 – all later than the Civil War ones and appropriate to a dating of *c.* 1644 and after (whilst Thomas Brewer's contributions – Nos. 360–1 – are earlier). Yet, if what survive of the elegant and beautiful manuscripts which Jenkins copied for Sir Nicholas are listed, the composer clearly must have spent an appreciable time at Hunstanton:

(1) 122 two-part airs in score (Christ Church, Mus. MS 1005);
(2) 84 three-part airs in score (Christ Church, Mus. MS 1005) add parts for 51 of these (Newberry Library, Chicago, Case MS VM.1.A.18.J.52c);
(3) (probably) a score of 21 three-part fantasias (British Library, Add. MS 31428);
(4) parts of 15 pieces for two bass viols and organ and of

[80] British Library, Harleian MS 6395, No. 578. Christ's Hospital Court minutes dated 9 December 1641 record that 'there hath bine Complaints by the porter of Mr Brewer for his late Coming in a Nights and Neglecting of his place'. It seems probable that Jenkins was the 'carrier' of works by Brewer which appeared later in manuscripts apparently associated with the North family, Bodleian Library, Mus. Sch. MS C.100, and British Library, Add. MS 31423.

17 pieces for treble, bass and organ (Royal College of Music, MS 921);

(5) organ part for 21 suites by Coprario, and an index (British Library, Add. MS 23779).

Jenkins completed work begun by other copyists, but no copyist continued work by him, apart from comments added by Sir Nicholas; he thus comes at the end of the line. The scores are fair copies, devoid of external markings except titles, but the parts are full of fascinating annotations concerning chronology, performance practice and notation.[81] From them it is learned that the 33 three-part airs by Jenkins copied first into Sir Nicholas's collection came from 'Mr. Derham's Blew Fol. Bookes', where their sequence was the same as the composer's 'origin[al]' order; presumably, then, he wrote these pieces at West Dereham. But

> All of Mr Jenkins his new composing in 1644 and 45 &c, have a pricke of Redd Inke set against them in the Catalogue

and prove to be entirely in Jenkins's own hand.[82] They are given a new 'origin' number, follow items copied by Sir Nicholas and would appear to have been written at Hunstanton. Further, from their position in the partbooks, from the curious numbering and pagination employed, and from their 'postinato' listing in the 'catalogue', it is clear that the last twelve of this group of 48 pieces were added after the rest of the music:

> After my score Booke was Bound, mr Jenk: at the importunitie of mr Derham made these new ones following, [...]

[81] These are discussed in the articles mentioned in note 78 on p. 53; *cf.* also Jane Troy Johnson, 'How to "Humour" John Jenkins' Three-part Dances: Performance Directions in a Newberry Library MS', *Journal of the American Musicological Society,* Summer 1967, pp. 197–208, and Andrew Ashbee, 'Towards the Chronology and Grouping of Some Airs by John Jenkins', *Music & Letters*, 55, 1974, pp. 30–44.

[82] Fully discussed in Andrew Ashbee, 'Towards the Chronology and Grouping'.

> And afterwards for 2T:2B & but Reduc'd into 1 Ba:2 TR: these Aires following [...].

To interpret 'importunitie' in this context is difficult. It could mean that Mr Derham pleaded for more pieces, or it could mean that Jenkins was prevented from returning to West Dereham because some crisis prevented Derham from receiving him there.[83] But one other oddity is resolved by these notes: the elaborate flourish incorporation 'Iohn Ienkins Fi=nis' after No. 45 expresses the composer's relief as he completes the copying of the last two suites in this collection of more than 200 dances.

Other music from West Dereham also found its way into Sir Nicholas's books: at least nine of Jenkins' airs for two bass viols and organ, and ten of Coprario's fantasia-suites for treble, bass and organ were examined by 'mr Derham's Bo:'. Jenkins clearly knew these Coprario pieces intimately and they were to prove a guiding star as he turned from writing traditional viol consorts to seek new colours and forms. In later years the fantasia-suite took pride of place in his own output and his impressive series of pieces in this genre incorporate a number of new developments. Sir Nicholas' notes show that Jenkins had made the organ parts of Coprario's suites at Hunstanton before the Derham texts were consulted. Sir Nicholas himself checked Jenkins' text with the Derham readings, recording the differences in music examples headed 'False and Doubtfull Places betwixt mr Derhams and my Organ Booke'.[84]

Invaluable though the L'Estrange manuscripts are for their musical contents, it is the annotations which make them uniquely important and beneficial to modern scholarship. In British Library, Add. MSS 39550–4, and Royal College of Music, MS 1145, these comments were at first perfunctory, increasing in elaboration as Sir Nicholas and his scribes searched for ever more perfect texts. But these

[83] Sir Thomas Derham died in May 1645.

[84] British Library, Add. MS 23779, ff. 63v–64.

two manuscripts do not yet contain the kind of remarks guiding performers or commenting upon notation like those in the Newberry books or in British Library, Add. MS 23779 mentioned below. Some of them, no doubt, are reminders, some concern corrections, but those on notation in particular suggest that the Newberry books (which can be dated from Sir Nicholas' remarks quoted earlier) and Add. MS 23779 date from soon after Jenkins' arrival. Why should Sir Nicholas give such detailed and elementary instruction to one of the major musical figures of his time – for these annotations all refer to Jenkins' copying? Would it be that Jenkins was new to the establishment and Sir Nicholas was offering him guidance as to how he liked things done at Hunstanton, having by this time developed particular views on how his music manuscripts were to be prepared?

> [*Newberry, Case MS VM.1.A.18.J.52c*]
> PA:46;Li:3.NO:15. In such a case as this, though the Notes be divided by the straines, yet Allowed to b or # the next Note, according to the common Rule.
>
> To All b or # tyed and Bound Notes, set the b or # only to the first Note: as Pag:35:L:4:NO:8 and P.47:L3:N:6: unlesse another Line or Page Intervene; then to b or # Both is Veniall; not of Necessitie.
>
> Prick no more Tripletts with black sembreves, as Pag: 5: and pag:53
>
> [*Add. MS 23779*]
> Places where b[s] and #[s] should be Affixt, (by my Rule of one Note betwixt) in respect of Distance, as to bting or #ping the Third Note: but not so proper and so forborne, because the Precedent and subseque[nt] Notes (though standing in one and the same pl[ace] yet spring or flow from severall parts; as from the B[ass] into the Meane, the Meane to the Base or the like. [Followed by a Table].
>
> Rarely that any Cleffe in D (unlesse # in F and C) key is Prickt without a b in B, but there being little odds in the

> number of Bbs and #s in the 7 Fancy, it may, passe as it is; if any change be upon faire Pricking, Flatt the Cleffe upon the 5: sembr: (and so to the end) Pag: 118:Lin: 4:Bar:8: The 7. Alm: and 7 Gal: may passe as they are, without any Alteration.
>
> The 8th Fancy is as the last. But upon Faire-Pricking, if any Change be; Flatt the Cleffe in B unto the 41 or rather 43 Sem-Breve, (Pag:124.Lin:2.Bar.I.Note 3d Low). There # the Cliff in F. and C. unto the 84 semBr: (Pag: 124.Li: 5:Bar:7.Note 2d) and from thence b it againe as Before, unto the end. The 8th ALM: may Passe as it is; Little Odds of s and s. The 8th GAL: also may Passe as it is; (the Odds of bs and #s not much) if any Change, b the Cleffe of the 2d straine.

Comments such as these show Sir Nicholas to have been a fastidious, even fussy, man. He evidently liked order, not only in such details, but equally in the distribution of the music. The beautiful scores copied by Jenkins arrange frequently haphazard sequences in the part-books into neat packets of pieces always in the same key-order: G minor, G major, D minor, D major, A minor, E minor, C minor, C major, F major, B flat major.

It would also appear that Sir Nicholas asked Jenkins to compose fresh pieces to ensure that each tonic was represented by a suitable selection of pieces.[85] This arrangement is at its tidiest in the seven groups of three fantasias making up Add. MS 31428 and in the eight sets of four pieces forming the series of 'Ayres' for two trebles, two basses and organ.[86] Though the later is absent from the surviving L'Estrange manuscripts, there can be little doubt that it was composed during the 1640s, for among the pieces is one called 'Newark Siedge'. At first it seems curious that Jenkins chose this event rather than the siege

[85] See Andrew Ashbee, 'Towards the Chronology and Grouping', especially p. 37. Sometimes the major-minor order is reversed.

[86] The 'Ayres' are published, ed. Andrew Ashbee, in 'John Jenkins: Consort Music of Four Parts', *Musica Britannica,* Vol. XXVI, Stainer & Bell, London, 1969, rev. ed. 1975, Nos. 1–32.

of Lynn, which was much closer to home. But Lynn, after all, was a Royalist defeat, and its moment of glory short-lived, while Newark had proved an indefatigable stronghold and rallying point for the Royalists throughout the Civil War. When, with Prince Rupert's intervention, the Parliamentarian besiegers were forced to abandon their positions and retreat, following the sharp battle on 21 March 1644, morale among the King's supporters must have received a tremendous boost. No wonder Jenkins seized this opportunity to cheer his Royalist patrons. Newark remained among the last pockets of resistance to the Roundheads, finally surrendering on 8 May 1646, by which time the War was virtually over.

Meanwhile, some nine months earlier, at Chester, the rout of the Royalist forces had dealt a severe blow to English music with the death of William Lawes, Jenkins's greatest contemporary, who was struck down in the mêlée. Poets and musicians joined in composing a series of elegies to him which were printed in a memorial volume compiled by his brother Henry[87] and boldly dedicated to the captive Charles I. Jenkins' 'Elegiack Dialogue on the sad losse of his much esteemed friend Mr. William Lawes, servant to His Majesty' is among the most elaborate and best of these tributes to one

> Who with harmonious numbers tame,
> could keep the Nemian Lion,
> force the Panther weep, melt the hard marble,
> [...] who nimbly hurl'd seraphick raptures
> and so charm'd th'incircled aire
> grew proud t'aspire, and court the spheres
> with musique of his lyre [...].

The text is doubtless the composer's own, for, as North says, he 'often proffered at poetry'; certainly the style is compatible with his known work. Another song by

[87] Henry Lawes and William Lawes, *Choice Psalms*, London, 1648.

Jenkins surely must also date from this time, although it was not published until 1672:[88]

> When fair Aurora from her purple bed arose
> and saw this Island drenched deep in gore;
> she wept
> and straight withdrew her rosy head,
> minding to see this mournful earth no more;
> Till that bright Star which ushers her,
> shall bring tidings of peace
> and Blessings in a King.

The sentiments here echo the actions of many of the King's supporters, particularly in an area like Norfolk where the strength of the Eastern Association defied any effective action to undermine Parliament's authority. The L'Estranges, Derhams and others had done what they could for the King, but could not break the grip of the Association. For years afterwards they were subject to crucifying taxes and monetary demands which left them impoverished. All they could do in the circumstances was to salvage what they could of their homes and estates, 'withdraw' their heads and look for 'tidings of peace and blessings in a King'. That music could be a solace at such times, they found ample proof:

> The Fantazia manner held thro' [...] the troubles; and when most other good arts languished Musick held up her head [...] in private society, for many chose rather to fidle at home, than to go out, and be knockt on the head abroad; and the entertainment was very much courted and made use of, not onely in country but citty familys, in which many of the Ladys were good consortiers.[89]

Even allowing for the various escapades undertaken by the L'Estranges and Derhams on the King's behalf, there is no reason to suppose that the internal social life of their houses was disrupted much beyond those few weeks

[88] John Playford, *The Musical Companion*, London, 1672, p. 106.

[89] North, *op. cit.*, p. 294.

of feverish activity, and the music manuscripts suggest that Jenkins was kept busy copying and composing. Many of the pieces require extraordinary virtuosity from two or three players and it is a shame that which of Jenkins' patrons or associates were capable of joining him in this demanding music remains unknown. Roger L'Estrange is said to have had a 'tolerable perfection' on the bass viol, but he was absent throughout this period. Clearly the musical resources at West Dereham and Hunstanton allowed performances of the virtuoso pieces in Royal College of Music MS 921 and it seems likely that most, if not all of Jenkins's brilliant fantasia-suites[90] (known today only in manuscripts of a later date) were also written for performance there. Elsewhere the majority, like the anonymous gentleman in Sir Nicholas's story, would have had to pass by these marvellous works, which partly explains why they survive in so few sources.

> A Gentleman being proffered his part upon the viole of an Aire which had many 𝄿 and some 𝅀 Rests, and full of a stirring Division; Excused Himselfe Thus, Vipers Tongues are Dangerous, I dare not come neere them; Besides, I see the Air Growes so Blacke, as I know there is a Storme and Tempest comming, and no Shelter or Refuge left for me, but your Indulgence and Dispensation from so Perillous a Taske.[91]

North remarks that 'in his latter time [Jenkins] could compose no otherwise than to the capacity of his performers, who could not deal with his high flying vein'.[92] But throughout his career he provided music for all shades of technique, and the 'horsloads' of dances transcribed into manuscripts like Christ Church MS 1005 were to prove a fruitful hunting-ground for John Playford – himself a Norfolk man – as he embarked on publishing

[90] Gordon Dodd (ed.), *Thematic Index of Music for Viols*, Viola da Gamba Society of Great Britain, London, 1980–7, Groups II, IV and VI.

[91] British Library, Harleian MS 6395, No. 589.

[92] *Op. cit.*, p. 347.

his series of music books 'fitted to the capacity of young practitioners'. The carrier of this music was probably none other than 'Thomas Derham esq. of Derham Grange, co. Norfolk', who, in company with Dr. Charles Coleman, was a godparent to Playford's son Thomas, christened at the Temple church on 22 April 1656.[93]

There is no record of how long Jenkins continued in service with the Derhams and L'Estranges; Thomas Derham's friendship with Playford tantalisingly hints that music loomed large in the life of the West Dereham household, although nothing other than the references in the L'Estrange books has come to light.[94] By good fortune a delightful letter (dated 14 June 1653) from Sir Nicholas L'Estrange to Sir Justinian Isham (1611–75) has survived among the latter's correspondence, lifting the veil fractionally on life at Hunstanton.[95]

> Noble Sr,
>
> My presenting my selfe thus to your eye in a white sheet, may seeme an Apparition or Phantasme (our wicked Age abounding with such) or looke like a Resurrection from the Grave: I confesse, these Barbarous and Calamitous Times have Layd to sleepe many Gallant Heroes; Interred an Armie of Glorious Martyrs, whose very

[93] Playford came of a Norwich family. A third godparent was 'Mrs Alice Hare, sister to Sir Ralph Hare of Stow Hall, co. Norfolk, knt.' The next son, Henry, baptised at the Temple Church on 14 May 1657 had Henry Lawes and Henry Playford as godparents.

[94] Thomas Derham (1634–97), son of this Thomas, became 'Carrier of letters and other Dispatches from his Maties Court or Place of Residence unto ye office of Post Master Generall in Ordinary' in January 1671/2, and ambassador at Florence in 1681 (when he was knighted). It was presumably he who supplied the text beginning 'I know that my Redeemer lives' which was set by Matthew Locke. *Cf.* Rosamund E. M. Harding, *A Thematic Catalogue of the Works of Matthew Locke with a Calendar of the Main Events of His Life,* Blackwell, Oxford, 1971, pp. 18–9.

[95] Northants Record Office, Isham Correspondence (I.C.) No. 323. I am much indebted to Lynn Hulse for supplying all the information about these three letters and for other references to the people they mention.

> Names are Monuments without a Tombe; and Buried other Devout soules alive [...].
>
> But Sr, to unvayle, and throw off all Disguises [...], give me leave in plaine English to tell you, that (after the cloystering of many yeares) having the Libertie the other Day to change Aire into Suffolke, and to that place where first I had the honour and Happinesse of your Acquaintance; There I understood, that (after all the strange vicisitudes of Fortune that we have seene) you were still, God be Praysed, among the Living; The Newes was a very high cordiall to my Drooping Soule [...].

No doubt the movements of any members of the L'Estrange family were carefully monitored by Cromwell's men, particularly during the War, and Sir Nicholas' 'cloystering of many yeares' was the least provocative line he could take. But by 1653, with the fighting over, he felt able to venture out again; it is perhaps some indication of his isolation that the purpose of the letter was to express his delight in finding that an old friend was still alive.[96] His Royalist sympathies obviously remain intact – as does his wit. A postscript to the letter suggests it was at Pakenham that the two men first met – either at the home of Sir Nicholas' brother Hamon, or, more probably, at that of his sister Elizabeth, married to Sir William Spring.[97]

Some two miles to the east of Pakenham, at Stowlangtoft, lived John Stuteville, two of whose letters to the Isham family are also of special interest. On 11 November 1650, he wrote to his 'Cosin Jane':[98] 'it is

[96] A 'Mr Isham', presumably Sir Justinian, contributed story No. 366 in Sir Nicholas's jest book, which might have been entered *c.* 1640–42.

[97] To judge by Sir Nicholas' jest book (British Library, Harleian MS 6395), his relationship with the Springs was particularly close; they contributed 84 stories to the collection – more than anyone outside the immediate Hunstanton household. Sir William supplied many of the bawdy jests! These stories spread throughout the book, with particular density between Nos. 201 and 275 (pre-Civil War).

[98] Jane, daughter of Sir Justinian and Jane Isham (1635–55). The younger Jane's sister Elizabeth married Sir Nicholas L'Estrange 2nd bart. (and son of Sir Nicholas, 1st bart.) on 14 October 1662. The

Musick to mee to heare you have proceeded soe farre in Musical Progression', and adding: 'If any of Jenkins his 4 part lessons can pleasure you, you may comand them'.[99] Music was evidently enclosed with another letter, dated 19 October 1657, sent to Sir Justinian Isham at Lamport, whom he had recently visited:[100]

> [...] Sr. I have taken the paines to pricke out ye Bels, both Peters & Jenkins his, ye Treble & Base parts, & I pricked them together, that Mr King may the better play them off upon the Harpsicorne: if they shall give you any content, I shall not thinke my labrs lost, but shall bee ready to communicate what Suff[olk] affords [...].

Presumably Stuteville obtained Jenkins' music through one of the Pakenham families, though

> of all his [Jenkins'] conceipts, none flew about with his name so universally as the small peice called his *Bells*. In those days the country fidlers were not so well foddered from London as since, and a master that made new tunes for them was a benefactor; and these *Bells* was such supply, as never failed to pass in all companys [...].[101]

In 1652 the title-page of Edward Benlowes' poem *Theophila* announced that 'Several parts thereof [were] set to fit aires by Mr. J. Jenkins'. Edward Benlowes (*c.*

---

match was suggested to John Stuteville by Lady Elizabeth Spring, and he endorsed the proposal, forwarding it to Sir Justinian.

99 Northant Record Office, Isham Correspondence (IC) No. 290.

100 *Ibid.*, (I.C.) No. 434.

101 North, *op. cit.*, p. 346. Playford published the piece as 'Lady Katharine Audley's Bells' in *Courtly Masquing Ayres* (1662), and I suspect the title was his since it does not appear thus elsewhere. On the mediaeval legend of St Katherine of Ledbury, Herefordshire, *cf.* Rev. Hugh Mountney, 'Lady Katherine Audley's Bells', *Bulletin of the Viola da Gamba Society*, 19, June 1963, pp. 4–7. Other sources for the piece are noted in Gordon Dodd, *A Thematic Index of Music for Viols*, pp. 121 and 128. In three sources 'St. Peter's Bells' are found nearby: Bodleian Library, Mus. Sch. MS D.220; Chetham's Library, Manchester, MUS MUN. MS A.2.6; Library of the School of Music, Yale University, New Haven, Connecticut, Filmer MS 3.

1603–76) was the son and heir of Andrew Benlowes of Brent Hall, Finchingfield, Essex, and he inherited the estate on the death of his father. Yet Wood notes that

> being a very imprudent man in matters of worldly concern, and ignorant as to the value or want of money [...], he did squander it (his estate and £700 a year) mostly away on Poets, Flatterers which he loved, in buying of Curiosities (which some call Baubles), on Musicians, Buffoons, etc [...]. He also very imprudently entered himself into Bonds for the payment of other men's debts; which, he not being able to do, he was committed to Prison in Oxford. [...] After he had been courted and Admired for his ancient Extraction, Education and Parts by Great Men of the Nation, who had been a Patron to several ingenious Men in their necessities [...], did spend his last days at Oxon; but little better than in obscure condition.[102]

Wood's comments paint a rather misleading picture. True, Benlowes was a somewhat visionary figure who set his sights beyond the world at large and, as such, made frequent financial miscalculations, but it was his ill-fortune that, on top of penalties resulting from sequestration of his estate – he too had been an active Royalist – Brent Hall was totally destroyed by fire in 1653. He lost all his personal possessions, including a stock of *Theophila*, his *magnum opus*, on which he had lavished so much expense and care, and he was to remain impoverished for the rest of his days. Wood's suggestion that Jenkins 'had been favoured much and patronised by Benevolus' may be no more than guess-work arising from the title-page, although it is true that Benlowes could count many distinguished men of culture among his friends.[103] No

[102] Wood, *Fasti Oxoniensis*, p. 359; *cf.* note 1, p. 13.

[103] *Cf.* Harold Jenkins, *Edward Benlowes*, Athlone Press, University of London, London, 1952, for an excellent account of the poet. Jenkins the writer found no evidence to show that Jenkins the composer stayed at Brent Hall, but draws attention to a musician called William Collins who may have been resident there. Among Benlowes' other

settings from *Theophila* have been identified among the composer's extant vocal music and it is likely that they perished in the Brent Hall fire. Yet there is an intriguing detail.

Benlowes evidently gave special presentation copies of *Theophila*, individually inscribed with his own exquisite penmanship, to particular friends. One surviving copy is headed 'For the trulie Noble Tho Durham Esq.' Surely this is Jenkins's patron, for, if Benlowes was friendly with Thomas Derham (the corrupt spelling 'Durham' is common in seventeenth-century sources), this acquaintance would explain how the composer became involved in setting parts of the poem.[104]

It must have been about this time, too, that Jenkins taught one Joseph Procter, whose death in Oxford on 22 July 1656 is recorded by Wood:

> Procter died in Halywell; and was buried in the church there. He had been bred up in the faculty of musick by Mr. John Jenkyns (the mirrour and wonder of his age for musick); was excellent for the lyra-viol and division-viol, good at the treble-viol and treble violin; and all comprehended in a man of three or four and twentie yeares of age. He was much admired at the meetings, and exceedingly pittied by all the faculty for his loss.[105]

A number of factors hint that Jenkins may have had more than a passing contact with the composer Christopher Simpson and his patron Sir Robert Bolles at Scampton in Lincolnshire. Bolles and Roger L'Estrange may have become acquainted when both attended Sidney Sussex College, Cambridge, in the mid-1630s. Though Roger fled to the continent in 1648 and did not return until August 1653, the Royalist sympathies of both families are likely to have bound them together during the

---

friends were the poets Phineas Fletcher, Francis Quarles and William Davenant.

[104] H. Jenkins, *op. cit.*, p. 232n.

[105] *Life and Times*, vol. I, p. 208. Andrew Clarke notes the burial entry.

Commonwealth. Certainly Roger calls Sir Robert his 'Familiar Friend' in commending Simpson's second edition of *The Division Viol* (1667) and in return received Bolles' 'silver possett Cupp with all the things belonging to it' from his widow in 1672. If Jenkins did stay at Scampton for a while, then the early 1650s seems the most likely time. North's remark that 'I never heard that he [Jenkins] articled with any gentleman where he resided, but accepted what they gave him'[106] suggests that the composer arranged his itinerary as circumstances dictated.

The elusive figure of John Barnard, perhaps the lay clerk from St Paul's Cathedral, adds a little to a bond between Jenkins and Bolles. Barnard has been suggested as associated with the copyist of three extant sets of viol books,[107] and a lost 'Barnard Score B:' was a major source from which Sir Nicholas L'Estrange gleaned five- and six-part consorts, including some of Jenkins' five-part fantasias, in what is now Royal College of Music, MS 1145. Above Nos. 15 and 16 in British Library, Add. MS 30487, a collection of all but two of Jenkins's five-part pieces, the copyist – tentatively identified as Barnard – has noted: 'This fancy is in Sr Robt Bowles his bookes wch I prickt in gamut key' and (a similar note) 'in B my key'.[108]

A further link in the chain is provided by the large collection of music manuscripts from the North family at Kirtling now mostly housed in the Bodleian Library, Oxford. This consists predominantly of Jenkins' music, but a small set of fantasias by Thomas Brewer (Mus. Sch. MS C.100) is likely to have made the journey from Hunstanton to Kirtling in Jenkins' portfolio. Four other fantasias for treble, two basses and organ by the obscure

[106] *Op. cit.*, p. 344.

[107] British Library, Add. Ms 30487: Library of Congress, Washington, MS M990.C66F4 (Vols. 1 and 2). *Cf.* Gordon Dodd, 'The Coprario-Lupo Five-part Books at Washington', *Chelys*, 1, 1969, pp. 36–40.

[108] Gordon Dodd (ed.), *Thematic Index of Music for Viols*, Fantasias Nos. 5 and 6. *Cf.* Chapter Six, pp. 245–7.

composer Richard Cooke are tucked away at the end of Jenkins' large set of similarly-scored pieces in Mus. Sch. MSS E.406–9. These books are dated 1654 and are believed to be among the earliest manuscripts in the collection.[109] The possibility that these pieces too were brought to Kirtling by Jenkins prompts an investigation into Cooke's life and work. The only other pieces currently known by him are some two-part airs first published by Playford in 1651.[110] According to Anthony Wood – our only informant – Richard Cooke

> was taken into the patronage of Sir Robert Bolles of [blank] in Lincolnshire, Bart., a great encourager of music in the times of affliction and sequestration and lived in his family with Christopher Simpson several years.[111]

It appears that at one stage Wood muddled him up with Captain Henry Cooke, from whose entry he deleted the following:

> at which time [after the wars] he had little left to maintain him, he was taken into the patronage of Sir Robert Bolles of [blank] who, being a most singular encourager of music, abode there also as before and after musicians John Jenkins, Christopher Sympson.[112]

Mention of Jenkins here is intriguing, but no reference to him or to Cooke has yet surfaced from the Scampton records.[113]

Nevertheless, Jenkins wrote commendations for both

[109] *Cf.* Margaret Crum, 'The Consort Music from Kirtling, bought for the Oxford Music School from Anthony Wood, 1667', *Chelys*, 4, 1972, pp. 3–10.

[110] *A Musicall Banquet* (1651); *Court Ayres* (1655); *Courtly Masquing Ayres* (1662).

[111] Bodleian Library, Wood MS D 19(4), f. 39.

[112] *Ibid.*, f. 37v.

[113] I am much indebted to Dr Margaret Urquhart who has kept me in touch with her research into Christopher Simpson and the Bolles family; *cf.* her 'Sir Robert Bolles Bt. of Scampton', *Chelys*, 16, 1987, pp. 16–29.

of Simpson's published books. Prefacing the first edition of *The Division-Violist* (1659) is a neatly-turned poem 'To his Excellent Friend Mr. Christopher Simpson, upon his most accurate Treatise of Division to a Ground':

Great Soul of Musick, who shall Sing Thy Praise
Give thee loud Plaudits; circle thee with Bayes;
Crown thy soft Numbers; who, at least incline
To treat or descant on this Treat of Thine?
For he that speaks thee home, 'tis fit he be
Familiar with Thy Soul, thy Worke, and Thee.

Some happy few that know, some that know not
Thy Worth, promiscuously throw in their Vote;
And why not I, who by Inspection see,
My Optick's clear by a Reflex from Thee.
Mix me i'th Chorus then, since to thy Praise
I bring no Flattery; Truth's my only Baise.

Thou art no God, and yet thou seem'st to be
A near Resemblance of some Deitie.
Witness that Excellent Scheme, thy Musick Sphere,
And those thy well composed Months o'th Yeere;
Which Months thy pregnant Muse hath richly drest,
And to each Month hath made a Musick-Feast,
Wherein the Graces do so subt'ly Play
As they conclude twelve Months within one Day.

And having rais'd this handsome Frame of thine
Thou also givest, Method and Designe
To work by: Rules to perfect, that t'will be
Stil'd Simpson's Grammar unto Harmony;
By which the Ingenious Scholar is both taught
To Play, and imitate what Thou hast wrought.

Pack hence you Pedants then, such as do bragg
of Knowledge, Hand, or Notes; yet not one Ragg
Of Musick have, more than what got by Theft,
Nor know true Posture of Right hand or Left;
False fingered Crew, who seem to understand,
Pretend to make when you but marre a hand.
You may desist, you'l find your Trade decay;
Simpson's great Work will teach the World to play.

How far Jenkins 'encouraged and probably assisted Mr Sympson in his edition of *The Devision Violist*'[114] is open to question, but certainly by 1659 the integration and exploitation of division techniques within fantasia-suites, as described by Simpson, is due more to Jenkins' example and influence than to any other composer; Simpson acknowledges as much in his conclusion:

> In these several sorts of Division of two and three Parts, my self, amonst others more eminent, have made divers Compositions, which perhaps might be useful to young Musicians, either for their Imitation or Practice: but the Charge of Printing Divisions (as I have experienced in the Cuts of the Examples in this present Book) doth make that kind of Musick less communicable. Howbeit, if you desire written Copies of that sort, (a thing most necessary for those who intend to Compose such like themselves) none has done so much in that kind, as the ever Famous and most Excellent Composer, in all sorts of modern Musick, Mr. John Jenkins.[115]

Both Matthew Locke and Jenkins wrote recommendations for the second edition of Simpson's *Compendium of Practical Musick* (1667).[116] Jenkins heads his letter 'To his much honoured and very precious friend, Mr. Christopher Simpson' and continues:

> Sir,
>
> Having perused your excellent *Compendium of Music* so far as my time and your pressing occasion could permit, I confess it my greatest concern to thank you for the product of so ingenious a work as tends to the improvement of the whole frame (I mean as to the least and most knowing capacities in the rudiments of that science). To speak in a word, the subject, matter, method, the platform and rational materials wherewith you raise and beautify this piece

114 North, *op. cit.*, p. 295.

115 *The Division-Viol* (1667), p. 61.

116 There is a modern transcription by Phillip Lord, B. H. Blackwell, Oxford, 1970.

Catledge (Kirtling) Hall, c. 1800, from a drawing by J. R. Thompson (courtesy of the British Library)

are such as will erect a lasting monument to the author and oblige the world as much to serve him, as he that is,

Sir,

Your most affectionate friend and servant,

JOHN JENKINS

By this time Jenkins, aged 75, had virtually reached the end of his teaching life and one senses that the old dog was unlikely to take up this new trick. He had recently been instructing young Roger North and had lent him 'Butler, with a comendation of it that it was the best in the kind'.[117] Although North later bought both Simpson books, and others by Playford and Morley, he persisted in praising Butler (against most contemporary and later opinion): 'I doe not know another in any language comparable to it'.[118]

Jenkins' association with the North family presumably

[117] Charles Butler, *Principles of Musik* (1636). *Cf.* also p. 97.

[118] *Op. cit.*, p. 137.

dates back to at least 1654, when the family's fine collection of his music began to be assembled,[119] and Kirtling seems to have remained his base until late in 1666, though apparently he continued to come and go as circumstances dictated. Certainly there was at least one major interlude in the early 1660s, when he took up his duties at the Restoration Court. The vivid reminiscences of Jenkins' most famous pupil, Roger North (*c.* 1651–1734), concerning his own musical upbringing at Kirtling, portray not only the musical aspirations of his family, but also present an endearing picture of Jenkins in the hierarchy of the establishment.

It was Roger's grandfather, Dudley the third Lord North who, having taken a liking to music while or a visit to Italy early in the century, had created 'a society of musick, such as was well esteemed in those time'. On 16 June 1658, Dudley wrote:

> God who had formerly raised unexpectedly some Musique unto me, hath since, after more than twenty years not touching an Instrument, restored me to take in hand for my pastime, (which hath proved a very useful divertisement to me), the Viol: and therein to do as much for my part as that little which ever I could. My Sons Children and their Masters have produced singing; and variety in that kind being the greatest delight of it, I fell by occasion and degrees to frame some words for composition and Consort [...].[120]

Roger was still an infant, but the other grandchildren were able to join in the instrumental as well as the vocal items:

> He [Dudley] played on that antiquated instrument called the treble viol, now abrogated wholly by the use of the violin; and not onely his eldest son, my father, who for the most part resided with him, play'd, but his eldest son

[119] *Cf.* Margaret Crum, 'The Consort Music from Kirtling'.

[120] *A Forest Promiscuous of Several Seasons Productions*, London, 1659, p. 311.

> Charles, and younger son the Lord Keeper, most exquisitely and judiciously. And he kept an organist in the house, which was seldome without a profes't musick master. And the servants of parade, as gentlemen ushers, and the steward, and clerck of the kitchen also play'd; which with the yong ladys my sisters singing, made a society of musick, such as was well esteemed in those times. And the course of the family was to have solemne musick 3 days in the week, and often every day, as masters supply'd noveltys for the enterteinement of the old lord. And on Sunday night, voices to the organ were a constant practise, and at other times symphonys intermixt with the instruments. [...] The consorts were usually all viols to the organ or harpsicord. The violin came in late, and imperfectly. When the hands were well supply'd, then a whole chest went to work, that is 6 violls, musick being formed for it [...].[121]

In fine weather music was sometimes made out of doors:

> This good old lord took a fancy to a wood he had about a mile from his house, called Bansteads, scituate in a durty soyl, and of ill access. But he cut glades, and made arbours in it, and no name would fit the place but *Tempe*. Here he would convoque his musicall family, and songs were made and sett for celebrating the joys there, which were performed, and provisions carried up for more important regale of the company.[122]

Texts of a number of the Bansteads songs, 'framed' by Dudley himself, were printed in his collection entitled *A Forest Promiscuous of Several Seasons Productions*, where he gives his own account of the site:

> I met within my little remaining limits near to my dwelling with either an open airey, or covert access; a parcel of delectable grounds graced with intermixture of pastures, woods, meadows, opportunity for waters, standing and flowing which much affected me; where I made a little shelter or grange against rain, between too paralel woods

[121] Roger North, *op. cit.*, pp. 10–11.

[122] *Ibid.*

> each within a small stone's cast of the grange, the one lately grown up, where are walks and seats to hear singing of Birds or voices, and turning at one end to a perspective, our Meadows, and through a pass of another wood by God's grace of like voluntary growth to reach a further great one. The other siding wood at equal distance is more ancient, having now a walk cross the nearest end, and divides plain and green grounds. In an obscure part of a little entertaining room is this inscription: *Inspinata auspicio Divino Tempe* [...].[123]

The book also includes texts of songs by Jenkins, but which of these were sung at Bansteads is unclear.[124] In a letter dated 28 August 1658, Dudley praises Jenkins

> whose infinitely flowing vein, in all kinds, I have as much admired, as been delighted in: but his Fashion promises no less; Spirit, Garb, and Air, shine in his first appearance. At his being with me lately, we had some speech of Fantasies, which he expressed capable enough to carry Air in their current [...].[125]

Among the other musicians in attendance at Kirtling were the organists Henry and George Loosemore and John Lillie the violist, all from Cambridge. Francis North (1637–85), Roger's elder brother, was a skilled performer on the bass viol and also attempted composition although, as Roger remarks, 'it was not to be expected he should surmount the style and mode of the great musick master Mr Jenkins, then in use where he came'. Around 1655 Francis moved to the Middle Temple, London, and embarked on what was to prove a distinguished career as a lawyer, but he would have delighted in the family music-making whenever he returned home.[126] Among

[123] *Op. cit.*, p. 307.

[124] *Cf.* also Bodleian Library, MS North e.37, which includes the bass part of an Echo corant 'to the Sherp Sute of Bansteds Ayres' by George Loosemore.

[125] From *A Forest Promiscuous*; *cf.* Roger North, *op. cit.*, p. 4.

[126] Pieces by him are in Bodleian Library, MS North e.37.

the servants particular attention might be paid to Francis White

> or perhaps Blanc, turned into English [...], a brisk gay spark that had bin bredd at court (such as it was) a page to Sr John Danvers [1588?-1655], one of the King's judges. He could dance, sing, and play very neatly on the violin, was good company, and served as a gentleman waiter, and was most acceptable in his musicall capacity.[127]

White, in fact, was steward at Kirtling and one wonders whether he copied any of the music manuscripts, remembering that the composer George Jefferies held a similar post in the household of Dudley North's brother-in-law, Sir Christopher Hatton, at Kirby, Northamptonshire.

Whatever Jenkins' connections with Kirtling in the 1650s, the new decade brought new responsibilities. Following the death of Cromwell, the 'unfriendly time' (in Dudley North's phrase) limped rudderless to its end, and on 8 May 1660 Parliament proclaimed the exiled Charles King. He landed at Dover on 23 May and made a triumphal progress to London, entering the city six days later. Even John Evelyn, whose *Diary* is normally so reserved in tone, waxed eloquent as he beheld the scene:

> This day, his Majesty, Charles the Second came to London, after a sad and long exile and calamitous suffering both of the King and Church, being seventeen years. This was also his birth-day, and with a triumph of above 20,000 horse and foot, brandishing their swords, and shouting with inexpressible joy; the ways strawed with flowers, the bells ringing, the streets hung with tapestry, fountains running with wine; the Mayor, aldermen, all the companies in their liveries, chains of gold, banners; lords and nobles, cloth of silver, gold and velvet, everybody clad in, the windows and balconies all set with ladies, trumpets, music and myriads of people flocking the streets, and was as far as Rochester, so as they were seven hours in passing the city, even from two in the afternoon till nine at night.

127 Roger North, *op. cit.*, p. 10. Some autograph letters of White survive at the Bodleian Library.

> I stood in the Strand, and beheld it, and blessed God [...]. Such a restoration [...], nor so joyful a day and so bright ever seen in this nation, this happening when to expect or effect it was past all human policy.[128]

Amid all the rejoicing was there among the musicians, one wonders, a Joseph able to foretell the years of financial famine which lay ahead?

Yet in June 1660 all seemed full of promise. No time was lost in re-constituting the court music. Former court musicians had their places restored and others were called to fill vacancies. Twelve new places for the violin consort showed where Charles' musical preferences lay. Thus, during the summer months, a whole succession of musicians came to Whitehall to take the oath and be admitted as members of the Royal Household. Among the earliest of them, on 19 June

> John Jenkins was sworne one of his Maties private Musick in the place of John Cocshall, by the Gent. Usher dayly wayters.[129]

The group of instrumentalists at court were known collectively as 'The King's Musick'; one contemporary list notes 'the recorders, the flutes, the hoboyes & sackbutts, the violins, the lutes & voyces, the trumpeters, drummers and fife'. The 'Private Musick' performed expressly for the King and, though built on the group known as the 'lutes, viols and voices', also included distinguished composers, violinists and keyboard players. Each group would have its own duties: concerts, dances, masques, Divine Service, dinner, plays (and, in due time, opera), or ceremonial gatherings all required music. A chosen few gave musical instruction to Royal children, or had charge of training and keeping boy apprentices. Each 'place' as a Royal musician carried with it an annual fee and a livery allowance, though some appointments were made 'with-

128 Evelyn's *Diary*, 29 June 1660.

129 Public Record Office, LC 3/33.

out fee', or 'extraordinary', whose occupants no doubt hoped for preferment later. Most court musicians were entitled to an annual income of between £40 and £60, but some were especially favoured by a higher fee – up to £200 – by allowances for training and keeping boys, or by the grant of more than one place, with the attendant increase in salary. A list made in about 1675 (but serving adequately for the whole Restoration period) puts the annual expense of maintaining the King's Musick at £5011. 19s.,[130] although additional charges arising when, for instance, a group of musicians was called to do duty outside London, or for instruments, music copying and similar incidental expenses, would push this figure very much higher.

An incredibly complex administrative jungle confronts the scholar as he attempts to map the lives of the Royal musicians from the plethora of court records still remaining. Only when the King had personally given his authority, expressed by one of the forms of Royal warrant, could a musician's appointment be confirmed, or he be paid. There were more pressing affairs than music requiring the King's attention in the first months of his reign, but on 31 December 1660 there was an order from the Lord Chamberlain to

> the Clerk of the Signet attendinge to prepare a Bill fit for his Maties Royal signature containing a grant unto John Jenkins one of his Maties Musicians in ordinary in the roome of John Coggeshall deceased with the yearly Fee of Forty pounds and unto John Lilly in the rooms of John Kelly in ordinary deceased with the like yearely Fee of fourty pounds payable out of his Ma:tis Excheqr to them severally respectively dureinge theire naturall lives, quarterly by even and equall porcions, that is to say at the feast of St. Michaell the archangel, the nativity of our Lord God, the annuncón of our blessed Lady the virgin

130 British Library, Add. MS 28080, f. 50v.

Charles II's 'Private Musick for Lutes, violls and voices' (1660-64)

Voices
Nicholas Lanier
Henry Cooke (Bass) (who also had responsibility for two boys)
John Harding (Bass)
Gregory Thorndell (Bass)
Alphonso Marsh (Tenor)
Edward Coleman (Tenor or Counter-tenor)
Stafford Darcy (Tenor)
Nathaniel Watkins (Counter-tenor)
John Clements (Counter-tenor)
Anthony Robert (Counter-tenor)
Henry Lawes (Counter-tenor) (replaced by Thomas Purcell, 1662)

Viols
Charles Coleman, senior and junior
William Gregory, senior and junior
Thomas Bates (Bass viol)
John Smith (Bass viol)
John Hingeston (Bass viol)
Henry Hawes (Bass viol)
Dietrich and Frederick William Steffkins (Bass viol)
Paul Bridges (Viol da Gamba)

Lutes
Lewis Evans (perhaps also Harp)
John Wilson
John Singleton (Theorbo)
John Jenkins (Theorbo)
John Lillie (Theorbo)
John Rogers (Treble lute)
William Howes (Treble lute)

Virginals
Giles Tomkins
Christopher Gibbons

Violins
Thomas Baltzar (1661–63)
Davis Mell (1660–62)
then
John Bannister (1662–79)

Composers
Matthew Locke
Henry Lawes (1660–62), then Charles Coleman (1662–64), then Henry Cooke

Musicians often bought instruments which they would use and reclaimed the purchase price from the Treasurer of the Chamber. These are usually named specifically in the warrants. The types of voice in the above list (when not specified in the documents) have been deduced in part from singers' predecessors or successors – assuming the place to be for a tenor, a bass, etc.

> and the Feast of St. John the Baptist last past, before the date hereof December 31st 1660.[131]

Even so, it was not until 5 February 1662 that the all-important Letters Patent were granted to Jenkins and a further fifteen months then elapsed until, on 20 May 1663, he received his first salary payment for the six months ending at Christmas 1660.

In the meantime a similar warrant had to be obtained in respect of his livery and on 17 July 1662 the Lord Chamberlain asked William Rumbold, Clerk of his Majesty's Great Wardrobe, to prepare one for the King's signature.[132] This procedure too took time, but was forwarded by the Lord Chamberlain to the Great Wardrobe on 4 November that year. It required that the musician should receive annually

> fourteen yards of Chamblet for a Gowne, three yards of black velvett to gard the same Gowne, One Furre of Budge for the same price foure pounds, [...] eight yards of Damaske for a Jacquet and three yards of velvett for a doublett [...].[133]

Although Jenkins' name appears regularly in the lists of court musicians until early in 1678, he was becoming too old to give more than token service. Roger North writes:

> He kept his places at Court, as I understand to the time of his death; and tho' he for many years was uncapable to attend, the court musitians had so much value for him, that advantages was not taken, but he received his salary as they were payd.[134]

Yet Jenkins' signature acknowledging receipt of his livery due at St Andrew 1661, but certainly not paid until after the November 1662 warrant could be produced, confirms

131 Public Record Office, LC 5/137, p. 246.

132 Public Record Office, LC 3/33, p. 74.

133 Public Record Office, LC 5/52, pp. 202–3.

134 *Op. cit.*, p. 344.

that he did spend some time at Whitehall.[135] Curiously, what appears to have been his signature receipting his 1662 livery has been wiped from the book, mute testimony no doubt to the confusion brought about by the chronic delays in paying these allowances.

In the year ending 29 September 1665, the declared accounts of the Treasurer or the Chamber record:

> to John Jenkin his Mats Musicón for the Lute, for strings by him bought and provided for one yeare ended at Midsummer 1661 by [...] warrant dated the 16th of July 1661: £20.[136]

A few other musicians – John Bannister, Thomas Baltzar, Charles Coleman and Henry Cooke – also received allowances for strings in addition to their salaries and liveries. That only one such payment appears to have been made to Jenkins again implies that the composer took little active part in the Royal service.

Yet he was at the height of his fame, worthy to be mentioned among the best lutenists of his time. Among his contemporaries at court was the lutenist John Rogers, who may have been the author of a Restoration tutor for the instrument used by Elizabeth Burwell.[137] In reviewing the 'severall Moodes and Tuneings of the Lute', he includes one by Jenkins:[138]

> Mr Jenkins alters all the Bases after a way of his owne because he uses a string more than the french which is the Twelfth. Hee tuneth the twelfth agreeable to our Eleaventh, The Eleaventh like unto our Tenth and soe the rest

[135] Public Record Office, LC 9/195, f. 21r.

[136] Public Record Office, E351/546, f. 40r and LC 5/137, p. 76. The latter has 'flute' in error for 'lute'.

[137] Facsimile, *The Burwell Lute Tutor,* with introduction by Robert Spencer, Boethius Press, Leeds, 1974. *Cf.* also R. Thurston Dart, 'Miss Mary Burwell's Instruction Book for the Lute', *Galpin Society Journal,* XI, 1958, pp. 3–62.

[138] *The Burwell Lute Tutor,* ff. 12v–13r.

> to the Sixth which is tuned like the ordinary Trumpet Tuneing [...].

By 1663 Jenkins would have attained his biblical 'three-score years and ten' and he seems to have felt that the time had come for him to withdraw from playing an active part at court. Whatever the reason, he placed his affairs in the hands of friends and appears to have retired again to Kirtling. Among the Lord Chamberlain's records are the official copies of two letters written by the composer. The first[139] dates from February 1663:

> I do hereby give full power and lawefull authority to my good Freind John Fisher gent. to receive my Debenturs from tyme to tyme from William Rumbold Esqr to enable him to receive my Liverie of Sixeteene poundes two shillings and sixe pence paieable out of his Maties great Wardrobe. Wittnesse my hand and Seale the 7th day of Februarie in the Fifteenth yeare of the Reigne of our Soveraigne Lord the King
>
> signed
>
> John Jenkins
>
> Sealed and delivered in
> the presence of
> John Lillie
> Thomas Batzor

Who this John Fisher was is unclear, but a man of that name was Auditor of the Duchy of Cornwall and thus singularly well placed to keep watch for a friend on the troubled financial affairs of the early Restoration court. Two or three John Fishers can be traced in Westminster records of the 1660s, of whom the most prominent was the well-to-do (and therefore heavily-taxed) 'Mr John Fisher' residing in the Great Sanctuary by the Abbey between about 1665 and 1687. His previous home has not been identified.[140] Next door lived Edward Braddock,

[139] Public Record Office, LC 3/33, p. 110.

[140] Westminster City Libraries, Archives Dept., holds rate-books, overseers account, highway rates, etc., for Westminster parishes. A

singing-man and Gentleman of the Chapel Royal, and others of the musical community were near-by. So was this the 'Mr Fisher' who was paid 7s. 4d. for his attendance at the funeral of the Princess Royal at the Abbey on 30 March 1661 'expecting a place in the choir but afterwards lost it',[141] or the 'Mr John Fisher' whose son Charles was buried in the Little Cloister there on 2 March 1663/4?[142] Jenkins may have lodged with him (whichever he was), but the issue is further confused because a 'Mr John Jenkins' paid similar rates to court musicians in St Margaret's parish on a tenement (or two) on the north side of St Peter's Street between about 1662/3 and 1671. It seems most unlikely that this was the composer, but the possibility must be admitted for the time being.[143]

More significant, though, is the presence of Thomas Baltzar's signature – the court scribes never could agree on a spelling! – which enables rather more to be read into Roger North's account of the impact which this prodigious violin virtuoso had on the elderly Jenkins:

> [...] one Baltazar a sweed came over over, and resided some years in England, and shewed us wonders upon ye violin ye like of wch were not knowne here before: his Hand was rough alla Tedesca, but prodigious swift, and clattering. This put our Master [Jenkins] on trying to Compass ye violin in his old Age, wch he did so far as to

particular search was made in surviving records of the early 1660s for St Margaret's, Westminster, and St Martin-in-the Fields, but a number of gaps because of the destruction of books in World War II prevents a full picture emerging.

141 Westminster Abbey Muniments 61228A, f.6, quoted in Franklin B. Zimmerman, *Henry Purcell, 1659–1695,* His Life and Times, University of Pennsylvania Press, Philadelphia, 2nd. rev. edn., 1983, p. 8.

142 Joseph Lemuel Chester, *The Marriage, Baptismal, and Burial Registers of the Collegiate Church or Abbey of St. Peter, Westminster,* The Harleian Society, London, 1876.

143 The composer may have kept a base in London, lodging in it as necessary, but generally musicians without immediate family who were in service at court would not have their own property. The tenement in St Peter's Street was 'empty' at the 1672 assessment.

> performe his part, but how well handed, any one may conceiv.[144]

If Baltzar inspired Jenkins to take up the violin, was it the latter, perhaps in league with his friend John Lillie, who encouraged the Swede to adapt the continental practice of *scordatura* tuning in performing lyra viol solos on the violin?

> He [Baltzar] often used a lira manner of tuning, and hath left some neat lute-fashioned lessons of that kind, and also some of his rough pieces behind him.[145]

Here, perhaps, was the starting-point for others in England to imitate the technique. Certainly it would help explain why a collection of lyra viol pieces in the Bodleian Library, Oxford: Mus. Sch. MS F.573, seems to be transcribed for violin. Among Baltzar's extant compositions is a large suite for three violins, bass and continuo which, it has been suggested, served as a model for the ten fantasia-suites for the same instrumentation attributed to Jenkins.[146] In any event, such a scoring would have proved both popular and useful at the Restoration court, where membership of the violin consort had been doubled. But Baltzar himself seems to have been employed as a soloist rather than as a member of the violin ensemble. Described as 'musician in ordinary to his Majesty in the private musick', he was given a new place and the munificent fee of £110 a year. He died suddenly in July 1663, only five months after witnessing Jenkins's letter, and was buried in the cloisters of Westminster Abbey.

Mus. Sch. MS F.573 also has strong connections with the Netherlands, and unique concordances for many of

[144] British Library, Add. MS 32536, f. 73v. For a full account of Baltzar, *cf.* Peter Holman, 'Thomas Baltzar (?1631–1663), The "Incomperable Luciber on the Violin" ', *Chelys*, 13, 1984, pp. 3–38.

[145] North, *op. cit.*, p. 301.

[146] Peter Holman, 'Suites by Jenkins Rediscovered', *Early Music*, VI, January 1978, pp. 25–35. *Cf.* also the correspondence ensuing in *Early Music*, VI, July 1978, pp. 481–3.

the violin/lyra pieces are found in other manuscripts originating there, but now in the library of Count von Goëss at Ebenthal, Austria.[147] The latter may have been compiled by another of Jenkins' colleagues in the King's Musick, Dietrich Steffkins, who is particularly well-represented in the books and who is known to have been in the Netherlands during much of the Interregnum.[148] Though a bass violist at court from 1635 to 1642 and again from 1660 to his death around December 1673, Steffkins, like Jenkins, seems to have spent much time as an itinerant musician.[149] He took part in *The Triumph of Peace* and may first have met Jenkins then. Two stories by him found their way into Sir Nicholas L'Estrange's collection,[150] which indicates some contact with the composer or his patron. Presumably it was after the Restoration that

> there was a particular freindship cultivated between old Mr Stephkins and him [Jenkins], and he often sent him kind tokens, which were peices of fresh musick, and the old gentleman (Stephkins) very much esteemed them.[151]

We learn from another version of this passage that these

147 *Cf.* Douglas Alton Smith, 'The Ebenthal Lute and Viol Tablatures: Thirteen New Manuscripts of Baroque Instrumental Music', *Early Music,* X, October 1982, pp. 462–7; Gordon Dodd, 'Matters Arising from the Examination of Some Lyra Viol Manuscripts', *Chelys,* 9, 1980, pp. 23–7.

148 W. J. A. Jonckbloet and J. P. N. Land, *Correspondance et oeuvres musicales de Constantijn Huygens,* Leiden, 1882.

149 Robert Bargrave heard Steffkins play on the bass viol at Hamburg in February 1653: *cf.* Michael Tilmouth, 'Music on the Travels of an English Merchant: Robert Bargrave (1628–61)', *Music & Letters,* 53, 1972, pp. 143–59. Thomas Isham noted in his *Diary* for 9 July 1672: 'Mr Jackson [...] came here with a gentleman named Stepkins, from the house of Sir William Langham; there is hardly his equal in England at lute playing' (modern edn., translated from the Latin, ed. Norman Marlow, Gregg, Farnborough, 1971).

150 British Library, Harleian MS 6395, Nos. 309 and 310.

151 North, *op. cit.,* p. 298.

same 'kind tokens' were 'not [...] useful where he resided', presumably because they were too difficult for amateurs. They probably took the form of solos for bass or lyra viol for Steffkins himself to play.[152] One wonders, too, whether Steffkins played any part in encouraging the Dutch editions of English consorts and airs, including a mysterious lost book: *J. Jenkins, Engels Speel-Thresoor* [...] printed in Amsterdam in 1664; he would appear to have been well-placed to do so.[153]

Certainly Jenkins' fame, and music, had travelled to the continent. Commenting on his prolific output, Roger North tells that

> A Spanish Don sent over to the late Sr P. Lely, the leaves of one part of a 3 part consort of his, with a desire to procure the rest *costa che costa* [= whatever the cost]; for his musick had got abroad and was more esteemed there than at home. I shewed him the papers, but he could tell

[152] Details in Gordon Dodd, *Thematic Index of Music for Viols,* p. 81. A particular interesting source is Bodleian Library, Printed Book MUS 184.c.8, Simpson's 1659 *Division Viol* with MS additions. Owned by John Covell of Christ's College, Cambridge, it includes works by 'R.L.', 'R.L.E.', 'R.L.S.' [Roger L'Estrange?], Jenkins (including two holograph pieces), and Simpson. Covell bought the book in 1660.

[153] Listed in C. F. Becker, *Die Tonwerke des XVI. und XVII Jahrhunderts,* Leipzig, 1885, as *J. Jenkins, Engels Speel-Thresoor van CC. de nieuwste Allemanden, Couranted, Sarabaden, Ayres etc. gesteld door elf de konstighste Violisten deser tydt in Engeland voor Bass en Viool, en ander Speel-gereetschap, mede LXVII Speelstucken als Allemanden. Couranten, etc. voor twee Violes en Bass, als mede een Bassus continuus ad placidum* [*J. Jenkins, English Treasury of Instrumental Music of 200 of the newest Allemandes, Courantes, Sarabandes, Airs, etc., composed by eleven of the most ingenious musicians of these days in England, for bass and violin, and other instruments, moreover 67 pieces such as Allemandes, Courantes, etc. for two violins and bass, also with a thorough bass if wished*], Amsterdam, 1664. Just as with the ghost collection of twelve trio-sonatas by Jenkins which both Hawkins and Burney assert was printed in London about 1660, no copy has been found. *Engels Speel-Thresoor* is thought to have been a pirated edition of Playford's *Courtly Masquing Ayres* (1662). *Cf.* Rudi A. Rasch, 'Seventeenth-Century Dutch Editions of English Instrumental Music', *Music & Letters,* 53, 1972, pp. 270–3.

> nothing of them, when or where they were made, or might be found, onely he knew they were his owne.[154]

Jenkins' second letter,[155] dated 4 January 1663/4, transfers and extends the duties of his attorney:

> Bee it knowne unto all men by these presents, That I John Jenkins one of the Gentlemen of his Maties private Musicke have constituted, and in my place appointed John Lillie of St. Andrewes Holborne, Gent. my true & laweful Attorney to aske, require, demand & receave in my name, and for my use all and singular the Arrerages of all Annuities, Fees, or other Sumes, due or paieable unto mee out of his Maties Exchequer, wardrobe or Treasury Chamber, And to give such acquittances & discharges for the same, as shalbe required. And all that my said Attorney shall happen to doe in and for thes premisses to allowe, ratifie, and establishe. And therto I bind mee, my heires & Executors by these prsents. In witnesse whereof I have hereunto sett my hand and Seale.
>
> Janu: 4th 1663
>
> Sealed and delivered to the use of the abovesaid John Lillie in the prsence of us — signed John Jenkins
>
> Robert North
> Francis Tompson

It is remarkable how often in the court records the names of Jenkins and Lillie are juxtaposed – from the first swearing-in on 19 June 1660 to the final sad 'ob. Oct. 1678' against both their names when their liveries for 1677 remained unpaid at the time of their deaths. (Lillie died just four days before Jenkins). Both were eminent lyra violists, though each was appointed as theorbo player at court. Their friendship was lengthy, since both were patronised by Dudley, third Lord North, during the later years of the Interregnum. Indeed, it may well stretch back much earlier if the story of 'Mr Saunders, who loved

[154] *Op. cit.*, p. 296.

[155] Public Record Office, LC 3/33, p. 114.

Musick so well', told by Jenkins to Sir Nicholas L'Estrange, refers to the violist/violinist who was a Cambridge colleague of Lillie's.[156] Once Lillie had removed to London, Francis North kept a watchful eye on his affairs:

> There was an old soker, that had lived in Cambridge, and so was his acquaintance, and had bin frequently with his grandfather for the purposes of his profession. This man, for the sake of places in the King's musick, removed to London; and having a reat expensive family, hardly maintained them. And his lordship [Francis] was so great patron to him, as almost to support his family; onely, to colour giving him pay, he set him to teach me on the theorboe lute, and to write musicke for him and others. He was free of his table as if he were of the house; and his lordship got him his salarys payed him, took a son into a good office. The old man was a peice of a droll, but very hearty and honest. He knew his lordship's family well, and particularly the tyranicall old lord, his grandfather; [...] and old Lilly (so he was called) used to say in his harsh

[156] British Library, Harleian MS 6395, No. 536:

> One Mr. Saunders, who loved Musick so well, as he could not endure to have it interrupted with the least unseasonable Noises; being at a meeting of Fancy Musick, only for the violes and organ; where many Ladyes and Gentlewomen resorted; some wanton tongues could not Refraine their chatt, and Lowd whispers, sometimes above the Instruments; He, impatient of such harsh Discords as they often interposd, The lesson being ended, riseth with his viole from his seate, and soberly Addressing himself towards them; Ladyes, sayes he, This Musicke is not vocall, for on my knowledge these things were never made for words, and after that they had not one word to say.

I am deeply indebted to Ian Payne who made a thorough search of Cambridge records on my behalf in an attempt to established whether or not William Saunders, court violinist between 1660 and 1674, could be linked with any 'Mr. Saunders' from Cambridge, but without success. For references to the latter *cf.* Nicholas Hookes, *Amanda* (1653), 'To Mr. Lilly, Musick-Master in Cambridge', and Pepys, *Diary*, 8 October 1667. The 'Mr. Saunders' whose family was shut up in Green Street, Cambridge, in the plague in October 1665 was a 'deep base': *cf.* J. R. Wadale (ed.) *Clare College Letters and Documents*, Cambridge, 1903, pp. 69–70.

> and lowd pronunciation in all places, that he was very sure the 2nd Dudley Lord North's children succeeded all so well in the world, and were blest by God Almighty, for the extraordinary duty of their father, and observance, payd to his father the old Lord North.[157]

Perhaps Jenkins' appointment of Lillie as his attorney was instigated by Francis North as one more piece of business to 'colour giving him pay', for it is tempting to identify one witness of Jenkins' letter among the 'good servants' of Francis: 'Mr. Robt. North [...] his cheif clerck for the confessions and other affaires of truth'.[158] But of Francis Tompson nothing is known, unless he was the Farmer of Excise (and later of Hearth Money) noted in the state papers.[159]

In any event, Lillie performed his duty most conscientiously, though the task must have been difficult. Given that the King felt it right to restore all the 'outward pomp and gilding' associated with the Crown, he received insufficient funds to remain solvent. This was in part due to the amount voted him by Parliament, but also to the inefficient collection of revenues, which lagged severely behind expenditure. As a typical result, by the early 1670s confusion multiplies, as administrators claim the dues of long-dead musicians and are paid by loans anticipated, but still not received by the Exchequer.[160] Inevitably, many musicians were forced into conditions of extreme hardship. Some years earlier Pepys, in conversation with John Hingeston, the 'Repayrer and Keeper of the Organs', heard that 'many of the Musique are ready to starve, they being five years behind-hand for their

[157] North, *op. cit.*, p. 37.

[158] Roger North, *The Life of the Right Honourable Francis North, Baron of Guildford*, London, 1742, p. 93.

[159] *Calendar of Treasury Books:* 26 July 1666 and 2 October 1669. His East Anglian connections may be significant.

[160] *Cf.* Andrew Ashbee, *Lists of Payments to the King's Musick in the Reign of Charles II (1660–1685)*, Ashbee, Snodland, 1981, p. xi.

wages'.[161] It is against such a background that Lillie systematically collects the payments for his friend and if (as the books show) these were eight-and-a-half years behind-hand at the last occasion – a mere month before the two men died – so were those of many of his colleagues; Jenkins did indeed receive his salary 'as they were payd'. The last payment assigned to Jenkins was on 3 September 1679, almost a year after his death, but the preceding entry is for Frances Lillie, widow of John, so we can be sure she collected both sums.[162] No doubt Jenkins, like many in court service at the time, bequeathed any arrears due to him to the colleague that had served him so faithfully. No executor seems to have claimed Jenkins' dues thereafter, but Mrs Lillie diligently pursued hers until, with relief, an Exchequer clerk wrote on 25 September 1683; 'theire is but one qrter of a yeare nowe due to Mrs Lilly for Mr Lillie was Buried on ye 28th of October 1678.[163]

The financial pressures of the time often resulted in the non-payment of liveries. As late as 30 November 1694 the Lord Chamberlain's records include 'An Abstract of Moneys [...] in part on Arreares due to Severall of the Servts of his late Maty King Charles the Second from Michás 1671 to Xmas 1684', listing debts of more than £2,000 due to eighteen musicians for their liveries. Generally records of payments for these are less complete than for the fees, though a series of Debenture Books indicates which were eventually received, each entry endorsed by the musician or his assign. Nevertheless, the many unsigned entries for the late 1660s testify to the upheavals resulting from the Great Plague and Fire, and especially from the Dutch War, all of which severely depleted the resources of court and country.

161 Pepys, *Diary*, 19 December 1666.

162 Public Record Office: E. 403/1793, p. 178.

163 Public Record Office: E. 403/1801, p. 175.

Table1

Payments of Jenkins' Salary by the Exchequer

P.R.O.: E.403/

Vol.				*for*		*ending*			*paid on*		
1763,	f.	21v	£20	6	months	25	Dec.	1660	20	May	1663
1764,	f.	85v	£40	1	year	25	Dec.	1661	7	Jan.	1664
1769,	f.	80r	£20	6	months	24	June	1662	30	July	1666
1770,	f.	76r	£20	6	months	25	Dec.	1662	12	Feb.	1667
1779,	p.	32	£40	1	year	25	Dec.	1663	11	Oct.	1671
1774,	p.	195	£20	6	months	24	June	1664	3	Sept.	1669
1776,	p.	158	£40	1	year	24	June	1665	18	July	1670
1776,	p.	169	£20	6	months	25	Dec.	1665	21	July	1670
1779,	p.	325	£40	1	year	25	Dec.	1666	27	Feb.	1672
1781,	p.	223	£40	1	year	25	Dec.	1667	24	Jan.	1673
1784,	p.	3	£40	1	year	25	Dec.	1668	30	Sept.	1674
1787,	p.	52	£10	3	months	25	Mar.	1669	8	May	1676
1789,	p.	75	£20	6	months	29	Sept.	1669	12	June	1677
1791,	p.	261	£20	6	months	25	Mar.	1670	3	Sept.	1678
1793,	p.	178	£20	6	months	29	Sept.	1670	3	Sept.	1679

Table 2

Payments of Jenkins' Livery

year	*signed by*	*P.R.O./LC.9/Vol.*		*paid on*
1660	John Lillie	195,	f.21r	
1661	John Jenkins		f.21r	
1662	[sig. removed]		f.34r	
1663	John Lillie		f.30r	
1664	–	196,	f.15	
1665	–		f.14	
1666	–		f.13	
1667	–		f.14v	
1668	John Lillie	197,	–	27 Feb. 1669
1669	Humphrey Madge		–	11 Nov. 1671
1670	–		f.14v	
1671	John Lillie	198,	f.13v	2 April 1672
1672	John Lillie		f.16v	19 Oct. 1675
1673	John Lillie		f.15	20 Oct. 1676
1674	John Lillie		f.14	9 June 1677
1675	John Lillie	199,	–	18 Dec. 1677
1676	John Lillie		f.17	9 July 1678
1677	– 'ob: Oct. 1678'			
1678	paid to John Mosse			

But the King's command for a 'retrenchment of payments out of our Treasury of our Chamber, bearing date 16 March 1667[8]' largely by-passed the musical establishment, which continued much as formerly. In common with many of the court personnel, though, most were forced to lend a year's salary to the Crown, receiving only six per cent interest in lieu at the time. Jenkins was one who helped in this way:

> [2 May 1671]
> J. Jenkins, gent. [received] 24s. [by way of] interest on £40 loaned by him to his Majesty on 18th July 1670 and by Tallies raised at the Receipt; dated the same day and debited for six months from 18th July 1670 to 19th January 1670/1. By letters of Privy Seal dated the last day of April 1668.[164]

In the 1670s money flowed more regularly and there were determined attempts to clear many of the debts which had accrued. Secure at Kirtling, Jenkins could leave these affairs to Lillie. There is indeed an impression that he did not press for his dues when others were facing more severe hardship and had more urgent claims on the money. Lillie, with his 'great and expensive family', apparently took every opportunity to draw his salary, while Jenkins received his portion much later. Livery payments present a similar picture; again it would appear that Jenkins was prepared to waive his claims to these during the lean years of the late 1660s so that his colleagues working at court would benefit more. Nevertheless, places in the King's Musick were for life, so he had every right to the money; security of tenure was a principal attraction for any aspiring to a court post – in theory, at least.

Whatever the financial burdens, the Restoration court was rich in musical talent. Regrettably fire at Whitehall in April 1691 seems to have destroyed music and documents, so that the present picture is far from complete.

[164] Public Record Office: E. 403/1778, p. 11. The original is in Latin.

Table 3
Exchequer Payments of Fees due to John Jenkins and John Lillie

Jenkins			*Lillie*	
1660	–		–	
1661	–		–	
1662	–		–	
1663	20 May	£20	20 May	£20
			26 May	£20
			24 Dec.	£30
			29 Dec.	£40
1664	7 Jan.	£40		
			8 Sep.	£30
1665	–		21 Feb.	£40
1666			12 March	£40
			28 July	£10
	30 July	£20		
			13 Nov.	£20
1667	12 Feb.	£20	–	
1668	–		–	
1669	3 Sep.	£20	3 Sep.	£20
1670			11 May	£20
	18 July	£40	18 July	£40
	21 July	£20		
1671	11 Oct.	£40	11 Oct.	£40
1672	27 Feb.	£40	27 Feb.	£40
1673	24 Jan.	£40		
			6 Nov.	£40
1674			20 May	£20
	30 Sep.	£40	30 Sep.	£20
1675	–		7 Aug.	£10
1676	8 May	£10	17 Aug.	£10
1677	12 June	£20	12 June	£20
1678			5 Aug.	£20
	3 Sep.	£20		
1679			21 March	£40
	3 Sep.	£20	3 Sep.	£20
1680			–	
1681			24 Sep.	£30
1682			19 July	£20
			7 Dec.	£20
1683			6 March	£20
			25 Sep.	£20
		£410 of £710		£720 of £730

Of course the grand occasions had their full share of music and, in the nature of things, are generally described by eye-witnesses, but little is known of the routine performances. What did the 'Private Musick' play, for instance, and how were they grouped? Surviving records are mute on this subject. When did they perform? Again it is not known. What is clear from the Lord Chamberlain's papers is that it was the Violin Band who were despatched to Portsmouth to receive the Queen, to attend her at Tonbridge, or to accompany the King to Hampton Court, Windsor, Newmarket, Oxford, Salisbury, or Bath, or wherever he decided to spend the summer months. The 'Private Musick' is never mentioned in the lists of the Household drawn up for these occasions, nor do its members claim for the extra expenses involved. Presumably, then, they were free from royal duties during these summer progresses, and Jenkins would have returned to Kirtling for lengthy periods, even when he was employed at court. To judge by Roger North's description (below), the new regime had little use for consort music of the traditional kind and the aging composer may have felt outmoded in London. The three-violin suites attributed to him are nonetheless an interesting and successful attempt to marry old and new styles, and there is every likelihood that they were written for the court musicians, but what else he produced for them cannot be identified.[165]

> The old way of consorts were layd aside at Court, and the King made an establishment, after a French model, of 24 violins, and the style of the musick was accordingly. So that became the ordinary musick of the Court [...], the

[165] The three-violin/continuo suites are in British Library, Add. MS 31423. Among other larger works which may date from this time are the Fancies and Airs (Group VII), Fancy-Almain-Corant sets (Group V), and two groups of pieces for which one bass only survives in Beinecke Library, New Haven, Connecticut, MS Osborn 515: fourteen pieces for treble, two lyra viols and bass; 29 pieces for treble and two basses (divisions). See Gordon Dodd, *Thematic Index of Music for Viols*, pp. 90, 91, 93 and 132.

> whole tendency of the ayre had more regard to the foot, than the ear [...].
>
> King Charles II was a professed lover of musick, but of this kind onely, and had an utter detestation of Fancys. [...] He could not bear any musick to which he could not keep the time, and that he constantly did to all that was presented to him, and for the most part heard it standing. And for songs he approved onely the soft vein, such as might be called a step triple,[166] and that made a fashion among the masters, and for the stage, as may be seen in the printed books of the songs of that time [...].
>
> This French manner is instrumentall musick did not gather so fast as to make a revolution all at once, but during the greatest part of that King's reigne, the old musick was used in the countrys, and in many meetings and societys in London; but the treble violl was discarded, and the violin took its place. [...] There were also divers societys and procured divers, as from Italy Cazzati and Vitali; and one from Sweden by Becker. [...] there was great flocking hither of forrein masters. [...] And they found here good encouragement.[167]

So Kirtling, where 'the violin came in late, and imperfectly', remained Jenkins' true base. The sympathy and comfort to be found there had to be balanced against making music in London with the best in the land. A young man would choose the latter, of course, but Jenkins was now seventy, with no welfare state to cushion his last years. The honour of a court post no doubt thrilled him, but what he could contribute to court music at his age would be uncertain for all concerned. Retirement from an active role at court was a rational and sensible decision; that he was to live on for fifteen more years was not to be anticipated, but in the event he was to receive the utmost kindness and care from all who looked after him.

[166] I.e., *Andante* in triple time.

[167] North, *op. cit.*, pp. 349–51.

Augustus Jessopp,[168] in introducing his edition of Roger North's 'Notes of Me', writes:

> The private account book of the fourth Lord has been preserved, in which every penny of his daily expenditure is minutely recorded during the last twenty years of his life [...]. He kept an organist in his house, one Mr. [George] Loosemore for many years, and it was in 1660 that the famous John Jenkins took up his residence at Kirtling, and remained there, as the account book shows, till young Roger matriculated at Cambridge [...]. For teaching the brothers Montagu and Roger, Mr. Catchpole received 7/- a week, and for their music lessons Mr. Jenkins was paid one pound a quarter.[169]

The whereabouts of this account book was unknown until recently, when Mary Chan discovered it among items still kept by the North family at Rougham.[170] It does indeed show regular payments to Jenkins 'for teaching ye children', 'for teaching my daughters', and, occasionally, 'for pricking lessons', although Jessopp's figure of 'one pound a quarter' for them does not bear close scrutiny. Between 1660 and 1663 Jenkins received from two to three pounds a year, but this suddenly increased to between five and seven pounds annually from 1664 to 1666. Here, surely, is confirmation that the composer divided his time between the court duties and the North family for the earlier years, but retired to Kirtling thereafter, as the court records suggest.

Roger, aged about nine in 1660, confirms that Jenkins was his teacher:

[168] Augustus Jessopp, *The Autobiography of the Hon. Roger North*, London, 1887.

[169] *Ibid.*, pp. v, vi and viii.

[170] At the time of writing I have not had the opportunity to see the book, but I am much indebted to Dr Chan for her kindness in sending her notes and extracts from it and for permission to use them here. A few smaller sets of accounts for Kirtling survive: Cambridge Record Office, L.95.12 (1661/2); Bodleian Library, MS North c.49 (1664/5), and MS Northb.12 (1666/7).

> I was instituted by that eminent master of his time Mr. Jenkins. He was a person of much easyer temper, than any of his faculty. He was neither conceited nor morose, but much a gentleman, and had a very good sort of witt, which served him in his address and conversation, wherein he did not please less than in his compositions. He was welcome to the houses of all lovers [of music], and particularly with us, being resident in the house for divers years.[171]

The easy-going temperament of Jenkins may have been partly responsible for Roger's lack of effort when he first took up music:

> I began in that intervall of time, as past between scool and Cambridge, and being at first backward, and averse to the paines of a new jargon, as the Elements of Musick were to me, and to be learnt and apply'd I knew not how or why, I fell lazy, and it was thought unaptness, which made my father and his freind Mr Jenkins almost give me over. But my mother, being for pushing me on, took opportunity to lett me know that my father took notice of my neglect of musick, and I should hear of it. This made me buckle a little closer, till I had the cord by the end, and left not to pull till I had the command of my little instrument the treble viol.[172]

North's reticent nature and youthfulness were responsible for him leading a somewhat secluded life at the university and he continued to practise regularly at Cambridge. He also notes that

> the wrighting of musick conduced as much to my learning as any thing could have done, for I was very sedulous and industrious at it, and began very early. I designed to write over all Mr Jenkin's compositions, and did execute my purpose upon a great many; but for want of good paper, and good directions in making the caracter black and regular, my first labours came to litle [...]. But I was not to stop here, but having wrote-over much musick, and some

[171] *Op. cit.*, p. 21.

[172] *Ibid.*, p. 22.

> in the score, I observed a litle of the composition, and offered at a litle of that kind, which Mr Jenkins seeing was so kind to correct it, and shew me the faults; then it was play'd, which was no small pride. But afterwards I got books, Mr Sympson's *Devision Violist*, and his *Compendium*. Mr Jenkins lent me Butler with a comendation of it that it was the best in the kind.[173]

So, in spite of his initial aversion to the art, it was not long before Roger 'became as fond of musick, as yong folks are of any thing they take to' and he never ceased to be grateful for his musical upbringing at Kirtling:

> Now to look a litle back, I cannot but wonder at the accidents of life; considering how very desirous, and at what charge some are, and withall of a good capacity, to learne musick, and cannot attain it; and without much formal teaching and that onely of the viol, it is my lot to master the art in such degree as I have here discovered. I neither esteem my self more capable, industrious inclined, or ingenious, but on the contrary much less than others; but ascribe it wholly to the accident of family, and company. My quality and relation gave me respect and admittance, where others could not so well have come; and not onely so but a foreward place in performance, which, joyned with a genius and inclination, was my advantage.[174]

In December 1666 Dudley North died. Included among 'My Lords Debts' is one for 'Mr Jenkyns: £50. 0. 0.', perhaps a monetary token of the esteem in which the composer was held by his patron.[175] Something of the affection with which Jenkins was regarded by Roger and by his grandfather is evident from their writings. Jenkins, for his part, reciprocated such feelings; in particular his poem 'In Memory of the Right Honble & truly Noble Lord, Ld: Dudley North who died Dec. 1666' is a fine

[173] *Ibid.*, pp. 22–3. *Cf.* also p. 71, above.

[174] *Ibid.*, p. 28.

[175] Bodleian Library, MS North b.12, ff. 355–6.

testimony to the encouragement, friendship and patronage which he had received from this 'good old lord'.

Infolded heer in silent dust doth lie
Large vertue shadow'd in Epitome;
Just, pious, prudent, Charitable, Good,
Right ancient Issue of a noble blood;
To Arte & Learning what might comprehend
A true Mecaenas and the Muses friend
Lyes sadly heer. And a great hope and trust
(fairly laid up) now crumbles into dust.
Who can not then in pity o'er his herse
Pay the just tribute of a weeping verse.
Eyes, if your springs are dry, at least impart
Some gentle moisture from a well-tun'd heart;
For hearts have strings and strings can sound relief,
As musick, when most elegant in grief.
Have we not cause a prodigie to fear,
When the North star declines our hemisphere.
May we not dread a fatal change and think
O[u]r Glory in his light to be extinct?
No; 'tis unjust; This star (not fixt alone)
Hast in its orb more glorious stars than one:
And such as can display a beam from him
On us, when our inferiour lights are dimm.
But, how this radiant flame should disappear,
Change its first station to another sphere,
This Globe of glory how it came eclips'd
To this dark world; say, To be better fixd,
Like Manoah's Angel wing'd with heavenly fire
As he in smoak of incense did aspire,
So this refulgent light ascends on high
Perfum'd with faith, zeal, praise and harmony;
No jarring sounds to bid the world farewell
But well-tun'd Anthems toll his passing bell;
Chime loud, ye spheres, And let yor musick ring;
Soule once enthroned true Hallelujahs sing.[176]

[176] British Library, Add. MS 18220, pp. 65–6; another copy at Bodleian Library, Rawlinson MS D.260, f. 34v. Add. MS 18220 has another poem by 'John Jenkins Mr of Musick' on p. 13, bearing the date 6 July 1665:

The death of Dudley in 1666 and the departure of Roger to Cambridge in the autumn of 1667 would obviously have put restraints on music-making at Kirtling; for the time being, at least, Jenkins' services were required there less. The younger Dudley's account book, though, still notes two payments to Jenkins 'for teaching of my son Roger' – one in 1667 and the other as late as 1669, while a recently discovered copy of a letter from the composer, authorising John Lillie to collect all his Court money for him, is dated 25 May 1668 from 'Catlidge in ye County of Cambridge'.[177] The composer's endearing character had made him many friends and he continued to be well looked after:

> The old gentleman had this singular happyness, that even in his last years, while he was but a bundle of infirmitys and as to musick utterly effete, he was acceptable to all ye familys where he had formerly frequented and finally made his owne choice where to lay his bones, wch was at Kimberly in Norfolk.[178]

Although evidence is lacking, it is reasonable to assume that Jenkins moved to Kimberley around 1670, there to spend the rest of his days at the home of Sir Philip Wodehouse (1608–81). Among Sir Philip's 'Anagrams and Toyes' is a verse 'Upon his noble kinsman ye Ld North: Ld Dudley North Duely Thron'd' and another 'Upon his

---

Tis late & time to rest, But, stay;
Sleep not, my soul, untill thou pray;
Night's Curtain o're the day is hurld:
Wellcome, my God, & farewell world.

O let my prarefull slumbers be
Now sweetned with fresh dews from Thee,
Such heavenly dewes as may advance
My soul into a holy trance:
Then in such blessed ecstacy
I shall not fear to sleep or dy.
Hallelujah.

177 Public Record Office, E406/50, f. 92.

178 British Library, Add. MS 32536, f. 73v.

son Mr Francis North (now Judge)', so clearly the two families were well acquainted.[179] Not many years before, in 1659, Sir Philip had demolished the old Hall and had built a new house at Downham Lodge. That was replaced by the present Hall (on the same site), which is believed to have been built in 1712 by William Tansman.[180] No trace of the house known to Jenkins remains.

Sir Philip dabbled in the arts with enthusiasm, though probably little skill, if his enjoyable but execrable verses[181] are anything to go by. Yet merely as a catalogue of his friends and acquaintances they are full of interest, and the re-appearance of names met elsewhere in this perambulation through Jenkins' life is intriguing. Who, for instance, was the Mrs Lilly who 'repayr'd the fortune' of Sir William Hovill, or the 'Mrs Mary Burwell now marry'd to my Coz. Walpole'? Perhaps more will come to light of 'Mr Hadly, my Lady Doyly's brothr, ye fine Musician', or of Sir Philip's own practitioners in that art: James Cooper and Matthew Stanton. Of course there is a poem 'Upon Mr J. Jenkins ye rare Musitian' which, like all the others, begins with an anagram on the composer's name:

John Jenkins: No key in sinn A key is a pitch in musick
This Coriphaeus in his Art
Of Music in its ev'ry part
prooves It all Purity within
No maide, No Cleff – No key in sin
John Jenkins: I ken no sin
Hee well may say I ken no sin
since Vertue is all Harmonye
of Truth combyn'd wth courtesye

[179] Beinecke Library, New Haven, Connecticut, MS Osborn b.131, Nos. 6 and 7.

[180] *Cf.* Nikolaus Pevsner, *North-West and South Norfolk, The Buildings of England,* Penguin, Harmondsworth, 1962, p. 220.

[181] Beinecke Library, New Haven Connecticut, MS Osborn b.131. The Jenkins poem is No. 170. *Cf.* also R. W. Ketton-Cremer, 'The Rhyming Wodehouses', *Norfolk and Norwich Archaeological Society Journal,* XXXIII, 1962, p. 35.

In all its Parts, Justice and Peace
Thro Musiques powr salute & kisse
A soule well tund do's disaffect each vice
as Discords, in ye eare of Paradize
They're Dissonants from Natures Law, ye rule
Of Reason rectify'd in Heavens high schoole
Tis Musiq wch sublyme's & elevates
The soule, from earth to its caelestiall state.

Not for the first time, allusions are found here to Jenkins' virtue. Such compliments run as a *cantus firmus* through all seventeenth-century accounts of him; their frequency and emphasis are such as to go well beyond conventional tributes and suggest that he did indeed seem to his contemporaries a rather saintly figure. It should be noted, though, that we have no descriptions of him as a young man, nor in his prime, and that benign old men invariably beget sympathy and honour. Quite how much should be read into North's comment that 'he was a good Christian, and truely religious' is difficult to say.[182] In all this it is worth recalling Dudley North's views on the music of his day:

> I am not against the short Airs that possess the present times; but before we can pass time enough in them, their very sweetness gluts, and grows fulsome [...]. The constant use of them is fit for common Consorts of pleasure, to tickle the ear, eat, drink, dance, or discourse, whilest they fill the Room and Ear, not the Soul [...].
> Our Frenchified Age requires rather a recollection and

[182] *Op. cit.*, p. 348. Certainly surviving vocal music by him is predominantly of sacred texts. These range from Latin prayers, through settings of George Herbert (another who, like Jenkins, shunned the glamour and clamour of court life), to such extraordinary subjects as the 'Song of the Woman's Cure in her Profluvion of Blood', the words of which are printed in *A Forest Promiscuous*. *Cf.* also the poem in note 176 on pp. 98–9.

> setling towards sobriety and gravity, than to be bubbled up to an over-Airy humour and lightness.[183]

With such sentiments Jenkins' bearing was well in tune. Yet his humility and complaisance was enriched by vivacity: 'Spirit, Garb and Air, shine in his first appearance' wrote Dudley North (in the same letter), while Roger added:

> Wherever he went, Mirth and Solace (as the song hath it) attended him [...]. He had neither vice nor humours, but formed his behaviour to complaisances, by sincere teaching, taking any part in consorts and encouraging yong beginners.[184]

Anthony Wood too had heard that 'though a little man, yet he had a great soul'.[185] Perhaps during his brief time at court Jenkins had made the acquaintance of the newly arrived Pietro Reggio, who, in the preface of his *Book of Songs* (1680), pays his tribute to the older master:

> I must not here forget the Friendship I have found from some, that were most Eminent in my own Profession; especially Mr. JOHN JENKINS, whose memory I reverence, as one of the best Masters of MUSICK in his time, and no less a Gentleman, who sometimes has communicated his Compositions to me, and Honour'd me so far, as to ask and take my Opinion; Yet, often I have heard this Great and Modest Man censur'd by some, who never could think to be talk'd of, if it had not been from their Arrogance, in presuming to tax so Great a Master.[186]

[183] *Ibid.*, p. 4. The original is in *A Forest Promiscuous.*

[184] *Ibid.*, pp. 297 and 348.

[185] Bodleian Library, MS Wood D.19(4), f. 73.

[186] Thomas Shadwell, in his poem 'To my Much Respected Master, and Worthy Friend, Signior Pietro Reggio, on the publishing of his book of Songs', includes the lines:

> Thy worth and Skill, great Jenkins lov'd, and knew;
> The Worthiest Master of my Youthful days.
> Whom Thou so justly honour'd with thy Praise.

In view of Jenkins' considerable reputation, it is curious that there

Our last, indeed the only glimpse of the aged composer at Kimberley is again provided by Roger North. For several years Roger accompanied his elder brother Francis, the Lord Chief Justice, around the various Assize Circuits. Twice in 1677 they followed the Norfolk Circuit, first in March – when their only stop in the county was at Thetford on the 22nd – and again in August. Progress was reasonably leisurely, and no doubt part of the time between their duties at the castle of Cambridge on Tuesday, 14 August, and St Edmondsbury on Friday, 17 August, was spent at Kirtling, conveniently half-way between. Their final appointments were in Norwich on Wednesday, 22 August, 'at the New-Hall' and later the same day 'at the Castle'.[187] here was an opportunity for Roger to renew acquaintance with the 85-year-old man who had first taught him the viol, since Kimberley was only a few miles to the west of the city. He took with him the newly published *Ayrs for the Violin* by Nicola Matteis, and later recalled the meeting:

> I toucht to his base the double stringed lesson, the 2nd or 3rd in Signr Nichola's 2nd book. He pulled off his spectacles, and clapt his hand on the table, saying he never had heard so good a peice of musick in all his life; which shewed his taste was just, and he would have served himself of such good patternes.[188]

Jenkins surrendered his court post in March 1678.[189] As early as 28 March 1676, the Lord Chamberlain had ordered a warrant to admit Richard Tomlinson as musician in ordinary without fee. He was to come in ordinary with fee 'upon the death or other avoydance of John

---

seem to have been no musical tributes such as survive for Locke and Purcell. He did, of course, outlive his close musical friends.

[187] *Cf. The London Gazette*, Nos. 1173 and 1213, for details of these Circuit itineraries.

[188] *Op. cit.*, p. 298.

[189] Andrew Ashbee, *Records of English Court Music*, I, Ashbee, Snodland, 1986, p. 178. (Public Record Office, LC 5/143, f. 68.)

Jenkins or William Howes'.[190] In the event Howes died on 21 April that year, so Tomlinson succeeded him.[191] Jenkins was eventually replaced by John Moss, sworn in on 19 April 1678.[192] Among the State Papers is a letter showing that Moss was recommended for the post by none other than Francis North:

> April: 1678. My Lord Chamberlaine desires that the right honable Mr Secretary Williamson would please to acquaint His Matie That John Mosse is the person whom His Matie was intreated to grant should bee one of His Musick in Mr Jenkin's place, at the humble request of the Lord Cheife Justice North.
> Rich. Colinge.[193]

Now ailing in health, the composer probably sensed that the end was near. Yet he remained philosophically cheerful:

> Mr Jenkins was a most happy person, for he lived and dyed beloved and unenvyed; and was sensible that he was capitall of his profession, during most of his life; and that made him amends for his living so long to be sensible of his being left behind, and almost wholly layd aside.[194]

Was it he so vividly pictured by the anonymous poet in his verse 'Upon a very old man playing excellent well upon the Lute'?[195]

> His Head retaines not haires enough to fitt
> a Lute with strings, nor teeth to peg a kitt.
> His stiff decrepit Limbs noe motion know,
> But wt ye courteous Palsy doth bestow.

[190] *Ibid.*, p. 158. (Public Record Office, LC 5/141, p. 377.)

[191] *Ibid.*, p. 159. (Public Record Office, LC 5/141, p. 389.)

[192] *Ibid.*, p. 178. (Public Record Office, LC 5/143, f. 68.)

[193] Public Record Office, SP 29/403, No. 120.

[194] North, *op. cit.*, pp. 298–9.

[195] I am much indebted to Harold Love of Monash University for drawing my attention to this poem in Beinecke Library, New Haven, Connecticut, MS Osborn, b.104, p. 91.

His bed's ye grave, each night he's buryed on,
Liveing to him's a resurrection.
Yet though ye function of his feet be gon
His posting hands runn swiftly on,
And in quick turnes, such nimble measures trace
Fayries on night-Mares sure begot his race.

Jenkins died on 27 October 1678, and was buried in Kimberley church two days later.[196] His grave in the centre of the chancel is still marked by a well-preserved stone. The epitaph on it may well have been written by Sir Philip Wodehouse:

Under this stone Rare Jenkyns lie
The Master of the Musick Art
Whome from ye Earth the God on High
Calld unto Him to bear his part
Ad'd eighty six October twenty sev'n
In Anno sev'nty eight he went to Heav'n.

In Sir Philip's book of poems the verse on the composer concludes with 'A kind of Epecedium of Him – J. J.':

This Rare Amphyon of Our tymes
Is toul'd to Heavn by his own chymes His Bells
Thes – and his Life's pure Harmonye
Conchording Truth with Courtezye,
And tuning it to Melodye
Have Winged his soule, up to the skye –
Call'd thither as A Chorister
(who was A Coriphaeus Heer)
'Mongst Cherubim & Seraphim There fixt to sing
Holy Hozannah's to Th'aeternall King.

Jenkins' life was a long one and had seen enormous changes, both musically and socially. He was brought up with the art of Byrd, Gibbons and their contemporaries; he died as the work of Purcell was beginning to appear –

196 The Kimberley burial register of this time has been missing for many years. The entry 'John Jenkins, Esq., was buried October 29th, 1678' was recorded by Charles Burney in his *History* and has since been repeated by others.

The grave of Jenkins in the chancel of Kimberley Church (courtesy of Robbie Buxton)

whose fantasias were to be the last great monuments of a glorious musical heritage which he himself had done so much to encourage and perfect; an art soon to be eclipsed by the flood of music and musicians which poured into the country from abroad, by the attraction of Italian opera and of Handel and Bononcini – but nevertheless an art which has an important place in the music history of England.

chapter two
The English Consort Fantasia before Jenkins

> The most principall and chiefest kind of musicke which is made without a dittie is the fantasia, that is, when a musician taketh a point at his pleasure, and wresteth and turneth it as he list, making either much or little of it according as shall seem best in his own conceit. In this may more arte be showne than in any other musicke, because the composer is tied to nothing but that he may adde, deminish and alter at his pleasure [...].[1]

There is no standard fantasia, no blue-print from which composers may work. The English consort fantasia seems hardly to have been born when Morley wrote his famous description of the genre. In it he draws attention to the freedom available to the composer of fantasias, his inspiration unconditioned by the shape and context of a text, the structure of a *cantus firmus*, or the traditions of the dance. Certainly one of the supreme strengths of the fantasia is its flexibility as a form, and, as Richard Nicholson has noted in the preface to our joint addition of Jenkins' six-part music,

> the all essential factor of unity depends on a right balance of parts, not on any prescribed and relatively external pattern.[2]

[1] Thomas Morley, *A Plaine and Easie Introduction to Practicall Musicke*, London, 1597, p. 180.

[2] *John Jenkins: Consort Music in Six Parts*, ed. Richard Nicholson and Andrew Ashbee, Faber Music, London, 1967, p. vii.

Jenkins was fortunate to arrive on the scene when the form to which he devoted most attention had attained moments of perfection – works by Byrd, Gibbons, Ward, Coprario and Ferrabosco the Younger spring readily to mind – and yet there was scope for his genius to enlarge upon that perfection. If a very few later composers like William Lawes, Locke and Purcell equalled his achievement in the field, they were unable to transcend it. By then the fantasia had changed in character, being coloured by the infiltration of florid melodic decorations (known as 'divisions') and dance patterns (a return to something approaching the medley concept of some early examples), by dramatic gesture, or by the adoption of other figures drawn from Restoration theatrical music.

The following summary of the main trends in sixteenth-century English consort music draws heavily on Oliver Neighbour's masterly account in his discussion of the consort music of William Byrd.[3] Neighbour suggests that interest in the viol waned after the reign of Henry VIII and again towards the end of the century. This fluctuation may be illusory in part, for I am sure that to some extent the modern view-point is obscured by the lack of sources. What is undoubtedly significant is that surviving manuscripts show clearly that in the mid-sixteenth century consort music was used for didactic purposes as much as for social recreation and that the principal composers of consorts were church musicians: Tye, Tallis, Taverner, Parsons and Robert White among them. Since choirboys required instruction to enable them confidently to hold their part in a complex polyphonic motet or canticle, what better means was available than to provide exercises based on chants familiar to them from their liturgical duties: *In Nomine*, *Christe qui lux es*, *Dum transisset*, or *Miserere*, or pieces based on the *ut re mi* to assist in the learning of solmisation. Of course,

[3] *The Consort and Keyboard Music of William Byrd*, Faber & Faber, London, 1978, especially pp. 26–35, 51–2, 61–2 and 65–6.

the didactic element may have applied as much to the composition as to the performance of such music, as is mentioned elsewhere;[4] one can only speculate since contemporary evidence is lacking. Yet it is worth remembering that records of seventeenth-century choirboys receiving instruction on the viol are plentiful and that this tuition may be a continuation of an earlier tradition.

Whether these *cantus firmus* pieces (and other sixteenth-century consorts) were sung or played is another question. Enough evidence survives to show that both methods of performance were acceptable, although clearly practical difficulties could arise.[5] In surveying contemporary performance practice, the scholar Warwick Edwards points out that several of Tye's *In Nomine*s copied among the 'sofainge sones' in British Library, Add. MS 31390 'could scarcely be performed by voices at all',[6] while in the late-sixteenth-century part-books, British Library, Add. MSS 30480–4, two warnings appear:

> If you c[an] not singe the seconds parte let it a lonne

and

> The seconde parte is good: but that is so hard: I will not singe this parte.[7]

Still, the tradition of singing textless pieces seems to have continued even into Jenkins' time, for as late as 1638 Michael East published some 'ayrie Fancies of 4 Parts, that may be as well sung as plaid'.[8] Increasingly, though, the restraints of a neo-vocal style gave way to more distinctive instrumental patterns. At the head of his

[4] *Ibid.*, pp. 27–8.

[5] *Cf* Warwick Edwards, 'The Performance of Ensemble Music in Elizabethan England', *Proceedings of the Royal Musical Association*. 97, 1970–1, pp. 113–23, for a full discussion of the evidence.

[6] *Ibid.*, p. 118.

[7] British Library, Add. MS 30481, f. 64; Add. MS 30483, f. 66v.

[8] Michael East, *The Seventh Set of Bookes*, 1638.

own score of the younger Ferrabosco's four-part fantasias Thomas Tomkins noted the change:[9]

> Alfonso 4 pts. Fancyes to the Vyolls: all of them excellent good. But made only one for the vyolls & organ wch is the Reason that he Takes such liberty of Compass wch he would have Restraynd: if it had Bin made for voyces only.

In the latter part of the sixteenth century all musical roads in England led to Byrd. No other composer of the time made so indelible a mark on so wide a spectrum of the contemporary musical scene. In consort music not only did he absorb and transmute the instrumental forms of his predecessors – the hymns, *In Nomine*s, pavans and galliards – but he also faced the challenge of creating larger abstract pieces: grounds, variations and fantasias.[10] Although his surviving consorts are few in number, their importance should not be under-estimated. It is true that in many respects they sit somewhat apart from the later English instrumental music. That is hardly surprising, for the bulk of them were written at a time when interest in such music appears to have been at a low ebb and before its madrigal-inspired revival in Jacobean times. Yet for all that they act as a pivot between old and new; while a place remained for traditional consorts, such as those arranged on a ground or around a *cantus firmus*, it was Byrd above all who showed that the free fantasia for viols offered diverse and exciting new possibilities in instrumental form, texture and colour. Only ten of the latter by him are known, as varied in style and outlook as the genius of the man would lead one to expect. Since the English choral tradition was his first home it is natural that initially he drew features from cathedral music.

[9] British Library, Add. MS 29996, ff. 72v–73.

[10] Although not abstract, being based on a *cantus firmus*, his *Browning* ranks in scale and invention with the most extended and complicated fantasias. For the music *cf.* Kenneth Elliott, *The Byrd Edition, 17: Consort Music*, Stainer & Bell, London, 1971, and for the fullest discussion of it, *cf.*, Neighbour, *op. cit.*, pp. 69–4.

Indeed, it is more than likely that some of the so-called instrumental pieces, such as the early six-part Fantasia in F and the four-part Fantasia in G, are in reality transcription of vocal pieces – with some adaptations.[11] Among features pertaining to contemporary motet or chanson styles may be noted the division of a subject into two phrases which can be used separately or in conjunction, a succession of overlapping imitative sections and the repetition of balanced phrases or strains in which parts interchange. In a sense the symmetrical structure resulting from this last scheme is the negation of 'fantasia' if defined as a 'flight of rhapsodic fancy', but, if nothing else, Byrd taught that the form required tight balance and control. Concluding the same six-part fantasia, the composer introduces a melodic ostinato reminiscent of one used by Richard Alwood in a keyboard piece (Ex. 1).

Ex. 1

Insistent repetitions of this figure in all parts brings the passage close to the character of a ground. Elsewhere, Byrd's five-part Fantasia in C employs a canon at the fourth in the top two voices, a device which may owe

[11] Neighbour's assertion that the text was a later addition to the music of the four-part Fantasia in G major is disputed by David Pinto. Pinto points out that the one manuscript source – British Library, Add. MS 29427 from Thomas Myriell's collection – was copied *c.* 1610 and is much more likely to be an adaptation of the motet *In manus tuas* published in *Gradualia*, 1605. He remarks that it is perverse to argue that Byrd, having taken features from the English choral tradition for his free-composed fantasias, then converted them back again, especially when both were published with texts on his authority. On these grounds he finds it equally questionable that the six-part Fantasia in F major began life in an un-texted version. But *cf.* also John Milsom, 'A Tallis Fantasia', *Musical Times*, cxxvi, November 1985. pp. 658–62, for another piece which, it is argued, began life as an instrumental consort before conversion to the texted *O sacrum convivium/I call and cry*.

something to a five-part song by Robert Parsons.[12] Richard Mico, close associate of Byrd in his old age, also composed a five-part pavan with two trebles in canon.

It is difficult to ascertain how far Byrd and his contemporaries were influenced by continental ricercars. The latter find virtually no place in contemporary English manuscripts, but perhaps a few printed collections accompanied the flood of Italian madrigals which poured into the country towards the end of the century.[13] At any rate some Italianate elements are evident in Byrd's little three-part fantasias.[14] Restrained in character, pure in harmony and line, concise in working-out, consistently polyphonic and with an equality of interest between the parts, they epitomise the best in small-scale abstract composition. They probably rank among the last of his consort works.

Larger ensembles required (and received) a different approach for their correspondingly larger forms. In two of his four-part fantasias, those in G minor and A minor, Byrd separates the three principal imitative sections by two little interludes. Here at least is a device which later composers (including Jenkins) seized upon when planning their own fantasias. The difference is that Byrd might find some unifying rhythm or motif to link his interlude with neighbouring sections, whereas his successors, including Jenkins, generally opted for complete contrast. Another scheme formulated by Byrd and developed by later composers – again Jenkins is among them – was the creation of one longer paragraph from

[12] Neighbour, *op. cit.*, pp. 74–5.

[13] Neighbour notes that ricercars by Willaert were to be found in the library of Lord Lumley, a patron of Byrd: *ibid.*, p. 96. Although the music itself is largely lacking, the presence of many alien musicians resident in England must surely have provided a bridge by which works crossed from the continent. *Cf.*, for instance, the few pieces by 'Mr. Renold', Ferrabosco the Elder and James Harden in British Library, Add. MS 30485.

[14] Neighbour, *op. cit.*, pp. 95–100.

two (or more) overlapping imitative sections and defined by a strong final cadence. But the most imaginative and far-reaching step he took was to bring the secular world into the fantasia through the introduction of dance patterns and popular song. The latter often grow out of earlier motifs so that their appearance, while a delightful surprise, is yet in keeping with the work as a whole. In the five-part Fantasia in C major, for instance, Byrd prepares for the tune called *Sicke, sicke and very sicke* with a phrase of similar line, life and length (Ex. 2(a)). Similarly, a lively dialogue with near-canonic upper parts in the second six-part fantasia suddenly breaks into *Greensleeves* (Ex.2(b)). On both occasions they are rhythmic as much as melodic patterns which prepare the way. In the wake of these tunes come triple-time sections ('triplas' in contemporary parlance), fully-fledged galliards, or both, with all three works closing in a common-time coda. If the results come close to a medley, which after all was a familiar genre in Elizabethan times, it must be emphasised that the overall structure is most carefully organised.

Ex. 2

Although later composers chose not to take up the medley idea *per se*, its legacy of juxtaposed metres, textures and phrase structures remained available to them to develop in different ways. At the time it was an innovatory step, challenging the traditional pattern of a succession of imitative points, but by the turn of the century the two forms should be seen as co-existing alongside each other, just as the *concerto grosso* lived with the solo concerto a hundred years later. During what Ernst Meyer calls 'the age of plenty'[15] – say, 1600 to 1630 – composers

[15] Ernst H. Meyer, *Early English Chamber Music*, Lawrence and Wishart, London, 1982, Chapter Five.

of fantasia for viols were at liberty to emphasise either plan, conceding only that such works should (almost invariably) begin in fugal style.

But music of another kind was to prove a crucial influence on the development of the fantasia. When, in 1600, Thomas Weelkes published his *Madrigals of 5. and 6. parts* he labelled them as 'apt for the Viols and Voices' – the first madrigalist to have done so, although many others soon adopted the formula, It seems likely that by this title he was acknowledging the undoubted upsurge in popularity in playing the viol which had followed close in the wake of the madrigalian explosion. Links between madrigal and consort music are close, although their full association has yet to be traced. Both, of course, must be viewed against the social change of the period.

During the reign of Elizabeth, England remained curiously apart from European developments in Renaissance art. In his fascinating study of Henry, Prince of Wales, Roy Strong writes:

> Stylistically England was a backwater, for Gloriana's reign had been a rock against change. It had almost glorified in its own insularity, producing during its last two decades a unique and archaic visual culture which had little to do with the mainstream of Renaissance art [...].[16]

Elizabeth's court was insular too in another sense. There the Virgin Queen was the sole patron of artistic activity; her taste alone prevailed. Only belatedly did the ideals of Italianate humanism gain acceptance in England. With the power of the state wrested from the clergy and transferred to the nobility, Elizabeth left patronage of the arts largely to the latter; the burgeoning of their vast country houses, as each lord vied with the others to assert his superior status, laid the base for artistic change, for it was the taste and learning of these men – the Herberts, Sydneys, Cecils, Sackvilles, and their like – which was to

[16] *Henry, Prince of Wales, and England's Lost Renaissance*, Thames and Hudson, London, 1986, pp. 87–8.

influence so much the direction taken by drama, literature, architecture and music.[17] It is no accident that, by James I's reign, English music mirrors this transfer of power emphasising the secular rather than the sacred forms, nor that within his court a group of composers emerge owing no allegiance to the church: Ferrabosco II, Lupo and Coprario, for instance.

Although the general musical life of the Jacobean court largely maintained the *status quo* – so far as surviving records show – the interests of individual members of the royal family allowed a much more diverse and adventurous cultural life to develop around this core. First there was Anne of Denmark's devotion to the masque, establishing the genre as a regular feature in the court calendar. More significant still was the brief but brilliant flowering of the establishment of Henry, Prince of Wales, which aspired to emulate the artistic patronage of the Medicis and their like, but which was brought to a premature end in 1612 at the youth's untimely and unexpected death. Among his close circle of friends and advisers were cultured men, including Sir Henry Fanshawe, Edward Cecil, Henry Wriothesley, Thomas Howard and Sir John Harrington, all of whom had a particular affection for Italian arts. The Prince's own musicians included Angelo Notari, whose *Prime Musiche Nuove* (1613) so sharply points to the contrast between contemporary English and Italian music, Thomas Lupo and, as teacher and extraordinary Groom of the Privy Chamber (a specially favoured position), Alphonso Ferrabosco. Although he appears to have had no regular court post at this time, John Coprario, as musician in the Cecil household, was very much in touch with court music; his *Songs of Mourning: Bewailing the untimely death of Prince Henry* (1613) to texts by Thomas Campion are among the most eloquent elegies produced in tribute. There was a four-

[17] *Cf.* Lawrence Stone, *The Crisis of the Aristocracy, 1558–1641*, Oxford University Press, Oxford, 1967, Chapter Twelve.

year gap before Henry's younger brother Charles was created Prince of Wales in his stead, on 3 November 1616. Records of Charles' establishment are extremely fragmentary, but it is clear that a number of Henry's musicians were re-appointed to serve him. These include Ferrabosco, Lupo and Notari, with Orlando Gibbons and Coprario among the new names. In spite of James' appointment of Thomas Lupo as

> composer for our violins, that they may be the better furnished with variety and choise for our delight and pleasure in that kind,[18]

it is likely that new musical development at court after about 1620 would emanate from the Prince's chambers. Playford's remark that

> For Instrumental Musick none pleased him [Charles] like those Fantazies for one *Violin* and *Basses Viol*, to the Organ, Composed by Mr. *Coperario*,

to which Charles 'could play his part exactly well on the *Bass-Viol*'[19] show that he delighted in the most bold and innovatory instrumental pieces of the period. Furthermore, Lupo, Gibbons and Ferrabosco all held double posts, serving both Monarch and Prince simultaneously. They too may have written their most modern pieces, such as the three-part fantasias with violins by Gibbons and Lupo, for the Prince rather than for the King.

Returning to the impact which foreign culture had on the English arts of the period, a number of lines of communication can be noted. Of considerable significance must have been the many aliens, particularly refugee Huguenots, who sought and found employment at Elizabeth's court. Some were artists and jewellers, like the Olivers and Hardrets, and some musicians, like the Laniers and Hardens, all tied up in an inextricable knot

[18] Public Record Office, LC5/115, dated 16 February 1621.

[19] John Playford, *A Brief Introduction to the Skill of Music*, 4th edn., London, 1664, p. xiii, and 10th edn., London, 1683, preface.

of intermarriages.[20] Such families, together with the previously settled players of Jewish and/or Italian origin – the Bassanos, Lupos, Comeys and Galliardellos[21] – virtually monopolised court music until after the Restoration. Emigrant catholics from England tended to settle in the Low Countries, where their musical influence was considerable. Numerous companies of English actors/musicians also earned their living there.[22] On the other hand relatively little Dutch influence can be detected in English music, although some popular tunes, like *Der Rommelpot* in Orlando Gibbons' second fantasia featuring the 'great dooble bass', were imported.

By the end of the sixteenth century foreign languages and foreign travel featured strongly in the education of the English elite, while English merchants played their part in bringing home Italian books and music. Although the number of people involved in this Italian connection was relatively small, the group nevertheless wielded a powerful influence on English cultural life. Thomas Morley, perhaps the most influential figure in the promotion of Italian music and musical style in England, even felt that an English composer was a prophet without honour in his own country:

> [...] such be the newfangled opinions of our countrymen, who will highly esteem whatsoever cometh from beyond the seas, and specially from Italy, be it never so simple,

[20] *Cf.* Mary Edmond, 'Limners and Picturemakers: New light on the lives of miniaturists and large-scale portrait-painters working in London in the sixteenth and seventeenth centuries', *Journal of the Walpole Society*, XLVII, 1980; Mary Edmond, *Hilliard and Oliver: The Lives and Works of Two Great Miniaturists*, Robert Hale, London, 1983.

[21] *Cf.* Peter Holman, 'The English Royal Violin Consort in the Sixteenth Century, *Proceedings of the Royal Musical Association*, 109, 1982–3, pp. 39–59.

[22] *Cf.* Alan Curtis, *Sweelinck's Keyboard Music*, E. J. Brill, 3rd edn., Leiden, 1987, pp. 10–34.

> contemning that which is done at home though it be never so excellent.[23]

David Pinto has drawn attention to the particular welcome given to the work of the Italian poet Giovanni Battista Guarini:

> It is far from fortuitous that the name of Guarini is prominent among [known English settings of Italian texts] since the educated circle around the Sidney and Herbert families, that took the initiative in directing the cultural activities of the new Stuart Court, had for some while kept a keen eye on Italy [...]. Guarini's style, though sensuous, was employed in the service of a moralising outlook on life that embodied in pastoral allegory of an archaic society a depiction of stoical Christian reliance on Providence – even outside the wake of the Counter-Reformation this, perhaps, explains the pull of his influence on thoughtful or sober-minded (but artistically cautious) patrons in England. For composers on the verge of a purely instrumental style the vogue could not have been more opportune, since it gave them license to merge usually incompatible dialects into an absolute language of greater potential resource.[24]

There is a substantial body of music with Italian texts or titles by English composers and of Italian madrigals 'Englished'. Clearly the five outstanding collections of Italian madrigals published in England between 1588 and 1598 exerted a profound influence, but while their impact on vocal music has been studied in some detail,[25] their links with instrumental music await full investigation. But it is already evident that incipits from some of these works

[23] *Op. cit.*, p. 179.

[24] 'The Fantasy Manner: the Seventeenth Century Context', *Chelys*, 10, 1981, pp. 26–8.

[25] *Cf.* Joseph Kerman, *The Elizabethan Madrigal; A Comparative Study*, American Musicological Society, New York, 1962.

were used as the basis for instrumental fantasias.[26] Much more problematical are the numerous textless pieces by Ward, Coprario and Lupo included in English manuscript collections of fantasias, but which are given Italian titles. Are these madrigals or fantasias? A mere handful are known with complete texts:

Ward:	Cor mio, deh! non languire	(Guarini)	*à 5*
Coprario:	Deh cara anima mia		*à 5*
	Udite lagrimosi spirti	(Guarini)	*à 6*
	Che mi consigli amore		*à 6*

Though Ward's piece appears in most instrumental collections, words are only supplied in Francis Tregian's vast anthology (British Library, Egerton MS 3665). But it is typical of Sir Nicholas L'Estrange's meticulous manner that he adds a note to his copy in British Library, Add. MSS 39550–4:

> This is called 'Cor Mio' in Mr Barn: B: [Barnard's book] and not numbered among the fancies because as well for voices and violles. Set for voices. Fan. b. [Fanshawe's book].

From this there can be little doubt that 'Cor mio' was a madrigal written for Ward's patron and employer, Sir Henry Fanshawe (d. 1616). Sir Henry's daughter-in-law relates that he was 'the favourite of Prince Henry' and 'a great lover of music, and kept many gentlemen that were perfectly well qualified both in that and the Italian tongue, in which he spent some time'.[27]

Texts for Coprario's three pieces are found in one of the earliest sources – Ellesmere MSS EL 25 A 46–51 at the Huntington Library, San Marino, California – in a

[26] *Cf.* Joan Wess, 'Musica Transalpina, Parody, and the Emerging Jacobean Viol Fantasia', *Chelys*, 15, 1986, pp. 3–25.

[27] *Memoirs of Lady Fanshawe*, ed. N. H. Nicolas, London, 1829, pp. 13–14, quoted in John Aplin, 'Sir Henry Fanshawe and Two Sets of early Seventeenth-Century Part-books at Christ Church, Oxford'. *Music & Letters*, 57, 1976, pp. 11–24.

group described as 'Madrigali', though again later manuscripts omit the words and set them in an instrumental context. Many other pieces preserve only Italian titles, but these too may have had vocal origins. By far the largest group in this category is the series of 49 five-part 'fantasias' by Coprario. Significantly 46 of these pieces were removed by Francis Tregian from his collection of madrigals and transferred to one of instrumental works.[28] Though some doubts remain, Richard Charteris presents convincing arguments in favour of considering these works as madrigals. He points out that texted and un-texted versions are largely identical and that such features as

> density of texture [...], the tessitura or the angular shape of the vocal line [...], the type of division writing in quavers (and less frequently semiquavers)

which would seem to indicate an instrumental origin, find their parallels in vocal items.[29] It has already been noted that Byrd drew upon vocal models in dividing a subject into two phrases which might be used separately, or in conjunction. This technique takes on a new lease of life in these pieces by Coprario, as is shown by the opening of No. 29 (*Ninfa crudele*), for instance (Ex. 3). Some two-thirds of the pieces go even further and open directly with a double theme. The completely texted (*Deh cara anima mia baciami tanto* (No. 32) show this device to result from the simultaneous rather than successive grouping of textual phrases (Ex. 4). Further tenuous links between

[28] 'John Coprario's Five- and Six-part Pieces: Instrumental or Vocal?', *Music & Letters*, 57, 1976, pp. 370–8.

[29] *Ibid*. For the opposite view *cf*. Clifford Bartlett's review of Charteris' edition of Coprario's five-part pieces in *Chelys*, 11, 1982, pp. 38–9; also Thurston Dart in 'Jacobean Consort Music', *Musica Britannica*, Vol, IX, Stainer & Bell, London, 2nd edn., 1962, p. 222. The music is published, ed. Richard Charteris: 'John Coprario, The Five-part Pieces', *Corpus Mensurabilis Musicae*, 92, American Institute of Musicology, 1981.

Coprario's six-part 'fantasias' and Guarini's *Il Pastor Fido* have been suggested by David Pinto, who also notes that 'Italian preference for lines of seven or eleven syllables in madrigalian verse is mirrored in the length of the often-recurring phrases of declamatory homophony in Coprario's fantasias'.[30]

Ex. 3

Ex. 4

The argument as to whether Coprario really did visit Italy early in his career remains unresolved, but there is no disputing either the Italianate nature of more than seventy of his works or the fact that this is an unusually large proportion of his output to adopt such an idiom were it intended solely for English consumption.

Thomas Lupo, on the other hand, belonged to a Jewish-Italian family long employed at the English court, so it is more natural to find him writing madrigal-fantasias. Although none survives with texts attached, five (in five parts) have Italian titles, some of which have been identified by David Pinto:

[30] David Pinto, *loc. cit.*, p. 25. For the music *cf. John Coprario: The Six-part Consorts and Madrigals*, ed. Richard Charteris, Boethius Press, Clarabricken, 1982. The fullest biographical account of Coprario and of his supposed visit to Italy is in Charteris' *John Coprario: A Thematic Catalogue of His Music*, Pendragon, New York, 1977.

> For the now textless madrigals 'Alte parole' and 'Che fia lasso di me' (five-part fantasias nos. 9 and 29), Lupo must have culled his poetry from Orazio Vecchi's *Libro Primo à 6* (Venice, 1583; reprinted 1588, 1591), where 'Alte parole e leggiadrett' accenti' functions as a seconda parte to 'Occhi soave'. His five-part fantasy 'Ardo' (no. 19) is nothing other than a double setting of a celebrated proposta and risposta: Guarini's 'Ardo si, ma non t'amo' (Madrigal 101) and Tasso's 'Ardi et gela a tua voglia'. Vocal settings like these are among the most spirited of Lupo's output.[31]

Ardo, indeed, is written in two balancing sections – a feature not lost on Jenkins when he came to compose some of his large-scale mature fantasias – and is a most effective work. As Ex. 5 shows, the chains of suspensions above a slow-moving bass and the moulding of the individual lines is truly vocal in style. Even some of the untitled pieces hint at madrigalian influence. The bold opening of No. 5 in six parts, for instance, offers a striking alternative to the usual imitative exposition (Ex. 6), and elsewhere there are plenty of similarly formed interludes giving some respite from polyphonic writing. But it would be wrong to look on Lupo primarily as a composer of madrigal-fantasias. Although his work is uneven in quality, he shows himself to be particularly imaginative in exploring new structural possibilities, new instrumental groupings and a more idiomatic instrumental style.

But neither Ward nor Coprario were unduly concerned with developing an instrumental idiom – at least

[31] David Pinto, *loc. cit.*, p. 24. He notes (in a letter to me) that some of Lupo's motets too appear without texts in instrumental collections: for instance, the 'songs fit for vials and organ in the great books' (e.g. British Library, Add. MSS 29372–7) listed by Thomas Myriell in Christ Church, Music MS 67. A complete edition of Lupo's consort music is in progress, ed. John Jennings and Richard Charteris (Boethius Press). For accounts of his music *cf.* John Jennings, 'The Fantasias of Thomas Lupo', *Musicology*, III, 1968–9 and *Chelys*, 3, 1971, pp. 3–15 (the same article); John Jennings, 'Thomas Lupo revisited – is Key the key to his later music?, *Chelys*, 12, 1983, pp. 19–22.

Ex. 5

Ex. 6

in their viol fantasias. The vocal parentage of Coprario's five- and six-part 'fantasias' is clear from the manuscripts, but the same cannot be said of his three- and four-part pieces, none of which acquired Italian (or even English) titles. Meyer comments that

> the number of sections in the three- and four-part pieces [by Coprario] even exceeds that in Lupo's fantasias [...]. Coprario's fantasias are full of variety, of changing musical pictures which pass by in constant succession.[32]

These sections are naturally short and section boundaries are generally clearly-defined. As it happens, this is exactly the principle which Coprario was to exploit in heightened form and so successfully in his pioneering Fantasia-Suites of the 1620s.[33] But for the time being he avoids the more sprightly and angular ideas which later so suited the violin, the excursions into triple time and the bolder use of instrumental colour. The relative brevity of the phrases is again suggestive of vocal patterns, whether in matching a line of poetry, or in allowing the 'singers' to

[32] *Op. cit.*, p. 162.

[33] Richard Charteris (ed.), 'John Coprario: Fantasia-Suites', *Musica Britannica*, Vol. XLVI, Stainer & Bell, London, 1980.

breathe. One of the three-part fantasias, No. 6, is monothematic. Its extreme simplicity in all parts, with abundant stepwise movement, hints that it was written for those taking their first tentative steps in playing consort fantasias.

Where Coprario's fantasias move rapidly through constantly changing ideas, those by John Ward are altogether more expansive. It is clear as much from his vocal as from his instrumental output that he preferred to work with the larger groupings of five and six parts, but that is not to deny the high quality and attractive manner of his six four-part fantasias, one of which old Dudley North praised for its 'brisk, lusty, yet mellifluent vein'.[34] But which John Ward wrote these pieces? Until 1984 it was assumed that one man wrote all music attributed to the name. My proposal in that year[35] that perhaps two men, possibly father and son, were active as composers seems to be bearing fruit, although scholars cannot yet agree how their works should be divided.[36] It seems likely that the younger man wrote the consort music.

Ward's fantasias have more breadth than those of Coprario because imitative work is expanded to create longer sections and there are numerous long slow passages full of telling suspensions and plangent harmony. Of all the parts the bass tends to be the least involved in imitative exchanges, in many instances clearly serving to underpin the harmony. Ward's use of chromaticism is generally cautions, although three of the five-part fantasias

[34] *Op. cit.*, p. 5.

[35] In a review of Craig Monson's *Voices and Viols in England, 1600–1650: The Sources and the Music*, UMI Research Press, Ann Arbor, 1982, in *Music & Letters*, 64, 1983, pp. 252–5.

[36] *Cf.* Robert Ford, 'John Ward of Canterbury', *Journal of the Viola da Gamba Society of America*, XXIII, 1986, pp. 51–63; Ian Payne, 'The Handwriting of John Ward', *Music & Letters*, 65, 1984, pp. 176–88.

toy with it for a while.[37] The most interesting of these is No. 1, where enharmonic movement round a circle of fifths anticipates the use to which Jenkins puts the device in his four-part fantasias Nos. 7 and 15.[38] But nowhere does he relish chromaticism to quite the same extent as Coprario in his six-part madrigal (fantasia) *Udite lagrimosi spirti* (Ex. 7), notwithstanding the fact that this example stands outside Coprario's normal practice. Ward's work can lack fluidity: rigid and somewhat mechanical imitations create a static effect rather than forward-flowing development, with both harmony and figuration tending towards undue repetition as in his five-part Fantasia No. 9 (Ex. 8). Nevertheless, the five- and six-part pieces are full of stunning contrasts, heightened by antiphonal interchanges and sometimes punctuated by dramatic silences.

As David Pinto points out,[39] one change directly attributable to madrigalian influence is a shift in instrumental scoring. Where earlier consorts tend to preserve a graded range of parts similar to that of sixteenth-century church polyphony – a single treble with alto, tenor, baritone, bass, or some parallel variant – later ones move towards a more brilliant and lighter ensemble featuring two equal trebles, alto/tenor, tenor and bass, while in three-part pieces composers increasingly neglect treble, tenor and bass textures in favour of two trebles and bass. By Jenkins' time the larger ensembles had settled into consistent combinations, but the Jacobeans still indulged in some experimenting and a number of unusual scorings can be found: some four- and five-part fantasias by Lupo and Coprario with two basses, or six-part ones by Ferrabosco II with three trebles, for instance.

Movement away from vocal models had to come, of course, if the fantasia was to develop, but might not the

[37] Nos. 1, 3 and 7. Ward's five- and six-part consorts are to be published, ed. Ian Payne, in the *Musica Britannica* series.

[38] *Cf.* Chapter Five, pp. 217 and 220.

[39] 'William Lawes' Music for Viol Consort', *Early Music*, VI, 1978, p. 19.

Ex. 7

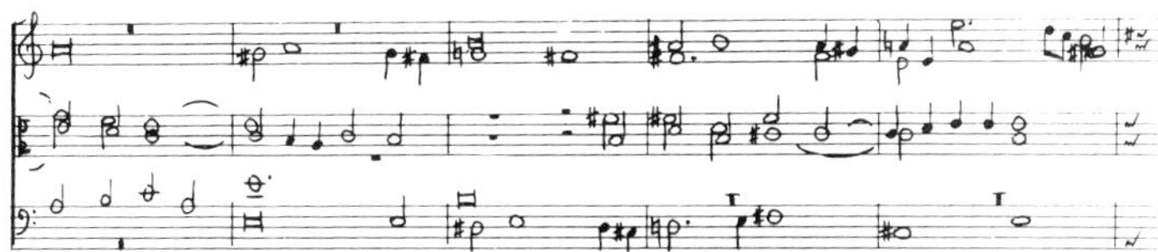

Ex. 8

turn be partly explained by Joseph Kerman's proposition that 'the English could never entirely reconcile themselves to the Italians' fundamental literary aesthetic'? He notes that

> behind modern elements in the style of the English madrigalists, one can always detect a tendency to write counterpoint for its own sake, forgetting for the moment the demands of text-illustration or declamation. [...] To be sure the Elizabethan madrigal was never a literary movement. It was imported and developed mainly by musicians, and poets did not play a dominant role in its history, as they had in Italy before.[40]

[40] *Op. cit.*, pp. 98 and 130.

The loss of madrigal texts, especially those in a foreign language, might also be explained by the same premise, re-inforced by the fact that by 1620 or so any waves of foreign emulation were temporarily receding – a tide which only turned again after the Restoration.

It has to be remembered that the work of this generation of composers – Coprario, Lupo, Ward, Gibbons, Ferrabosco II, Dering and others – overlaps with the early part of Jenkins' life. Their work and his first pieces cannot be placed in any chronological perspective; the question of who influenced whom becomes difficult to probe and answer. Although of this group only Ward lived beyond 1630, many of them must nevertheless have remained active composers well into the 1620s, by which time Jenkins had reached maturity as a composer.

As a violinist at court, Thomas Lupo was in the forefront of musical development in England. While most of his larger fantasias for viols are written in a traditional way, a good many of his pieces for smaller groupings break fresh ground. Throughout Lupo's work capricious rhythmic patterns and irregular phrase structure show a marked movement away from vocal style. He was especially fond of employing a double-subject to open his fantasias (like Coprario): about half of his five-part pieces, for instance, open in this way. Imitative treatment of themes seems rather looser than in the work of most of his contemporaries. Many pieces present a lively succession of ideas, none of which settles for very long, and Lupo is equally adept at ringing the changes with regard both to the interchange of slower and faster sections and to the instrumental groupings within the chosen ensemble. Textures are relatively open, with plenty of rests. Occasionally, though, he aims for a more integrated structure. One fine example is the four-part Fantasia No. 1, whose double theme serves for the whole piece (Ex. 9(a)). It is a master-stroke to form the slower-moving central section from augmented versions of the subjects (in combination with other ideas (Ex. 9(b)) and bring all together again at normal speed as the piece draws to its lively close (Ex. 9(c)). The concluding imitative exchanges at the unison or octave over a dominant pedal are another feature which Jenkins adopted most effectively (Ex. 9(d)).

Ex. 9

It seems likely that Lupo's most progressive pieces were written towards the end of his life, after his appointment as composer to the violins to James I in February 1621, or as musician to Prince Charles.[41] Certainly the treble parts of a number of his consort pieces are suited to performance by violins, especially some of the three-part fantasias for two trebles and a bass. How much such works owe to Italian examples of the kind and how far they can be rated as an English breed is open to question; surely, though, Gibbons was a significant influence here, since the two men must have worked closely together at court for a decade or more. But Lupo tried a variety of scorings in his music and among the three-part pieces are fantasias for two trebles and tenor, or treble and two tenors in addition to the usual treble, tenor and bass. There are even two remarkable works for three equal instruments; one appears in various manuscripts scored for trebles

[41] The same is true of Gibbons; *cf*. pp. 133–5.

or tenors, the other for basses. Like Gibbons, Lupo introduces *tripla* sections in some of his three-part fantasias.

Four of the five- and six-part works,[42] absent from the earliest sources, bring in 'divisions', another feature which was to play a major part in later seventeenth-century consorts. Perhaps these pieces were written with specific players in mind, for the likelihood is that they were performed by the 'private musick' at court. In the six-part works the two bass parts only are florid – as is the case in Gibbons' six-part variations on 'Go from my window' – while in the five-part pieces, like Fantasia No. 16 (Ex. 10), these are joined by a *concertante* treble (probably a violin) leaving the two middle parts in a supporting role.

Ex. 10

Six of Lupo's four-part fantasias ought really to be called 'Air', for they bear little resemblance to the traditional fantasia. In character they come close to the masque dances which were so popular by this time, though they are not divided into true strains. No doubt these pieces too originated at court as Lupo fulfilled his obligations as composer for the violins

> that they may be the better furnished with variety and choise for our delight and pleasure in that kind.[43]

Here again, he varies the scoring and among the genuine viol fantasias in this group are three for two trebles and two basses which seem to be the earliest works for this

[42] Nos. 16–17 *à 5* and 9–10 *à 6*.

[43] Public Record Office, LC5/115.

scoring. If so, their example was to bear rich fruit in years to come as Jenkins built up several very fine collections with two basses, but especially his magnificent series of 32 'Ayres' for this particular combination.[44]

Perhaps it is an acknowledgement of the pervasive Italian influence in English musical life which in the 1580s caused the wait William Gibbons to call two of his sons by Italian names: Ferdinando and Orlando. Yet of all the major Jacobean composers of consort music it is Orlando Gibbons who owes least to the Italian style and who benefits most from Byrd's legacy. Like Byrd, of course, he held a post in the Chapel Royal, being appointed organist there on 21 March 1604/5, but later he also became 'one of his Maties Musicians for the virginalles to attend in his highnes privie Chamber' which would have brought him into more direct contact with the work of James I's Private Musick, including such figures as Ferrabosco II and Lupo. Around forty pieces of consort music by Gibbons survive, richly varied in style, the majority being fantasias. Again, though only nine years Jenkins' senior, Gibbons can hardly be though of as belonging to an earlier generation, but the timing of those nine years seems crucial. While none of Jenkins' mature work can be attributed to the first decades of the century, the bulk of Gibbons' consort music seems to have been written then.[45]

To some extent he trod the same path as Byrd. Beginning with a series of youthful *cantus firmus* pieces (four-

[44] *Cf.* Andrew Ashbee, 'John Jenkins: Consort Music of Four Parts, *Musica Britannica*, Vol. XXVI, Stainer & Bell, London, rev. edn., 1975, Nos. 1–32.

[45] On Gibbons' consort music *cf.*: Francis Baines, 'The Consort Music of Orlando Gibbons, *Early Music*, VI, 1978, pp. 540–3; Oliver Neighbour, 'Orlando Gibbons (1583–1625): The Consort Music', *Early Music*, XI, 1983, pp. 351–7; John Harper, 'The Distribution of the Consort Music of Orlando Gibbons in Seventeenth-Century Sources', *Chelys*, 12, 1983, pp. 3–18; John Harper (ed.), 'Orlando Gibbons: Consort Music', *Musica Britannica*, Vol. XLVIII, Stainer & Bell, London, 1982; Michael Hobbs (ed.), *Orlando Gibbons: Six Fantasias for Viols in Six Parts*, Faber Music, London, 1982.

and five-part *In Nomines*), he moved on to works planned on the lines of ricercar or madrigal and eventually experimented with the introduction of *triplas* and popular tunes. His magnificent six-part fantasias are likely to be among the first works of his maturity and exploit the rich resources of the full consort, at times bending towards a vocal style, with voice-leading (Ex. 11(a)) or homophonic interludes (Ex. 11(b)), but at others building (Ex. 11(c)) a complex web of polyphony from wide-ranging melodies or drawing out long expressive lines with chains of suspensions and rich harmony (Ex. 11(d)). Three other six-part 'fantasias' attributed to him stand apart; they seem to have begun life as verse anthems and should be viewed in the same light as other Jacobean consorts which once may have been vocal.

Ex. 11

(a)

(b)

(c)

(d)

Consort music was rarely published, but Gibbons bravely had nine of his three-part fantasias 'Cut in Copper, the like not heretofore extant', as the title-page proudly announces. This little book proved to be influential not only in providing a stylish copy-hand for others to imitate, but also as an advocate for consorts of smaller groupings. The large series of three-part fantasias by Lupo may in part have been inspired by Gibbons' collection – and initially were presumably played by the same group of musicians – but there can be little doubt that Jenkins, too, was encouraged by this example to begin both his splendid series of three-part fantasias. Gibbons' three-part consorts are particularly interesting because they are so diverse in character and scoring. The publication begins with a group of four fantasias scored for treble, tenor and bass viols, all in the traditional format of a succession of imitative 'points'. The remaining five works are for two trebles and bass; at court at least the upper parts may have been taken by violins. As with some of Lupo's consorts, there is a definite move towards a more popular manner. Regular phrase-structure and shapely melody, like that opening Fantasia V (Ex. 12), hint that the masque dance is hovering nearby, and in Fantasias VII and IX contrast is further increased by the introduction of triple-time passages. At the same time canonic and sequential passages which feature prominently in all Gibbons' instrumental work (Ex. 13) probably owe much to the composer's church activities since both disciplines are equally evident in his anthems and services.

It has been suggested[46] that the printed collection was published around 1620, but the span of composition cannot be determined on available evidence. Family resemblances within the various groups of pieces may point to a relatively short gestation period.

[46] First by Thurston Dart, in 'The Printed Fantasias of Orlando Gibbons', *Music & Letters*, 37, 1956, p. 342.

Ex. 12

Ex. 13

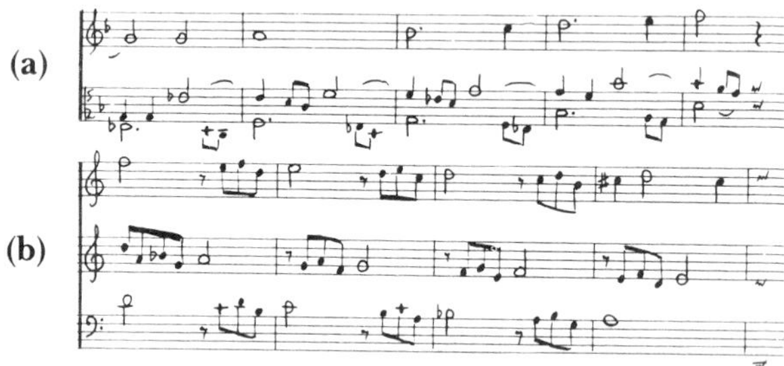

Perhaps contemporary and with these printed works, or even later, are a remarkable group of pieces written for the unusual combination of treble, bass, 'great dooble base' and organ. The precise contribution of the latter is indistinct, its notated part being restricted to a few extra lines in the texture, particularly in the opening bars, making a four-voice ensemble. Two of the group are in four parts with an added tenor.[47] More than one commentator has remarked that this series forms

> a new experiment in texture, providing also a new dimension in sound. Sometimes the top and bottom parts are separated by four octaves, so that the middle part stands out with startling clarity; the parts never cross.[48]

Peter Holman has suggested that these works may be

[47] Some doubt exists as to whether Nos. 5–7 of this three-part group are by Gibbons; *cf.* Neighbour's article cited in note 45, p. 131.

[48] Francis Baines, 'Fantasias for the Great Dooble Base', *Chelys*, 2, 1970, pp. 37–8.

connected with Gibbons' patrons, the Hatton family. They seem to have owned a 'great dooble base' since the instrument is also called for in some pieces by the steward, George Jeffries, later in the century.[49] Gibbons' pieces continue the trend towards increasingly well-defined sectional structure through increased exploitation of contrasting elements, and the 'popular' vein is further developed. Two *tripla* sections occur in No. 2, while the strains of *der Rommelpot* are to be heard in No. 3 and *Rufty-Tufty* in the first four-part fantasia. These works are altogether larger in scale than the other three-part pieces.

It is interesting that the introduction of an organ here stems from a composer who helped forge that instrument's independence in verse anthems and it seems to coincide with a general move towards providing a written part for the instrument in all or major consort pieces. Where fantasias for viols were concerned, there was little attempt at exploiting the organ for its own sake; rather it merely doubled the string parts, serving, in Thomas Mace's words,

> in stead of Holding, United-Constant-Friend; and [...] as a Touch-stone, to try the certainty of All Things; especially the Well-keeping the Instruments in Tune, &c. And in This Service the Organ should be Equally Heard to All; but especially to the Performers Themselves, who cannot well Perform, without a Distinct Perceivance Thereof.

Mace, of course, was writing with amateur performance in mind, and, moreover, having listed the advantages of a table organ, which

> standing in the midst, must needs be of a more certain and steady use to Those Performers, than if It stood at a Distance; They all Equally Receiving the same Benefit, no one more than another [...].

[49] 'George Jeffries and the "great dooble base"', *Chelys*, 5, 1973–4, pp. 79–81.

goes on to advertise his own for sale, for '(by Reason of my Deafness) [...] I have (of Late Years) parted with It [...]'! Notwithstanding his personal preferences and circumstances, he is at pains to emphasise that

> the Organ in This Service [is] not [...] Eminently to be Heard, but only Equal with the other Musick.[50]

Earlier manuscripts of consort music (before the 1620s) generally exclude any part for the organ. Provision of an organ book did not become standard practice until late in the Jacobean era, although the instrument went on to make its mark much more distinctly in the fantasia-suites and consort music of the Caroline years. Yet it would be injudicious to suppose that it was excluded from earlier performances, especially those which were in any way 'public', or which required extra body for the sound to carry sufficiently to auditors. Clearly the organ was an established part of the furniture in many of England's magnificent houses at the turn of the new century: the ancient instrument still at Knole (1623?), the numerous references in the Cecil papers to tuning and moving organs between 1607 and 1611, and Thomas Dallam's purchase of 'a portative wind instrument which stands at Court at my Lord Chamberlain's' all testify to its regular use.[51]

Of the major Jacobean instrumental composers there remains Alphonso Ferrabosco the Younger. Son of an Italian musician employed at the Elizabethan court, he himself evidently showed musical promise as a child and gained several places in James I's (and later Charles I's) establishment. Although he was active as a singer and composer for masques – and published a book of songs in 1609 – his principal claim to fame now rests with his

[50] *Musick's Monument*, London, 1676, p. 242.

[51] *Cf.* particularly Richard Charteris, 'Jacobean Musicians at Hatfield House, 1605–1613', *Royal Musical Association Research Chronicle*, 12, 1974, pp. 115–36.

instrumental work, particularly his fantasias for viols. More than fifty consorts by him survive, in four, five and six parts, compared with a mere dozen attributed to his father. Curiously enough, where five parts are concerned he does not seem to have composed any true fantasias on the lines of the four- and six-part collections, but the eight outstanding pavans in five parts more than compensate for the absence of fantasias. He had no interest in following the path chosen by his contemporaries of adapting and transferring madrigalian characteristics to their consorts; rather his fantasias are consistently polyphonic, with hardly a trace of other textures. His was a real attempt to break away from vocal patterns and establish a truly idiomatic instrumental corpus: the first to provide substantial collections of consorts to match the size and scope of contemporary books of madrigals. The venture proved highly successful, for surviving manuscript sources contain more copies of Ferrabosco's consorts than of any others. Twenty or more transcriptions of each work are common for his very fine series of four-part fantasias, for instance, compared with only eight or less for those by Jenkins. On first acquaintance some of Ferrabosco's themes may seem a trifle austere – especially when compared with Jenkins' 'true musicall ayre' – but in practice they prove both pliant and adaptable for their purpose. As Gordon Dodd points out, Ferrabosco 'was an architect (like his father) rather than a tone-painter'.[52] It is the architectural aspect of fantasia writing which Ferrabosco mastered so brilliantly and which Jenkins in particular was to develop in the next generation. The paramount feature which affected many smaller scale initiatives was the movement away from the accepted pattern of a succession of half-a-dozen or so imitative points towards a structure based on two balancing sections. The increased exposure of subjects because of the expansion

52 'Alfonso Ferrabosco II – The Art of the Fantasy', *Chelys*, 7, 1977, pp. 47–53. *Cf.* also Raymond Vaught, *The Fancies of Alfonso Ferrabosco II*, unpublished Ph.D. dissertation, Stanford University, California, 1959.

of sections demanded considerable resource if mere long-windedness was to be avoided, but Ferrabosco proved equal to the challenge. Commentators have noted that the best of the composer's works 'display an extraordinary quality of controlled excitement'[53] and that his 'groups of quavers have a determined onward drive, giving an impression of bubbling energy and a copious head of steam'.[54] To achieve this momentum the composer takes particular care in building individual sections so that they culminate in a climax which often involves some feat of contrapuntal ingenuity. To give one example: the pure and simple exposition of his four-part Fantasia No. 17[55] with its regularly-spaced entries is decidedly motet-like in style, but successive introduction of dotted rhythms, stretto, rhythmic modifications to the theme and some separate emphasis of its (descending) tail maintain interest, eventually leading to a close combining all these elements with augmented and diminished forms of the subject (Ex. 14).

Constant rhythmic alteration to the subject is much more natural in an instrumental than in a vocal context and is a device of which Ferrabosco – and later Jenkins – was particularly fond. Both use it to sustain interest in their more expansive paragraphs.

A particularly distinctive feature in Ferrabosco's fantasias is his use of pedal points in the bars leading up to an invariably well-defined cadence at the close of all substantial sections. In the middle of a work these will normally be on the dominant (as shown by the relatively brief example in Ex. 14), but the composer was fond also of employing a long tonic pedal to conclude his fantasias,

[53] Robert Donington, *Grove's Dictionary*, 5th edn., Macmillan, London, 1952.

[54] Dodd, *loc. cit.*, p. 51.

[55] *Musica Britannica*, Vol. IX, No. 21. *Cf.* Dodd, *loc. cit.*, for another example of a complex and ingenious conclusion in four-part Fantasia No. 20.

Ex. 14

around which other parts weave in intricate counterpoint (Ex. 15) – a characteristic which was hardly new, since it is readily found in many early madrigals by Arcadelt and others.

Ex. 15

A unity may be given to the whole work by thematic links between subjects of different sections. In Ex. 14, for instance, the upward scale pattern of the new subject in the last bar bears a strong family resemblance to that of the opening section, its livelier character driving the music forward while also contrasting effectively with the relatively smooth motion of the earlier part. More obvious still is the limited rhythmic adjustment to the subject of four-part Fantasia No. 16 (Ex. 16(a)) which, as part of a double act, serves also as the basis for the second half of this work (Ex. 16(b)). Employment of such double themes is common in Ferrabosco's fantasias.

Ex. 16

(a)  (b)

So, too, are subjects which divide into two phrases, as in Fantasias Nos. 5 (Ex. 17(a)) and 7 (Ex. 17(b)). Either form of construction gives the composer a wealth of material from which to build his fugues.

Ex. 17

(a)

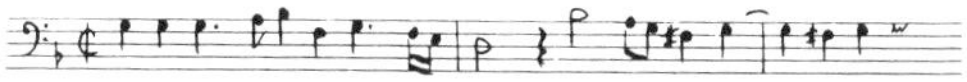

(b)

Some fantasias have double expositions, one perhaps introducing instruments from the treble down and the other from the bass up (as in the four-part Fantasia No. 18), or vice versa (as in the four-part Fantasia No. 4). Where these employ double themes, invertible counterpoint is put to good use, as indeed it is also in the works of Coprario and Lupo. Antiphonal effects are quite common – again Fantasia No. 17 provides a splendid example of paired duets between the two inner and two outer parts, but Ferrabosco's six-part consorts do not feature the device to anything like the same extent as those by Coprario, Ward or William White.

Although his use of tonality is more adventurous than the guide-lines laid down by Morley and Butler would countenance, Ferrabosco does not generally explore its full possibilities. It is nevertheless apparent that the longest sections of his fantasias are the most varied in their treatment of key, showing that he appreciated the value of key-colour as a structural feature.[56] While it was

[56] *Cf.* Fantasias Nos. 8 and 16 *à* 4.

Jenkins who with supreme mastery developed this aspect of fantasia writing, Ferrabosco II left three remarkable works every bit as adventurous as the later composer's essays in the genre. His four-part Fantasia No. 21 – and his only true monothematic consort – may have influenced Jenkins' experiments in modulating round the key circle,[57] while the two hexachord fantasias, known in both four- and five-part versions, display tremendous skill in modulation which accommodates a chromatically raised or lowered *cantus firmus*.[58]

Of all the Jacobean composers, Jenkins learned and took most from Ferrabosco II, but not exclusively so, as will be seen.[59] It is clear from this brief survey (whichomits several important consort composers, like Richard Mico and Thomas Tomkins) that the Jacobean fantasia was Hydra-headed, its burgeoning forms supplying a wealth of possibilities for further development. It was Jenkins' good fortune that he arrived on the scene at such an opportune moment and posterity's that he displayed such consummate skill in building on the work of his predecessors.

[57] *Cf.* Chapter Five, p. 207.

[58] *Musica Britannica*, Vol. IX, No. 39. *Cf.* also Edward Lowinsky, 'Echoes of Adrian Willaert's Chromatic "Duo" in 16th- and 17th-century Compositions', *Studies in Music History: Essays for Oliver Strunck*, Princeton University Press, Princeton, 1968.

[59] *Cf.* pp. 213–5.

chapter three
Music and Manuscripts in Seventeenth-century Oxford

Of paramount importance in the history of viol music is the musical activity in Oxford during the third quarter of the seventeenth century. From the mid-1650s a number of regular music meetings were held in the city, supported and largely directed by members of the University. These meetings are significant because many of the manuscripts used at them have been preserved. The first had been set up under the terms of William Heather's will in 1621.[1]

> Imprimis, [I ask] that the Exercise of Musick be constantly kept every week, on Thursday in the afternoon, afternoons in Lent excepted.
> Secondly, I appoint Mr. Nicholson, the now Organist of Magd. Coll. to be Master of Musick, and to take charge of the Instruments. [...]
> Thirdly, I do appoint that the said Master bring with him two boys weekly, at the day and time aforesaid, and there to receive such company as will practise Musick, and to play Lessons of three Parts, if none other come.
> Lastly, I ordain that once every year the Instruments be viewed and the books: and that neither of these be lent abroad upon any pretence whatsoever, nor removed out of the Schools and place appointed.[2]

[1] Heather (1563–1627) founded the Oxford music professorship by a deed dated 2 February 1626/7, and endowed it with £17. 6s. 8d., of which £13. 6s. 8d. was for the professor's salary, with the remainder to be paid to the reader of a theoretical lecture.

[2] Anthony Wood, *The History and Antiquities of the University of Oxford*, ed. John Gutch (1796), II, pp. 358–9. *Cf.* also Bruce Bellingham, 'The

It is interesting to note that Heather expected the Master and his boys to *play* rather than sing, since in his bequest of 48 sets of music only 'One sett of Fancies and In'omines of Alphonso Ferebosco' is specifically instrumental[3]. Yet among 'Instruments & other goods given by Dr. Heather' were 'A Harpsichord with a winde instrument of two stops' and 'Tenne Vialls'. How far, if at all, this collection was increased in succeeding years is unclear, but certainly the instruments suffered 'in the time of rebellion and usurpation'. Miraculously the books survived virtually intact; presumably they could be shut away out of danger. Between 1643 and 1646 the Music School became 'the magazin for cloth for soldiers' apparrell and coates' and the music meetings stopped entirely. In 1654 Seth Ward, Oxford Professor of Astronomy, replied to a tract by John Webster which attacked practical music-making as degenerate (pleading instead for more attention to be paid to the theoretical aspects), in these terms:

> The Theory of Musick is not neglected, indeed the Musick meeting by the Statutes of this University appointed to be once a weeke hath not of late been observed, out instruments having been lately out of tune, and our harpes hanged up.[4]

Two large sets of consort music – Bodleian, Mus. Sch. MSS C.64–9 and E.437–42 – proved fruitful sources for musicians in post-Restoration Oxford when they were forming their own collections and at least one of these seems to date from the 1640s. The six books of C.64–9 are each inscribed 'George Stratford 1641'. He may have

---

Musical Circle of Anthony Wood in Oxford During the Commonwealth and Restoration', *Journal of the Viola da Gamba Society of America*, XIX, 1982, pp. 7–70 (especially pp. 55–6).

[3] Heather's bequest is listed in Margaret Crum, 'Early Lists of the Oxford Music School collection', *Music & Letters*, 48, 1967, pp. 23–4.

[4] Seth Ward, *Vindiciae Academarium* (1654), quoted in Richard L. Greaves, 'Music at Puritan Oxford', *Musical Times*, January 1969, p. 26.

been the son of George Stratford, gentleman, of Thornton, Gloucestershire, whose progress at Oxford can be traced from his Matriculation entry to Magdalen Hall on 28 January 1624/5, aged 14, to the award of a B. D. degree on 2 July 1639.[5] On 15 May 1648 he was included in a list of 'The Names of such Persons as have not submitted to the Authoritie of Parliament in the Visitation, and are expelled the University by the Committee of Lords and Commons for regulating the University of Oxford'.[6]

Oxford, of course, was the Royalist headquarters between 29 October 1642, when the King rode into the city in state at the head of his troops, and 27 April 1646, when he left it disguised as a servant. Music undoubtedly maintained a place in the life of the court, which in turn must have influenced and supported the musical life of the city. At the same time Wood found many of

> The young men of the city university [...] to have been debauch'd by bearing armes and doing the duties belonging to soldiers, as watching, warding, and sitting in tipling-houses for whole nights together. I have had the opportunity (I cannot say happiness) to peruse several songs, ballads, and such like frivolous stuff, that were made by some of the ingenious sort of them, while they kept guard, [...] which [...] I shall pass [...] by, as unworthy to be here [...] mentioned.

With organs silenced and cathedral and collegiate choirs disbanded during the Commonwealth, many church musicians were thrown out of work. Wood records how William Ellis, previously organist of St John's College, Oxford, established a weekly concert after he had been deprived of his living:[7]

[5] *Cf.* Joseph Foster, *Alumni Oxoniensis: The Members of the University of Oxford, 1500–1714*, Oxford, 1891, four vols.

[6] Montague Burrows, *The Register of the Visitors of the University of Oxford from A. D. 1647 to A. D. 1658*, London, 1881.

[7] *The Life and Times of Anthony Wood*, Vol. I, p. 129.

> After Cathedrals & Organs were put down in the grand rebellion, he [Ellis] kept up a weekly meeting in his house opposite to that place where the [Sheldonian] theatre was afterwards built, which kept him and his wife in a comfortable condition. The meeting was much frequented and many masters of musick were there, and such that had belonged to choires, being out of all employ, & therefore that meeting as all other musick meetings did flourish.[8]

Wood himself joined the circle in 1656, by which time he professed 'some genuine skill in musick'. His financial jottings at this time frequently include 'at Elleses 6d' – the cost of admittance and refreshment. Yet one suspects that at first he attended as a listener only; he had been indifferently taught on the violin by three Oxford musicians, finally acknowledging

> there was yet no compleat master in Oxon for yt Instrument, because it had not been hitherto used in consort among Gentlemen, only by common musitians who played but two parts. The Gentlemen in our private meetings play'd 3, 4 & 5 parts with Viols [...] with either an organ or Virginal or Harpsecon with them: and they esteemed a violin to be the Instrument only belonging to a common Fidler and could not endure it to come among them for feare of making their meetings seems to be vaine and Fidling.[9]

Elsewhere he emphasises again that

> Mr Low, a proud man, could not endure any common musitian to come to the meeting, much less to play among them.[10]

But in succeeding years violins did infiltrate the meetings, in large measure because of the appearances there of

[8] Bodleian Library, Oxford, MS Wood D 19(4), f. 46v. *Cf.* John D. Shute, *op. cit.*

[9] British Library, Harley MS 5409, ff. 46r–v.

[10] *The Life and Times of Anthony Wood*, Vol. I, p. 205.

Davis Mell and Thomas Baltzar, both of whom played 'to the wonder of all the auditory'. Indeed, one of the benefits of Ellis' gatherings was to provide a platform for the best musicians. Apart from Mell and Baltzar, Wood also mentions others, including John Gamble and Thomas Pratt,

> two eminent Musitians of London [...] who entertain'd him with most excellent musick at the meeting house of William Ellis. Gamble had obtain'd a great name among the musitians of Oxon for his book before publish'd, entit. 'Ayres and Diologues to be sung to the Theorbo-Lute or Bass-Viol'. The other for several compositions, which they played in their consorts.[11]

Thanks to Wood, Ellis' meeting is the best documented, but some occasional members of the group also organised their own consorts.

Thomas Janes, a theorbo player, held weekly meetings in his chamber at Magdalen College and later Narcissus Marsh (1638–1713) did the same at Exeter College and afterwards at St Alban's Hall. In his diary Marsh notes that

> I had before this [1664], betaken myself to the practise of musick, especially of the viol, and after the fire of London I constantly kept a weekly consort (of instrumental musick, & sometimes vocal) [...] on Wednesday, in the afternoon, & then on thursday, as long as I lived in Oxford.[12]

Surviving music books and manuscripts in Marsh's splendid library in Dublin (built in 1701–3) were surely used at his music meetings and were compiled by many

[11] *Ibid.*, vol. I. p. 256. July 1658 was a vintage month. Wood was at Ellis' on 6, 9, 13, 14 July: 'spent with Mr Gamble and Mr. Pratt at Tavern, 4s; at Elleses for a lodging 1s.'; 15, 20, 24: 'spent att Mr Elleses on Mr. Baltzier, Mr. Low, etc. 1s.'; 27 July. On 17 August: 'spent on Mr Mell, 3s. 6d.'

[12] Quoted in Alec Hyatt King, *Some British Collectors of Music*, Cambridge University Press, Cambridge, 1963, p. 14.

copyists.[13] His two major collections of consorts containing fantasias by Jenkins (EIR-Dm, MSS Z.3.4.1–6, Z.3.4.7–12 and relevant basso continuo parts in Z.3.4.13) mostly duplicate Bodleian, Mus. Sch. MSS C.64–9 and E.437–42 mentioned earlier; the bleak news that 29 sets of music, at least ten of which contained pieces by Jenkins, were missing from the library by the mid-eighteenth century[14] is softened by the thought that many of these could equally easily have been copied from the still extant manuscripts in the Oxford collections.

Meanwhile, John Wilson had been appointed Heather Professor (or *Choragus*) in 1656 to assume supervision of the weekly music meetings. At Ellis' Wilson 'sometimes played on the Lute, but mostly presided at the Concert', which suggests that those meetings may have been looked upon as fulfilling Heather's wishes for a time, especially since they were held 'first on Thursday, then on Tuesday'. At any rate surviving papers for 1656–7[15] show that Wilson supervised repairs to instruments and copying of music for the Music School and that the 'scholastical musitians' soon held their own meetings. Wood remarks that

> After his majestie's restoration, when the masters of musick were restored to their several places, [...] the weekly meetings at Mr Ellis's house began to decay, because they were held up only by scholars who wanted directors and instructors, &c. so that in few yeares after,

[13] *Cf.* Richard Charteris, *A Catalogue of the Printed Books on Music, Printed Music and Music Manuscripts in Archbishop Marsh's Library, Dublin*, Boethius Press, Clarabricken, 1982; Richard Charteris, 'Consort Music Manuscripts in Archbishop Marsh's Library, Dublin', *Royal Musical Association Research Chronicle*, No. 13, 1976, pp. 27–63.

[14] Richard Charteris, 'Music Manuscripts and Books missing from Archbishop Marsh's Library, Dublin', *Music & Letters*, 66, 1980, pp. 310–17.

[15] *Cf.* Mrs R. Lane Poole, 'The Oxford Music School and the Collection of Portraits formerly preserved there', *Musical Antiquary*, IV, 1912–13, pp. 143–59; also Bellingham, *op. cit.*

> the meeting in that house being totally layd aside, the chief meeting was at Dr. (then Mr.) Marshe's chamber, at Exeter Coll., and afterwards at St. Alban's hall [...].
> Besides the weekly meetings at Mr. Ellis's house, which were first on Thursday, then on Tuesday, there were meetings of the scholastical musitians every Friday night, in the winter time, in some colleges; as in the chamber of Henry Langley, or of Samuel Woodford, in Wadham Coll.; in the chamber of Christopher Harrison in Queens' Coll.; in that of Charles Perot in Oriel; in another at New Coll. &c. – to all which some master of musick would commonly retire, as William Flexney, Thomas Jackson, Gervas Westcote, &c.; but these meeting[s] were not continued above 2 or 3 yeares, and I think they did not go beyond the yeare 1662.[16]

Which manuscripts were used at the various meetings cannot yet be said with precision. Certainly Bodleian, Mus. Sch. MSS C.64–9 and E.437–42 between them carry a comprehensive collection of Jacobean and Caroline fantasias and associated works, a repertory very much in tune with the ideals of Ellis and his friends. Margaret Crum suggests that Bodleian, Mus. Sch. MSS E.431–6, a large collection of three- and four-part airs, was compiled for 'the Schooles' by Thomas Jackson, though other manuscripts in the same hand have led to the suggestion that they might have been copied by Ellis himself.[17] In their day even these unpretentious airs were highly regarded: more than thirty years later Wood remembers the effect which some of them (by Benjamin Rogers) had on the assembled company:

> His [Rogers'] compositions for instrumental music [...] have been highly valued, and were always, 30 or years ago or more, first called for, taken out and played as well in

[16] *The Life and Times of Anthony Wood*, Vol. I, p. 275.

[17] Crum, 'Early Lists [...]', p. 27. For the suggestion that this copyist might be Ellis, *cf.* J. Buncker Clark, 'A Re-emerged Seventeenth-Century Organ Accompaniment Book', *Music & Letters*, 47, 1966, pp. 149–52.

> the public music school as in private chambers: and Dr. Wilson the professor, the greatest and most curious judge of music that ever was, usually wept when he heard them well perform'd, as being wrapped up in an ecstacy, or if you will, melted down, while others smiled or had their hands and eyes lifted up, at the excellency of them.[18]

Wilson returned to London in 1660 at his re-appointment to the King's Musick and his place as Choragus was taken by Edward Lowe, the organist of Christ Church. Lowe was a most conscientious curator of the Music School collection; many volumes were indexed, annotated and in some cases copied by him, and his diligence brought him honour from at least one of his contemporaries, John Hingeston:

> This set of Bookes & works of mine [Mus. Sch. MSS D.205–11] I freely give to ye Musique School at Oxon whereto I was ye more incouraged, from what I have heard & seene of ye care, Dilligence & industry, of ye present thereof in ye Universitie, Mr. Edward Lowe, my ever honored frind and fellow servant.

Under Lowe's direction a large collection of manuscripts and instruments was acquired between 1665 and 1675 as part of a scheme for 'refurnishing the publique Musique Schoole' in the University. Accounts quoted by Hawkins of the 'disbursements [...] in the year 1667' record the original purchase:

> Sets of choice books for instrumentall music, ii [= eleven] whereof are the composition of Mr. John Jenkins, for 2, 3, 4, 5 and 6 parts for the organ and harpsecon and 6 setts more composed by Mr. Lawes, Copprario, Mr. Brewer, and Orlando Gibbons, all bought of Mr. Wood, which cost £22. 0. 0.[19]

[18] *Fasti Oxoniensis*, Vol. II, pp. 305 and 307.

[19] *Cf.* Margaret Crum, 'The Consort Music from Kirtling, brought for the Oxford Music School from Anthony Wood, 1667'. *Chelys*, 4, 1972, pp. 3–10.

Other volumes were added from time to time. Many of the books bought from Mr Wood are bound in old deeds belonging to the North family of Kirtling, Cambridgeshire, Jenkins' patrons in the 1650s and 1660s. It therefore seems probable that the collection was dispersed from Kirtling following the death of Dudley, third Baron North, in December 1666. 'Mr. Wood', it has been assumed, is the Oxford chronicler Anthony Wood. Perhaps one can go further and suggest that he may have bought the books during his first visit to London: 14–28 June 1667, although he admits

> It was the first time that A.W. was at London; and the truth is, his time being short, he only took measures what to doe at his next going to that place.[20]

Furthermore, there is no evidence in Wood's carefully kept accounts of any such purchase.

At first it seems extraordinary that the Oxford musicians continued to collect, copy and play music which largely had been written between fifty and a hundred years earlier. Both Wilson and Lowe were getting on in years – Wilson was in his sixties and Lowe could not have been much younger – and they naturally may have been drawn towards the music of their younger days, but this is unlikely to be the only reason for such conservatism. Oxford, Cambridge and the 'Third University of England' – the Inns of Court in London – brought together young men who were the heirs to families for whom the performance of fantasias, pavans and *In Nomines* on viols had been a treasured part of home life. Abstract music of this subtlety and complexity requires a receptive and sympathetic mind. Some scholars have emphasised 'the importance of the training in listening to the sustained expression of complex modes of thought and feeling' of that time. The universities and Inns were a particularly favourable environment for the development of this

[20] Andrew Clark, abridged by Llewelyn Powys, *The Life and Times of Anthony Wood*, Oxford University Press, London, 1961, p. 170.

aural culture, whether through the formal disputation, 'which kind of exercise doth both whet their wits and strengthen their memory', or through informal 'conference with others' which, as Edward Coke so perceptively remarked, 'is the life of studie',[21] or through the sermon. 'Conference with others' is a marvellous description of consort music for viols. But it was, and is, more than that. If it were intended merely for social diversion, its recipients readily acknowledged that it often filled them with a spiritual elevation and relief from the 'hurry of action' of those troubled times. The oft-quoted words of that old Cambridge cleric Thomas Mace express this better than most:

> We had for our Grave Musick, Fancies of 3, 4, 5, and 6 Parts to the Organ; Interpos'd (now and then) with some Pavins. Allmaines, Solemn, and Sweet Delightful Ayres; all which were (as it were) so many Pathettical Stories, Rhetorical, and Sublime Discourses; Subtil, and Accute Argumentations; so Suitable, and Agreeing to the Inward, Secret, and Intellectual Faculties of the Soul and Mind; that to set Them forth according to their True Praise, there are no Words Sufficient in Language; yet what I can best speak of Them, shall be only to say, That They have been to myself, (and many others) as Divine Raptures, Powerfully Captivating all our unruly Faculties, and Affections, (for the Time) and disposing us to Solidity, Gravity, and a Good Temper; making us capable of Heavenly, and Divine Influences.[22]

But in Cambridge by 1676 viol consorts had faded from the scene:

> Whereas now the Fashion has Cry'd These Things Down, and set up others in their Room; which I confess make a Greater noise; but which of the Two is the Better Fashion, I leave to be Judg'd by the Judicious [...]. Very little of

[21] Sir Edward Coke, chief-justice, in *The First Part of the Institutes of the Lawes of England*, London, 1628, quoted in Prest, *op. cit.*, p. 170.

[22] *Op. cit.*, p. 234.

> This so Eminent Musick do we hear of in These Times (the Less the Greater Pity).[23]

Yet in Oxford the medium continued to flourish and manuscripts were still copied in the 1660s and '70s. Marsh's meeting has already been mentioned, but others too played their part, prominent among whom were Matthew Hutton and members of the Withy family.

Hutton was a close friend of Anthony Wood and is frequently mentioned in the latter's writings, where he is described as an 'excellent violist'. Quite a number of manuscripts copied or collected by him have survived and several of these contain fantasias by Jenkins:

(a) York Minster Library: MSS M3/1-4(S). A set of four part-books in Hutton's hand in which the seventeen pieces are numbered in two series.[24] Nine four-part fantasias by Jenkins are included; a copy date 'Dec 7. 1667' is written in the bass book after No. 7 of the first series – Jenkins' Fantasia No. 12. A large number of distinctive textual variants link this source with Christ Church, Music MSS 468–72, whose readings of the Jenkins items are virtually identical.[25] Jenkins' Fantasias Nos. 5 and 6

[23] *Ibid.*, pp. 234 and 236.

[24] *Cf.* Richard Charteris, 'Matthew Hutton (1638–1711) and his Manuscripts in York Minster Library', *Galpin Society Journal*, XXVIII, April 1975, pp. 2–6; David Griffiths, *A Catalogue of the Music Manuscripts in York Minster Library*, York Minster Library, Sectional Catalogue 2, 1981; John A. Irving, 'Matthew Hutton and York Minster MSS. M.3/1–4(S)', *The Music Review*, Vol. 44, Nos. 3/4, 1983, pp. 163–77.

[25] The unknown copyist of Christ Church, music MSS 468–472 would also appear to have known scribes working for Narcissus Marsh, since the 20 four-part fantasias by Ferrabosco II in this source occur in the same order in Marsh's score Z.2.1.12, now in his library in Dublin. In this article mentioned in note 23 above, John Irving concludes that at least some pieces in Hutton's MSS M.3/1–4(S) were copied direct from Marsh's MSS: Z.3.4.1–6 (also in Dublin). Nos. 1–11 of the five-part pieces in MSS 468–472 (all ascribed to Ward) seem to have been copied from Nos. 16–26 of Bodleian, Mus. Sch. MSS C.64–9 (where No. 8 is correctly ascribed to William White). This same sequence of

are not included in the York books, though the selection otherwise matches the Christ Church collection. This suggests that Hutton already owned

(b) British Library: Add. MSS 17792–6: five part-books from a set of six, containing Jenkins' four-part Fantasias Nos. 5 and 6 (but none of the others).[26] The books were originally made by John Merro (d. 1639), a singing-man at Gloucester Cathedral from as early 1609.[27] Two other sets of books copied by Merro are known to have survived: Bodleian Library, Mus. Sch. MSS D.245–7 and New York Public Library, Drexel MSS 4180–5.[28] Several sequences of pieces in Merro's collection are duplicated; thus a group of seven four-part fantasias by Ives, Jenkins and Ferrabosco II at the end of the New York books also appear in Add. MSS 17792–6, where they are numbered 19–25. An entry in Gloucester's Dean and Chapter Account Book for 1628/9 suggests one reason for these duplications: 'Repayed to John Merro for a Roome which he rented of John Beames to teach the Children [the choirboys] to playe uppon the Vialls: 10s'. It was Hutton who identified Jenkins as the composer of the two fantasias by adding his name in the altus and bassus books.

---

pieces occurs in Marsh's MSS Z.3.4.1–6, although with the last two items reversed.

[26] Pamela J. Willetts, 'Music from the Circle of Anthony Wood at Oxford', *The British Museum Quarterly*, XXIV, Nos 3–4, London, 1961, pp. 71–5.

[27] The most detailed account of Merro yet given is in John Sawyer, *An Anthology of Lyra Viol Music in Oxford, Bodleian Manuscripts Music School D.245–7*, unpublished Ph. D. dissertation, University of Toronto, 1972.

[28] Philip Brett ('Consort Songs', *Musica Britannica*, Vol. XXII, Stainer & Bell, London, 1967, p. 173) writes of Drexel MSS 4180–5: 'Like [Add. MSS 17792–6] it may subsequently have belonged to Matthew Hutton since it contains annotations which appear to be in his hand'. But Craig Monson (*Voices and Viols in England*, p. 138) could not trace Hutton's hand in the books and therefore disputes his ownership. John Irving (*loc. cit*) includes the Drexel books in his tally of Hutton manuscripts.

Merro's work is inaccurate, but his books are among the earliest known sources for Jenkins' music.

How did they come into Hutton's hands? It seems likely that there is a connection here with Dr Thomas Isles (1588–1649), the ale-drinking canon of Christ Church, Oxford, who had been installed as a Prebendary at Gloucester on 13 July 1622. Isles would thus have known Merro and may have brought the books to Oxford, where he settled in 1632.[29] It is clear that Anthony Wood's family were on friendly terms with Isles and his wife Martha: one of the earliest memories of the chronicler (then aged four) was his being taken to the canon's lodgings to see the royal family ride into Oxford on 29 August 1636. Thomas Isles died in 1649, although Martha lived on until February 1674/5.[30] It was a William Iles who gave some of Merro's books to the Oxford Music School. A note in both Mus. Sch. MSS D.245–7 and F.575 reads:

> Mr William Iles sent thes ten Bookes to Dr Fell Deane of ch: ch: in Oxford for ye use of the publick musick scoole whereof 5 of them are of one sort, & the other 5 of another, they are markt with ye 10 first figures at the topp of this page that soe it may bee discovered which is wantinge. William Iles 1673.

The relationship, if any, between Thomas and William Isles is not known. All ten books: 'Two sets [...] given by Mr Iles' are recorded in the 1682 catalogue of the Music

[29] This may not have been until after Merro's death in 1639. Merro wrote on the flyleaf of D.245–7 in 1633.

[30] *Cf.* Wood's *History and Antiquities of Oxford*, p. 449, for Thomas Isles' memorial; also p. 507 and various references in Clarke's edition of Wood's *Life and Times*. Other references, including some to his son Thomas, occur in Burrows, *op. cit.*, and Thomas Fosbroke, *An Original History of the City of Gloucester*, London, 1819. Fosbroke also mentions Merro and his wife Elizabeth, but there seem to be inaccuracies in his dates.

School collection.[31] but only Nos. 7–10 survive today as D.245–7 and F.575. A second note by Iles:

> There is 6 bookes in partes of one sorte of Binding and 4: more several sortes: in all 10: bookes.

contradicts the first and suggests that it is a set of six part-books which has become lost. The differing bindings of D.245–7 and F.575 lend credence to the idea. If so, a suspicion takes root that perhaps the New York books (which have lost their original binding) once belonged to the Iles collection. Like many other Drexel manuscripts, they are thought to have been purchased at the sale of the Victorian antiquarian Edward Rimbault's library in 1877. Rimbault, it is known, helped himself to some items from Oxford libraries, and it may be that this set belongs among his ill-gotten gains.[32]

(c) British Library: Add. MSS 30488-90. A set of three part-books containing Jenkins' 21 fantasias for two trebles and a bass, in Hutton's hand. Various copying dates are included ranging from 'Dec 18 1661' to 'Jan 27 1665/6'. Later Hutton made a score of the pieces, now

(d) York Minster Library: MSS M20(S), evidently completed on 'Jan 21 1667/8'. A memorandum on the front cover confirms the link with Oxford which could be assumed from the dates:

> 11 Octo: 1671. This score I borrowed of Mr. Hutton of

[31] Crum, 'Early Lists', p. 30.

[32] *Cf.* Alec Hyatt King, *op. cit.*, p. 62, and Monson, *op. cit.*, pp. 138–9. Rimbault himself, in his introduction to *A Collection of Anthems* [...], Musical Antiquarian Society Publications, Vol. 14, London, 1846, states that they 'were formerly in the possession of the celebrated John Evelyn', though then in his own library. Evelyn's books were kept at Christ Church, but this set is not listed in his manuscript catalogue. Rimbault goes on to say they retain 'the original binding [...] with the Arms and Badge of Edward the Sixth stamped on the sides', but in the sale catalogue of his library (lot 1337) they are simply described as 'old calf'.

> Brazen-nose. Who bidd mee keepe it 'till hee calld for it. Ed. Lowe.

This appears to be the 'Mr. Jenkins' 3 part Fancies in score covered with white paper' now missing from 'The Gift of Mr. Lowe late Professor' in the 1682 catalogue of the Music School manuscripts.

Another West Country connection, between Worcester and Oxford, is apparent in investigating the Withy family.[33] They first appear on the musical scene quite early in the seventeenth century. the third of Tomkins' published *Songs of 3. 4. 5. and 6. parts* (1622) is dedicated to 'Humphry Withy', while in Bodleian Library, Mus. Sch. MSS E.415–8 are two pavans by Tomkins 'made for J. Withy' and on the flyleaf of the tenor book 'Mr Thomas Tomkins, Mr Humphry Withy 1642'. Humphrey does not seems to have been a composer, but there are over forty compositions extant by John Withy – there may well have been two composers of this name. In the Sibley Music Library, Rochester, New York, are three part-books headed 'Jo. Wythie his booke' which include five of Jenkins' fantasias for two trebles and a bass, but at present there is no reason to connect this manuscript with Oxford. In the 1690s Anthony Wood wrote that John Withy was

> a Roman catholic and sometimes a teacher of music in the city of Worcester. Father of Francis Withie of Oxon, composed several things for 2 violins.

[33] The appropriate 'Withy' entries in *The New Grove Dictionary of Music and Musicians*, Vol. 20, Macmillan, London, 1980; also John A. Irving, 'Consort playing in mid-17th-century Worcester: Thomas Tomkins and the Bodleian partbooks, Mus. Sch. E.415–8', *Early Music*, XII, 1984, pp. 337–44, and 'Oxford Christ Church MSS. 1018–1020: a valuable source of Tomkins's Consort Music', *The Consort*, 40, 1984, pp. 1–12; and Robert Thompson, '"Francis Withie of Oxon" and his common-place book, Christ Church, Oxford, MS 337', *Chelys*, 20, 1991, pp. 3–27.

> John Withie was excellent for the lyra-viol and improved the way of playing thereon much.[34]

In Christ Church library is a copy of Christopher Simpson's *A Compendium of Practical Musick* (1667), which Francis Withy 'baught of Mr Jons in Worster for 2s. 1d.', bearing the date 12 October 1667. At some time Bodleian Library, Mus. Sch. MSS E.437–42 also came into his possession and he added music to the ends of some sections in the books. Four of Jenkins' three-part fantasias were already included; Withy added the second of the composer's four-part set.[35] He seems to have taken up a post as lay-clerk at Christ Church in June 1670 and remained as a singing-man at Christ Church until his death in December 1727. One of the attractions laid on by the University of Oxford at the visit of Cosmo de' Medici in May 1669 was 'a division by Mr [...] Withie on the base viol'.[36] This might have been Francis, six of whose sets of divisions for bass viol have survived,[37] or it might equally have been the John Withy whose works appear in several Oxford manuscripts.[38]

There was to be one more chapter in the story of the Oxford manuscripts before they were allowed to rest on the library shelves. Henry Aldrich (1647–1710) became a canon at Christ Church in 1681 and was installed as Dean

[34] Bodleian Library, Wood MS D 19(4), f. 136r. There are nine pieces by him for lyra viol in Playford's 1661 and 1669 published collections of music for the instrument.

[35] Confirmation of Francis Withy's hand is given on the front flyleaf of MS Mus. Sch. E.430 by Edward Lowe: 'Bassus Continus: Mr Simpsons little Consort: Prickte and given mee by Mr Francis Withye: 11 Jan. 1672/3'. He also copied Bodleian, Mus. Sch. MSS C.59–60, C.61 and MS parts of bass viol and other music added to a printed copy of Playford's *Cantica Sacra*, 1674, now at the University of Illinois. *Cf.* Thompson, *loc. cit.*

[36] Wood, *Life and Times*, Vol. II, p. 158.

[37] Bodleian, Mus. Sch. MSS C.61 and C.71.

[38] *Cf.* Gordon Dodd, *Thematic Index of Music for Viols*, pp. 199 *et seq.*

on 17 June 1689. He accumulated a very fine library of music which he willed to the college at his death.

> I make it my request to the Dean and Chapter [...] that they will be pleased to take such care of my Prints and books of Musick that they may not be exposed to common usage nor to any man without their leave and appointment, because they are things of value in themselves, and to be found in very few libraries.

Contemporary with Aldrich was Richard Goodson senior, who succeeded Lowe as Choragus in 1682 and who, like Aldrich, left his music to Christ Church in 1718. Fortunately a catalogue of both bequests was made by J. B. Malchair in 1787,[39] which helps identification of most of the remaining Oxford sources for Jenkins' fantasias. Christ Church MSS 468–72 (noted earlier as a source known to Hutton) is the only set relevant to this study which came to Goodson.

Aldrich's collection was enormous and impressive in its scope. Although it is not clear how he came by all the books, previous owners and some copyists of all his manuscripts containing Jenkins' fantasias can be identified; they fall into two particular groups.

One collection belonged to Christopher, First Baron Hatton (d. 1670) and includes Music MSS 2, 397–400, 403–8 and 436. Stephen Bing wrote the score-book (MS 2) and organ book (MS 436), but both sets of part-books were copied by John Lillie, Jenkins' old friend.[40] Hatton's steward at his Northamptonshire estate was the composer George Jeffries whose son Christopher became a student at Christ Church in 1659, progressing to M.A. in 1666.

The second collection was originally formed by John

[39] Royal College of Music, MS 2125.

[40] *Cf.* Pamela Willetts, 'John Lilly, Musician and Music Copyist', *The Bodleian Library Record*, VII, No. 6, February 1967, pp. 307–11; David Pinto, 'The Music of the Hattons', *RMA Research Chronicle*, 23, 1990, pp. 79–108.

Browne (1608–91), Clerk of the Parliaments.[41] Again there are Oxford links. Browne's brother-in-law (by his second wife) was Robert Packer, M.P. for Wallingford; and Christ Church MS 430, an organ part for fantasia-suites by William Lawes, is inscribed by Browne: 'This for Robert Packer Esqr at Shellingford'. But there is another possibility. Browne was first married to Temperance Crew (d. 1634), whose family also owned estates in Northamptonshire. One of them, Nathaniel Crew (1633–1721), was in Oxford from 1652 to 1674, eventually becoming bishop there. Wood notes him as a member of the music meetings shortly before the Restoration: 'a violinist and violist, but alwaies played out of tune, as having no good eare'.[42] I have suggested elsewhere[43] that MSS 423–8 may have originated in the Crew household and come to Browne in the 1630s, but this is pure speculation. Nevertheless, Browne's own hand appears in MSS 423–8 and 473–8, so it is reasonable to assume that he owned both sets at some time. The organ book (MS 1004) clearly belongs with MSS 423–8[44] Of MSS 716–20 one cannot be so sure: all that can be said at this stage is that one of Browne's copyists wrote four fantasias by Lupo in these books and that there are interesting similarities regarding the sequence of pieces and the attribution of works between MSS 716–20 and 423–8. In any case, it is highly probable that the alto and tenor parts of three four-part fantasias by Jenkins (the only items by him in

[41] *Cf.* Andrew Ashbee, 'Instrumental Music from the Library of John Browne (1608–1691), Clerk of the Parliaments', *Music & Letters*, 58, 1977, pp. 43–59; Nigel Fortune and Iain Fenlon, 'Music Manuscripts of John Browne (1608–91) and from Stanford Hall, Leicestershire', in Ian Bent (ed.), *Source Material and the Interpretation of Music: A Memorial Volume to Thurston Dart*, Stainer & Bell, London, 1981, pp. 155–68.

[42] *Life and Times*, Vol. I, p. 2.

[43] 'Instrumental Music from the Library of John Browne', p. 57.

[44] It is also connected with Rowe Music Library, King's College, Cambridge, MSS 114–7.

the books) were written to supplement another set of parts or replace missing ones. but it is not clear when.

It is a remarkable story, much of which remains to be researched and written. A tremendous debt is owed to those seventeenth-century Oxford musicians who so assiduously collected this consort music, no less than to the curators of the Bodleian, Christ Church and other libraries who have cared for it ever since. The extent of posterity's debt to them is shown by the five collections of Jenkins' music discussed in this book. Of the 30 known sources for them at least 23 passed through Oxford. If only the remaining seven sources had survived, all 28 works for treble, two basses and organ, all the four-part fantasias and two associated pavans would be lost and the six-part pieces would be known only by the organ part (losing Fantasia No. 12 entirely).

chapter four
The Six-part Works

The fame of John Jenkins as a composer has rested almost entirely on his magnificent series of fantasias for viols. There are more than 100 of them, embracing a variety of instrumental groupings and differing styles. The quality of the music and the pre-eminence of the fantasia as an instrumental form in the early seventeenth century makes these works a natural starting point in assessing Jenkins' contribution to the development of English instrumental music. But the composer's prolific output runs to around 1000 compositions. Naturally many of the remaining works, though competently written, are musically of small consequence, yet it was these little pieces – mostly dances – which were printed at the time, rather than the more substantial fantasias and fantasia-suites. Both John Playford and Christopher Simpson note that, with a relatively small potential market, to have gone to the inordinate expense of publishing the larger works was not economically viable. The bulk of seventeenth-century consort music, including Jenkins' finest pieces, was therefore circulated in manuscript copies. Some 130 manuscripts and seventeen printed sources contain his work, the large number reflecting the esteem in which it was held during his lifetime.

Of course, his contemporaries knew him not only as a composer but also as a teacher, a performer, and a man of delightful personality – facets of his life which, at best, we can reach out for imperfectly. Nevertheless, these other roles and the various duties and circumstances surrounding them must often have had a considerable bearing on the kind of music which he and others like him produced. The number of people available for performance, their individual techniques, the type and number of instruments available, the ratio of professional and gifted amateur performers to second-rate players and even 'learners': all these factors doubtless played a part in influencing aspects of style, standards of technical difficulty, or the specific scoring of a work or series of works, quite apart from any special commissions from the patron. Most of Jenkins' consort music is geared to amateur performance. It is ideally suited to the talents of the less able performers he was likely to muster in consorts at the country households of the nobility: the aristocratic amateurs, a musical servant or two, and, if he was lucky, another professional like himself similarly employed in the house or nearby.

Jenkins provided them with hundreds of airs and dances, which were often grouped into suites. These were scored for two, three and four parts with continuo. For variety there were some fifty pieces for one, two and three bass viols, many containing florid passage-work called 'divisions', and more than 200 solo and ensemble pieces featuring the lyra viol – a small bass instrument employing tablature notation like the lute, and tuned in a variety of ways. All this was their staple fare, but their most delectable musical dishes were the fantasias and pavans.

The single fantasias written relatively early in the seventeenth century by Coprario, Lupo, Gibbons, Ferrabosco II and others were repeatedly transcribed throughout some seventy years, but the composers themselves increasingly focused their attention on the fantasia-suite – once Coprario had led the way. In these pieces the fantasia heads a group of two or three movements, usually a common-time air and a concluding triple-time dance. From the first there were striking differences between the fantasias for viols and those in the suites, perhaps the most important of these being the integration of 'division' techniques in the latter, dispelling the equality of tone and character between voices which was so distinctive a feature of the traditional fantasia. The use of violins in place of treble viols and the emergence of an obbligato organ part led composers to exploit the differing instrumental timbres and explore idiomatic writing to a larger degree than hitherto, and the whole work was divided into more-clearly defined, contrasted and varied sections. Jenkins' early fantasia-suites seem closely modelled on those by Coprario: this is scarcely surprising since he helped copy and perform them at both the Derham and L'Estrange households.[1] As time went on, however, his predilection for 'division' writing got the upper hand, and his fantasia-suites for treble with two basses, and two trebles with one bass to the organ require prodigious techniques from players. These 'division' passages are a summation of the techniques expounded by Christopher Simpson in *The Division Violist*, and in their use Jenkins went much further than his contemporaries, including William Lawes. Just as the fantasia for viols holds pride of place in Jenkins' earlier career, it is the fantasia-suite – of which he wrote more than 70 – which dominates his output later on.[2] Indeed, as his friend Christopher Simpson remarked,

> In these several sorts of Division of two and three parts [...] none has done so much [...] as the ever Famous and most Excellent Composer, in all Sorts of Modern Musick, Mr. John Jenkins.[3]

Jenkins' extant six-part pieces comprise twelve fantasias, two pavans and two *In Nomine*s. They are found in two groups of sources, neither of which includes holograph

[1] *Cf.* p. 56.

[2] I intend to discuss these works in the second volume of this study.

[3] Simpson, *The Division-Viol*, p. 61.

copies, so their value in assessing the origin and date of the music is extremely limited. The earliest group, comprising Music MSS 423–8, 473–8 and 1004 at Christ Church, Oxford, all belonged at one time to John Browne (1608–91), Clerk of the Parliaments from 1638 to 1649 and again from 1660 to 1691.[4]

Browne's books contain what appears to be exclusively pre-Commonwealth music and also demonstrate a bias towards Court and London-based composers. He apparently set up house in the early 1630s and, with the help of several copyists, began forming a large collection of consort music. One or two of the manuscript sets – including both 423–8 and 473–8 – seem to have been begun before Browne gained possession of them and the collection as a whole was probably completed by the early 1640s. Browne himself copied Jenkins' six-part Fantasias Nos. 1 and 2 into MSS 423–8 while Nos. 8 and 12 were added by the next scribe. Organ parts for these last two pieces were included in MS 1004. MSS 473–8 apparently came into Browne's ownership in an almost complete state; they can be identified among the manuscripts bequeathed to Christ Church by Richard Goodson in 1718 and listed in the eighteenth-century catalogue by J. B. Malchair.[5] MSS 473–8 are among the best sources for viol music, but Browne's books otherwise seem to be at some remove from Jenkins himself: their versions of his pieces are not particularly accurate and one work was even first ascribed to another composer.

It is very disappointing that the surviving manuscripts from the L'Estrange library contain none of Jenkins' four- or six-part music, since their presence there might have thrown considerable light on contemporary texts and sources. It seems inconceivable that the L'Estranges played only his five-part pieces, virtually all of which

[4] *Cf.* p. 159.

[5] Royal College of Music, MS 2125.

occur in Royal College of Music MS 1145; presumably the other sets were present in books now lost.[6]

The most complete sources of Jenkins' six-part music belong to an even later period. Both Bodleian, Mus. Sch. MS C.83 (a set of seven parts: viols and organ) and British Library, Add. MS. 29290 (an organ book) contain all the pieces except Fantasia No. 12. C.83 was one of the 'North' manuscripts 'all bought of Mr. Wood' in 1667. In Mus. Sch. MSS C.89, C.90 and C.101 the principal scribe for this whole collection completed various sets of music by Lawes and Coprario, which had apparently been begun by an earlier hand; the rest of the work he shared with assistants, probably four in number. In Mus. Sch. MS C.83 the music falls into two groups, the first series comprising Fantasias Nos. 1–9 and the second series the remaining works. This division is bibliographically as well as musically significant. In the viol parts the paper for the first group is ordered as quires of eight with one leaf added and the music is entered by one of the assistant copyists and marked 'exam'(ined) by that hand, but with the title 'Fantazia' inserted throughout by the principal scribe. To these first sets of quires was added a second set of eight leaves of a different paper on which the principal scribe himself wrote out the six pieces making up the second series; he was also responsible for the whole organ part. In the latter, as in other manuscripts from the collection, are to be found textual queries and corrections which Margaret Crum tentatively suggests may be in the hand of old Lord North himself. The music scribes remain at present unidentified, but in the light of her evidence their work seems to belong in the period between 1654 and 1665.[7]

[6] A note by Sir Nicholas concerning the text of a Ward five-part fantasia 'in my first coppy' (p. 8 of British Library, Add. MS 39550) hints at such a loss.

[7] *Cf.* Margaret Crum, 'The Consort Music from Kirtling [...]'.

It is likely that British Library Add. MS 29290 was also connected with the North family and is of roughly similar date.[8] Two of the five copyists – Jenkins himself (the third scribe) and George Loosemore (the fourth) – are known to have lived at Kirtling, and all the music in the book, except for Jenkins' five-part fantasias and pieces by Mico, is found in the collection to which C.83 belongs. Jenkins' six-part works are here divided into the same two series, the first copied by George Loosemore and the second by the final scribe, although the order of the 'Series II' pieces differs from that in C.83. In both sources, then, changes of paper, quiring, or copyist suggest that the second group was added to the first at a later stage.

With so few sources on which to draw, dating is problematical. It may be significant that no music by Jenkins is found in Francis Tregian's comprehensive score-books,[9] although Tregian's imprisonment[10] probably imposed some limitation on the form of his collection, quite apart from his preferences. So far there is no indication that any of Jenkins' music was in general circulation before Tregian's death in 1619, yet surely the 27-year-old composer would have begun composing before then? On the other hand, composition of six-part viol consorts seems to have died out around 1640 – once William Lawes had contributed his masterly series. In the light of available evidence, which must rely more on stylistic criteria than on external features, it is reasonable to propose a dating of *c.* 1615–35 for Jenkins' six-part music as a whole. The division of these works into two series in the North manuscripts nonetheless requires further consideration.

C.83 is not the only source from Kirtling to show evi-

[8] *Cf.* Pamela J. Willetts, 'Autograph Music by John Jenkins', *Music & Letters*, 48, 1967, pp. 124–6.

[9] British Library, Egerton MS 3665; New York Public Library, Drexel MS 4302.

[10] *Cf.* p. 28.

dence of later additions to Jenkins sets.[11] In some cases the additions may (in part anyway) comprise works composed at Kirtling, but the possibility that others are hitherto uncollected works from earlier times is always present. It cannot be assumed therefore, that late additions necessarily imply a late composition date. In the past I have inclined to the view that at least some of the 'Series II' pieces might be placed among Jenkins' earliest compositions. Such a view seems supported by features such as the possible parody of a Palestrina madrigal in Fantasia No. 10, the medley-type structure of the piece called the Bell Pavan' and the continued interest in the *In Nomine*, all of which seem more at home in Jacobean rather than Caroline times. Moreover, a number of technical infelicities occur throughout this group which are generally uncharacteristic of the composer and perhaps imply that he was still refining his craft. Yet these are superficial arguments which, on close examination, carry no real weight. It may even be too simplistic to separate the dating of the two series; the latter, after all, are known only in manuscripts from one household. Indeed a convincing case can be made for assigning a *late* rather than early date to some 'Series II' pieces – in spite of a few unresolved doubts.[12]

David Pinto has noted points of resemblance between Fantasia No. 11 and the Fantasy in William Lawes' six-part Set VI in G minor sufficient to suggest that Jenkins

[11] Others are Mus. Sch. C.98 (32 Ayres for two trebles, two basses and organ), Mus. Sch. C.99 (the four-part Fantasias discussed in Chapter Five; *cf.* p. 207), and Mus. Sch. C.88 (Lyra consort). For details, *cf.* Margaret Crum, 'The Consort Music from Kirtling [...]'.

[12] Lawes' Fantasy is published, ed. David Pinto, in *William Lawes: Consort Sets in Five and Six Parts*, Faber Music, London 1979, pp. 59–67. The proposition that a link exists between Lawes' Fantasy and Jenkins' Fantasia No. 11 á 6 was first floated at a Viola da Gamba Society meeting in June 1985. I am much indebted to David Pinto for developing this idea and for arguing in favour of a late dating for some 'Series II' pieces. The case as expressed here stems largely from his work and I

was exploring something of the newer manner of his younger contemporary. (That it was not Lawes imitating Jenkins is evident from the fact that many stylistic features in Fantasia No. 11 run contrary to Jenkins' normal mode of expression.) There are a number of reasons that an established composer as Jenkins certainly was by the 1630s should undertake such an enterprise. Having helped to bring the fantasia to a peak of development, he witnessed others injecting into it a plethora of new effects fundamentally transforming its idiom and form. He was still young enough to have to respond to such change, but characteristically circumspect in doing so. Indeed, one senses that he did not find it easy to adapt to the new manner: the extravagant gestures, angular lines and dissonant harmony promoted by Coprario and Lawes were foreign to his own essentially understated lyrical style, based as it was on the most fluent contrapuntal technique. There are many works by him, apparently dating from the 1630s and 1640s, which do little more than dip a toe into this turbulent sea of change. Yet eventually he did steer a successful course into the new regions, where his splendid fantasia-suites stand out among the prominent landmarks. Fantasia No. 11 might be placed among those works cautiously toying with the new language, although why it should emulate the Lawes piece is more difficult to determine. This was an age in which a pupil might imitate the work of a master, either as a didactic exercise or simply in homage, composers might engage in friendly rivalry – perhaps in mastering a particular contrapuntal problem – or might draw themes from recognised models, such as *Lachrimae*, perhaps for symbolic intent, or as some form of parody. None of these seems appropriate in this particular case and it may simply be that Jenkins, perhaps on the prompting of a patron, set out to

---

am grateful to him for allowing me to hijack it in discussing the relevant pieces below.

produce (on his own terms) a counterpart to a favourite piece from the family's collection.[13]

Both pieces open with similar themes (Ex. 18(a)) – not blatant imitation certainly, but bearing a family resemblance – and continue by alternating tonic and dominant entries, capped by a matching high treble statement at the eighth breve. So regular a scheme is contrary to Jenkins' normal practice, in which subject entries undergo supple and subtle modifications to pitch and rhythm. A further uncharacteristically mechanical imitation bulldozes its way through all the parts in bars 13–14 (Ex. 19), where a curious feature is the double-stopped note in Bass II, perhaps hinting at a seventh imitation which does not materialise. This bold stroke marks the end of the fugue and can again be matched in Lawes' Fantasy where a similar regular procession of subject entries serves the same purpose.[14] Jenkins tacks on three more bars to his section to steer the music away from C minor to a cadence in G minor. One imaginative touch here is the imitative dialogue in the upper voices, picking out the arpeggio figure from the initial subject. (Ex. 20(a)). This type of motif, with its leap of a sixth, appears frequently in Jenkins' three-part fantasias and early fantasia-suites, supporting the view that this fantasia may, like them, be of a relatively late date. Equally significant in this respect is the bass part at the same point, whose leaps of a ninth and octave must surely be interpreted as 'divisions' on the simple line given to the organ. This angularity too runs contrary to Jenkins' usual pre-occupation with smooth polyphony.

It should be noted in passing that the organ part of these 'Series II' pieces differs markedly from that provided for 'Series I'. Maybe this difference should be viewed with caution. Organ parts which were essentially a

[13] *Cf.* the discussion of Fantasia No. 15 *à 4* in Chapter Five, p. 220, for another example where such prompting may have occurred.

[14] Bars 17–20.

Ex. 18

Ex. 19

Ex. 20

skeleton short-score of viol consorts were not necessarily devised by the composers and even in these 'Series II' pieces the independent (and obligatory) role given to the organ by Lawes in his consorts is not attained. The organ parts of 'Series II' pieces in Mus. Sch. MS C.83 and Add. MS 29290 – both apparently from Kirtling – differ quite substantially from each other, suggesting that they were produced by two separate musicians. But the interesting common denominator lies in the way both pay more of a complementary rather than subsidiary role to the string parts. Independent fragments are woven into the upper strands and there is much octave doubling, particularly of lower lines – practices which emanate from the obbligato role given to the organ in the emergent fantasia-suites of the 1620s and 1630s.

In Fantasia No. 11 a second fugue (bars 17–31) introduces a dance-like subject, whose compound groupings brings lively new interest into play. This is worlds apart from Lawes' centre-piece, where *concertante* treatment of two basses is boldly contrasted with the rest of the ensemble. Yet the initial figure here features repeated notes like Jenkins' theme (Ex. 18(b)) and declamatory figures at its conclusion (Ex. 20(b)) link up with the fragmented motifs in Jenkins' work (Ex. 20(a)).

The majestic final section of Fantasia No. 11 (Ex. 18(c)) is especially beautiful. Here the simplest of figures generates an expressive stream of suspensions and allows rich harmony to develop – even augmented chords, normally so sparingly used (Ex. 21(a)). Again the spark which ignited this section may be traced to Lawes' piece, where a similar descending figure over an identical rising semitone initiates his final section (Ex. 18(c)). But where Jenkins persists in working out the motif. Lawes moves on to derivative ideas which eventually turn into a recognisable variant of the first subject (Ex. 21(a)).

Fragmentary chromatic lines of the type seen in Ex. 21 occur in most 'Series II' pieces – the parallel with the Lawes extract here is striking – but are largely absent from Fantasias Nos. 1–9. Such passages are common enough in this period: the semitonal steps act as passing notes, usually forming the third of a triad, changing the harmony from major to minor, or vice versa. Chromaticism of this kind is especially visible in the second strain of the 'Bell Pavan' which, as will be suggested below (p. 179), may be a memorial piece; the conventional link between chromaticism and expression of grief may therefore be

Ex. 21

the *raison d'être* here. Joseph Kerman notes the general conservatism of the English madrigalists in using chromaticism[15] (notwithstanding a few notable examples to the contrary), so it is interesting to find Jenkins introducing a number of highly effective harmonic shifts in these six-part works, considering that they may not date from much later. In Ex. 22, from the Pavan in F major, the clash between Treble I, Tenor I and Bass I on the penultimate beat is uncharacteristic of Jenkins; perhaps this, like one or two other similar collisions in the 'Series II' pieces, may have been a response to the bold individuality of Lawes' part-writing. But the placing of the G major triad within the E flat major frame-work here is beautifully managed for maximum effect. The progression itself is one which recurs a number of times in the collection, sometimes acting as a pivot for modulation (Ex. 23), although at others, providing a point of colour within a single key.[16] In reverse it is also used as a striking link between sections where a cadence in a major key is fol-

[15] *Cf.* Joseph Kerman, *The Elizabethan Madrigal: A Comparative Study*, pp. 212–20.

[16] Some other examples are: (a) Fantasia No. 8, bars 31–2: (b) Bell Pavan, bars 12–14; (c) *In Nomine* No. 2, bars 16–19.

lowed immediately by another in the relative minor, the mediant of the first binding the two together (Ex. 24).

Ex. 22

Ex. 23

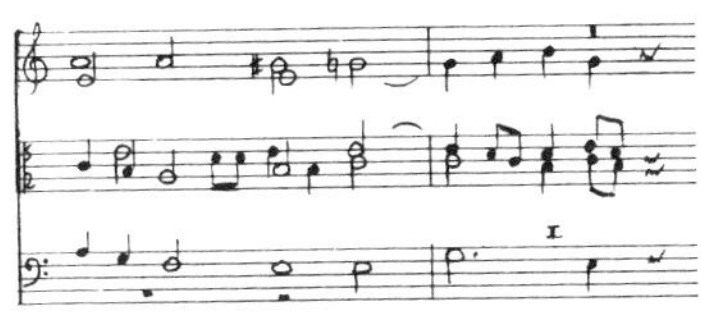

Ex. 24

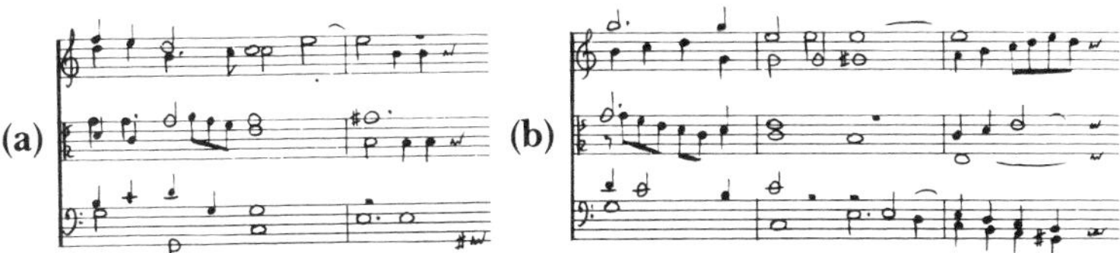

Jenkins' two *In Nomines* are his only essays in a form which, by then, was close to extinction. His was perhaps the last generation to show any concern for the art of 'discanting upon a plain-song', which had been a favourite exercise for training sixteenth-century composers and one which gave the best a chance to show their paces. The principal sixteenth-century composers, of course, were nurtured in the bosom of the Church, whose tradition of composing around a *cantus firmus* had been established for centuries. The movement from vocal to instrumental music in the Jacobean era must be attributed in part to the rise of a group of composers whose first allegiance was to state (or private patron) rather than the Church. This humanistic turn owed much to the concept of 'The Compleat Gentleman' among those Renaissance ideals firmly established in England during the later sixteenth century. Yet 'discanting upon a plainsong' remained a fine discipline all the while music retained its contrapuntal bias. Jenkins, Ferrabosco II, Ward, Tomkins, Gibbons, Mico, and apparently Dering all contributed instrumental *In Nomine*s or hexachord fantasias, but after them only William Lawes and Purcell felt inclined to add to the genre.[17]

The mention of Lawes here may again be significant. Three *cantus firmus* pieces appear in his five- and six-part sets as part of larger groupings of three or four movements,[18] so in noting that Jenkins' Fantasias Nos. 10 and 11 are in the same keys as his two *In Nomine*s, one wonders whether they too ought to be paired. In view of the close relationship between the opening themes of the two G minor pieces (Ex. 26(a)) this pairing seems highly probable. If so, one might conclude that such attachment is part of the general trend towards forming sets of pieces around a single tonic evident in the fantasia-suites, dance suites and other similar groupings of the Caroline period and lends further support to the proposed late dating of 'Series II' pieces. If there is indeed a link between Lawes' G minor Fantasy and Jenkins' Fantasia No. 11, it should be noted that Lawes' six-part pieces are thought to have been written *c.* 1636–41[19] and that these particular Jenkins works are likely to bear (at earliest) a corresponding date.

Jenkins' *In Nomine*s are, as North says, 'most elabourate'. The G minor work is structured as a fantasia with

[17] *Cf.* Oliver Neighbour, *The Consort and Keyboard Music of William Byrd,* pp. 26–50 for a survey of the *In Nomine* during the sixteenth century.

[18] Set I: 'On the Playnsong'; Set IX: 'Inominy'; Set X: Inomine'.

[19] *Cf.* the introduction to David Pinto's edition, pp. viii-ix, mentioned in note 12 on p. 167.

two sharply contrasted sections. Like others before him, Jenkins treats the *cantus firmus* with some freedom, particularly towards the close (Ex. 25).

Ex. 25

(a) Taverner (transposed)

(b) Jenkins

The broadly spaced fugal exposition hints that the work is planned on a grand scale, as does the lengthy delay before the entry of Treble II with the plainsong. Jenkins soon seizes on the lively tail of his subject to provide a volatile backcloth to the chant and a foil to the correspondingly slow harmonic changes. Once the initial subject disappears from view (bar 37) another lively figure is brought into play (Ex. 26(b)), whose rhythm as much as its melody provides a focus for imitative treatment. The writing becomes more florid still, launching into agile division techniques for which Jenkins, among others, was praised by Christopher Simpson in *The Division Violist*. The gradual build-up to this exciting climax is splendidly managed, and so it is sad to find the second half of the work falling short of such initial promise. The abrupt change of mood at bar 66 is unconvincing and the overuse of an unenterprising subject (Ex. 26(c)) makes for a dull section. One feels too that the restrictions imposed by a rigid *cantus firmus* cramp Jenkins' normal freedom in exploring structure and key. Indeed, his most ambitious attempt to break away from the nearly related key-circle – touching on F minor – comes at the point where he disrupts the normal line of the plainsong, but this is clumsy work when compared with his usual fluency in such matters.

Ex. 26

(a)

(b) **(c)**

Such criticisms cannot be levelled at the E minor *In Nomine*, which is endowed with a unity lacking in the G minor work. A simple canzona-like motif provides the initial 'point' (Ex. 27(a)), but all continuations from it are treated with complete freedom. But from time to time a subsidiary motif in one part is taken up in imitation by others, bringing some discipline to the otherwise loose polyphony. A three-crotchet pattern replaces the canzona rhythm at the head of a livelier subject (Ex. 27(b)), but this pattern too is liable to change and develops a still more energetic tail (Ex. 27(c)). Once again the mercurial division patterns employed so effectively in the G minor *In Nomine* are brought into play, but are much more happily placed here to provide a fine climax before the relatively brief majesty of the coda. Harmonic bonds, too, are loosened a little, with one or two characteristic touches of the tonic major enlarging the tonal palette.

Ex. 27

(a)

(b)

(c)

Fantasia No. 10 is also a fine piece. Joan Wess has drawn attention to a number of English instrumental works in which thematic material seems to derive from madrigals printed in the 1588 edition of *Musica Transalpina*, among them the initial motif of this fantasia, which echoes Palestrina's five-part madrigal 'Vestiva i colli' (Ex. 28, transposed).[20] Whether this is more than

Ex. 28

[20] *Cf.* Joan Wess, *loc. cit.*, pp. 3–25.

coincidence must remain an open question, since both theme and counter-subject are conventional. Allusion to a Palestrina piece also seems to call into question a late dating for the work, although possibly the composer was satisfying the whim of a patron. Musically this fantasia gives every appearance of belonging among the 'Series II' pieces already discussed and, whether inspired by a vocal model or not, is truly instrumental in style, fully exploiting the textural contrasts available with six parts. After a conventional opening fugue, Jenkins introduces a novel passage featuring dotted rhythms, where various instruments are highlighted in turn and where there is a much more fragmented sense of line. The insistent repeated-note figures of this section surely link up with similar passages in Jenkins' fantasias for treble, two basses and organ[21] and his early fantasia-suites. Rhythmic inconsistencies abound in the notation here, causing problems for editor and performer alike. It is interesting to note a tendency to write a dotted-rhythm for a leading instrument and non-dotted notation for imitating parts (Ex. 29). Were the latter expected to copy the leader?[22]

Ex. 29

The beautiful progression at bars 27–8 has already been noted (Ex. 24). Two trios provide a welcome change from the six-part texture and Jenkins matches the practice of contemporaries such as White and Ward in making the second trio an exact transposition of the first and by giving it to the three instruments rested initially. Usually sequential repetition in Jenkins' music is on a smaller scale, but here the long phrases creep higher and into

[21] *Cf.* Chapter Seven, pp. 304–6.

[22] Some players make all the figures dotted. David Pinto suggests that they might alternatively be performed as gentle triplet patterns.

progressively sharper keys before an arresting entry for all six instruments leads back down again. In bar 43 Jenkins lands himself in a tight corner from which there is no escape through conventional part-writing – hence the minim rest in Tenor I (Ex. 30).

Ex. 30

The lovely final section is built from descending scales – a recurring finger-print in the composer's consort music.

A number of reasons, then, suggest that these four pieces come late in the chronology of Jenkins' six-part *œuvre*: their absence from early sources, possible links with Lawes' music, the character of the organ part, and stylistic features such as repeated-note figures, fragmented or declamatory motifs and a heightened use of chromaticism. To these may be added bass parts whose tessitura is far less restricted than in the 'Series I' pieces, making much more use of the higher register.

But what of the technical 'errors' which appear more extensively in this second group of pieces than elsewhere in the collection? Undoubtedly some result from careless copying rather than careless composing. Yet, given the paucity of sources, it may be that these works passed out of Jenkins' hands before he had proper opportunity to refine them; there must have been many occasions when consort composers like him were pressed for new pieces and lacked ample time to perfect them. Sometimes variants, as in Fantasia No. 3 discussed below (pp. 193–6) and the four-part Fantasia No. 7, even seem to catch this refining process in action.

As with the *In Nomine*, the era of the pavan was passing and all Jenkins' examples come late in the development of the form. No longer was it necessary to heed Morley's advice to

> cast your music by four, so that if you keep that rule it is no matter how many fours you put in your strain for it will fall out well enough in the end.[23]

The pavan had passed from the dance floor into the realms of pure chamber music, where it was to hold an honoured second place to the fantasia: 'very Grave, and Sober; Full of Art, and Profundity'. Although Morley allowed two, three, or four strains, three was the norm and was always used by Jenkins. Nevertheless he took considerable liberties with the length of the strains, tending to make the middle one comparatively short while drawing out the last well beyond the length of the other two. So it is with the two six-part pavans where, in performance, repetition of the final strain seems best omitted, not only on grounds of the elaborately extended musical content, but also because the effect of the concluding bars in both instances is so very final.

Thurston Dart was perhaps the first to suggest that named pavans like Byrd's and Gibbons' 'Earl of Salisbury' may have been memorial pieces for the person mentioned in the title.[24] It is difficult to escape the belief that at least some of Jenkins' 'bell' pieces may have had a similar origin.[25] Indeed, Sir Philip Wodehouse's little verse 'Upon Mr J. Jenkins ye rare Musitian'[26] says as much:

[23] Thomas Morley, *op. cit.*, p. 296.

[24] *Cf.* his Notes on p. 39 of his edition of *Parthenia*, Stainer & Bell, London, 1960, rev. edn. 1962.

[25] These are 'The Sixe Bells' (Bodleian Library, Mus. Sch. MS C.84); 'Lady Katherine Audley's Bells' (many sources, including Bodleian Library, Mus. Sch. MS C.88); 'St Peter's Bells' and 'Bow Bells' (both attributed to Jenkins in Chetham's Library, Manchester, MS MUS. MUN. A.2.6.); 'Bells' *à 2* in F (several sources, including Christ Church, Music MS 1005).

[26] Yale University, Beinecke Library, MS Osborn b.131, No. 170, quoted in *Roger North on Music*, p. 348n.

This rare Amphyon of Our tymes
Is toul'd to Heaven by his own chymes* *his Bells

Of course, in 1678 this is more likely to have been the popular *Lady Katherine Audley's Bells* (published by Playford in *Courtly Masquing Ayres* (1662) and which exists in numerous manuscript copies) rather than an outmoded pavan for viol consort. Yet how wonderfully apt seemed the elegiac beauty of the 'Bell Pavan' (played by the English Consort of Viols circled round the composer's grave) at the Tercentenary Commemoration Service for Jenkins held in Kimberley Church on 27 October 1978; some words of Edward Taylor serve as a remembrance of that day:

Methinks I see Heaven's sparkling courtiers fly,
In flakes of Glory down him to attend,
And hear Heart-cramping notes of Melody
Surround his Chariot as it did ascend;
Mixing their Music, making ev'ry string
More to enravish as they this tune sing [...].[27]

Morley's budding composer was advised, when writing a pavan, that

> In this you may not so much insist in following the point as in a Fantasy, but it shall be enough to touch it once and so away to some close.[28]

A few years later and he could have cited the 'Bell Pavan' as an example of how to do it: the opening strain is built from two loosely imitative 'points' (Ex. 31(a) and (b))

Ex. 31

[27] Ed. Thomas H. Johnson, *The Poetical Works of Edward Taylor*, Princeton University Press, Princeton, 1943.

[28] Morley, *op. cit.*, p. 296.

before the threads are drawn together and we are reminded of the basic pulse traditionally associated with the form: ♩♩♩ The anguished chromaticism which opens the second strain has already been mentioned.[29] Yet the elegiac mood is broken immediately after by music of delightful buoyancy and suppleness (Ex.32).

Ex. 32

Tonality is somewhat ambiguous here, tacking between A major and E major with the Mixolydian mode also floating in the background. At the start of the third strain all participate in another imitation of a 'point' before peals on the trebles herald the 'bells' to come. These are clearly derived from the so-called 'Whittington Chimes' (Ex. 33), which, since the Whittington story is connected with Bow church, may have been played by the clock there.[30]

Ex. 33

It is intriguing to note that St. Mary-le-Bow stands opposite the south end of Milk Street. Here lived Baldwin Derham, mercer (d. 1610), whose family became Jenkins' patrons. Maybe the church was also for a time a focal

[29] *Cf.* note 28, p. 224.

[30] *Cf.* Chapter One, note 28, p. 27.

point in the life of the young composer. But there certainly was a tradition linking the theme with a memorial role which can be clearly traced in English music between about the 1580s and the 1650s. A full investigation lies beyond the scope of this book, but one only has to cite works like Vautor's 'Sweet Suffolk Owl', Johnson's 'Full fathom five' and familiar keyboard pieces from the *Fitzwilliam Virginal Book* to show that the tradition was well-established.[31] Vautor uses the peal in setting 'and sings a dirge for dying souls', while two of the keyboard pieces place it as a 'passing' or 'burial' knell after a 'battle'. The 'Bell Pavan', then, might have served as a memorial piece for one or other of Jenkins' parents, who died in 1617 and 1623 respectively; neither was eminent enough to be named in the title. Maybe too much is being read into the significance of the bell passages in Jenkins' music; perhaps they merely are his particular means of filtering a musical experience of the commonalty into consorts intended for 'persons of quality'. Such, presumably, was the aim of Byrd, Gibbons and others in quoting 'cries' and snatches of ballads; Jenkins' bells may have been a part of this tradition. One further reference to the Whittington Chimes, which can hardly date from any earlier than the second quarter of the seventeenth century, is to be found in the third movement of Jenkins' Fantasia-Suite No. 10 for treble, bass and organ (Ex. 34). Only the

[31] Thomas Vautor, *The First Set: Beeing Songs of divers Ayres and Natures* [...] (1619), No. 12. For a transcription of Johnson's song *cf.* John P. Cutts, *La Musique de Scène de la Troupe de Shakespeare: The King's Men* [...], Centre National de la Recherche Scientifique, Paris, 1971, p. 24. *Fitzwilliam Virginal Book* No. 69 is Byrd's 'The Bells', and No. 173 is a medley ascribed to him, but which is known in other forms certainly not composed by him. For a mixed consort version (and information on sources) *cf. Musica Britannica*, Vol. XL, Stainer & Bell, London, No. 24. There is also the spurious 'Burying of the dead' attached to Byrd's 'Battle' in Elizabeth Rogers' Virginal Book (British Library, Add. MS 10337). *Cf. Neighbour, op. cit.*, p. 166, for a discussion of the last two pieces and p. 122 for 'The Bells'.

first few bars quote the Chimes directly, but other bell resonances continue to sound throughout the movement. In view of the relatively late date of this work, caution must clearly be exercised before assuming that the 'Bell Pavan' belongs to an earlier period.

Ex. 34

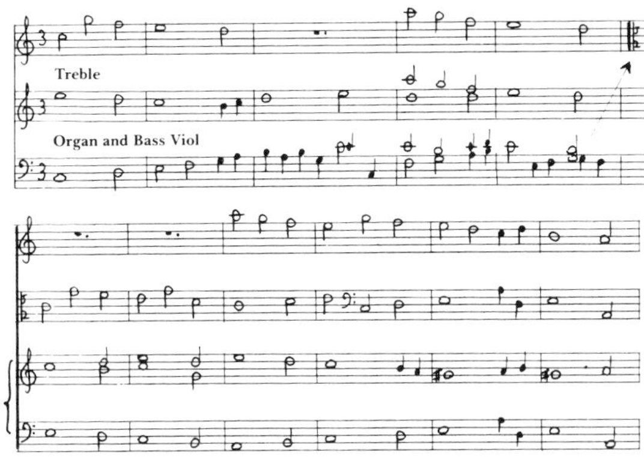

Jenkins was a prolific and fluent composer who, it seems, would sooner write a new piece than adapt an old one; his five-part Pavan No. 3 also exists in a three-part version.[32] Yet so, with this duplication in mind, it is interesting to note how easily the main content of his six-part Pavan in F could similarly be reduced to a trio. The two treble parts in particular are closely imitative – more obviously so than in the 'Bell Pavan' – and, with the lowest bass, mostly give a text as harmonically complete as any in his true three-part dances. Yet a six-part texture was in the composer's mind from the start: the rich inner parts and their voice-leading would be sorely missed in any reduced version.

Serene and mellow, this pavan ranks among Jenkins'

[32] *Cf.* Chapter Six, pp. 259–60.

finest works. The secret of its beauty derives especially from an unusual tonal plan in which probes towards the brighter, sharper keys are eschewed in favour of those seeking the sub-dominant and even warmer regions beyond. This tendency is firmly established by the dramatic E flat chord in bar 7, pulling the music into the sub-dominant from where, by a circuitous route touching on several keys, it eventually finds its way back to F major at the close. A new tonal area is explored in the second strain with keys centred on the relative minor: F major, D minor, G minor, A major.

The trio-voicing changes into two groups each comprising a treble, tenor and bass; but their antiphonal treatment of a two-bar phase is disguised because the first group continues to play once the second has entered. Nor are these additional parts very convincing in themselves and only serve to muddle the neat opposition of the slow-moving treble and its lively fellows. At bar 22 comes another editorial/performance problem in the shape of groups of repeated quavers, some of which are slurred in pairs. The slurs appear to be bowing marks (indicating two notes to one bow) and may be adopted in the unmarked groups too (Ex. 35). Their tremulous fluttering certainly brings an imaginative touch of colour to the proceedings, heightened by the urgency of the upward-

Ex. 35

striving melodies which settle in A minor – the sharpest tonality in the piece – at the close (Ex. 35). The final strain equals the length of the other two combined and the work here assumes something of the character of a fantasia, though again, in keeping with Morley's *dictum* cited earlier,[33] imitation is not fully developed. Once more the tonal journey is interesting, with the briefest hint of the dominant soon transformed firmly into its minor mode and allowing Jenkins to set up a tonal argument between C minor and E flat major as the centre-piece of the section (the beautiful passage quoted in Ex. 22). It is the subdominant again which acts as the pivot whereby the music regains the tonic to underpin the pealing bells of the coda.

Having surveyed the 'Series II' pieces, it is easier to consider the content of the isolated Fantasia No. 12. Why was this work omitted from the otherwise complete six-part collections of Mus. Sch. MS C.83 and Add. MS 29290? If it had been written years before, it is quite possible that no copy was available at Kirtling, or even that Jenkins had absent-mindedly forgotten about it, as happened to some other works:

> A great Don from Spaine sent over the papers of one part of a consort of 3, all fantasies, to Sr P. Lely desiring to have the consort compleat *costa che costa* ['whatever the cost']. I shewed the old gentleman [Jenkins] ye papers; he sayd he beleeved ye composition was his, but when made and where to enquire for them he knew not and they could never be found.[34]

A third possibility, that the piece is by someone else, seems unlikely on stylistic grounds.

Fantasia No. 12 is a fine work, lacking the impact only of the best 'Series I' fantasias. The counterpoint is skilfully managed and is certainly not the work of a novice. Features typical of Jenkins' writing include the generally

33 *Cf.* p. 180.

34 North, *op. cit.*, p. 344.

broad scale, smooth-flowing lines (completely avoiding the angular twists of Lawes' style) and a relative freedom in the imitation in which intervals and/or rhythms are not necessarily matched exactly. Some of Jenkins' contemporaries were critical of what seemed to them to be an insipid style 'wholly devoid of fire and fury' – but this was a matter of taste and there is no doubt that much of the lyrical fervour of his music arises from his contrapuntal fluency. Subtle modifications to the shape and rhythm of his themes enable him to incorporate as many contrapuntal tricks as he pleases without the part-writing ever appearing forced. Ex. 36, for instance, shows the double subject of the expansive opening section and the respective forms of their next three appearances. Theme B goes against the *tactus* (the underlying beat) at first in order to kick against theme A, but later appearances are with the *tactus*, causing the harmonic gear to slip momentarily at bars 7–8 (Ex. 37). Jenkins largely ignores theme B at first, which only gets properly under way at bar 8. The *x* figure incorporated in both themes carries the music forward and binds the whole section together.

Ex. 36

Donald Peart comments on the 'rather severe Aeolian modality' of this work and remarks that 'A minor is a key in which Jenkins seems particularly at home'.[35] So it is,

[35] Donald Peart, 'John Jenkins: Consort Music of Six Parts', *Musica Britannica*, Vol. XXXIX, Stainer & Bell, London, 1977, p. xiv.

Ex. 37

and the composer chooses not to stray far from his tonal centre here: though there are brief excursions to the dominant, sub-dominant and F major in this first section, none is allowed to settle.

Two features in particular suggest that this work is relatively early: the range of the parts is restricted and joins between sections are heavily disguised. Although lively new patterns emerge at bar 25, these still weave round remnants of the initial subjects. But eventually this new, and (as it turns out) central, episode reduces to a texture reminiscent of Jenkins' four-part fantasias, with the treble mostly keeping its distance from an intricate web woven by two tenors and a bass (Ex. 38). No attempt is made to link the voices by a common motif, although the interplay of dotted rhythms is a striking element.

Ex. 38

The theme of the final section has been met already in Fantasia No. 10, where it is presented in a kind of miniature set of variations (bars 46–53): (a) two-part imitation at the fifth between treble and bass, (b) harmonised with block $^{6}_{3}$ triads and imitated at the sixth by the bass, (c) as a four-part fugato, and (d) as one strand in a free-voiced six-part contrapuntal texture. But in Fantasia No. 12 the subject is treated more as a constantly recurring *cantus firmus* with less (though not negligible) emphasis on imitative possibilities. The two tenors hint at inversion in bars 40–42 and a sudden burst of bass divisions in bars 46–47 causes Tenor II to jig in sympathy. Yet generally, the unfussy rhythms and extreme smoothness of the parts ensure that this is a serene and tranquil conclusion to the work. There is enough emphasis on key colour to maintain interest, moving from a hint of G major (the brightest point in the work) to a warmer F major at the other extreme. Altogether this work reveals the hand of a mature Jenkins in its assured technique, in the confident and successful planning of large-scale sections, and above all in its lyricism.

Possible links between viol consorts and *Musica Transalpina* have already been mentioned.[36] The influence of Alphonso Ferrabosco I on English music might be cited to reinforce these connections since there are more works by him in *Musica Transalpina* than by any other. Morley pays tribute to Ferrabosco's 'deep skill' and more than forty years after the composer had left England Henry Peacham pronounced that 'for judgement and depth of skill [he] was inferior unto none.[37] Among the distinctive ploys which Kerman identifies[38] in Ferrabosco's work in his habit of breaking a madrigal

> after the first three or four lines, coming to a strong full-cadence with a *longa* in all parts, followed by a vertical stroke through the whole staff – a double bar. Thereafter he generally starts up again homophonically, often with three or four voices only.

[36] *Cf.* p. 119.

[37] Henry Peacham, *The Compleat Gentleman*, London, 1622, p. 101.

[38] *Op. cit.*, p. 88.

On at least one occasion his son Alphonso Ferrabosco II transferred the procedure to consort music;[39] so could it be this practice which is echoed by Jenkins in Fantasias Nos. 1 and 5 (Ex. 39(a) and (b)), where double-bars mark the end of the first section at a 'strong full-cadence' and change of mood? The structure of each work is distorted if these repeats are taken literally[40] and both do move off homophonically after the double-bar.[41]

Ex. 39

There is a family relationship between several of the themes in the six-part works, 'wrought with no small industry, yet easy and familiar', as North remarks.[42] Apart from the common *canzona* trademark (𝅗𝅥 ♩ ♩) in works such as Fantasias Nos. 10 and 11 and the E minor *In Nomine*, a striking similarity also exists between the initial subjects of Fantasias Nos. 1, 4 and 9 (Ex. 40(a), (b) and (c)) The counter-subjects shown are soon discarded,

[39] In his Fantasia No. 2 *à 6*, published as No. 78 in *Musica Britannica*, Vol. IX, pp. 119–22.

[40] Since these double-bars are notated in six different ways, no precise interpretation seems possible.

[41] Other Jenkins fantasias with double-bars at this point are No. 21 for two trebles and bass and No. 20 for treble, two basses and organ.

[42] *Op. cit.*, p. 296.

though their independent rhythms help to energise the opening bars of their respective pieces.

In Fantasia No. 1 the counter-melody is displaced by imitative treatment of the *x* motif shown in Ex. 40(a), matching the first episode in a fugue and similarly serving to take the music into the relative major preparatory to further statements of the subject. But Jenkins quickly steers the music towards the sub-dominant, tacking between this key and the tonic before coming to rest in the latter at the double-bar. So striking is the change of mood here that one can be forgiven for not realising that the new section is still derived from the opening theme. Jenkins has cleverly disguised this relationship by inversion, by changing to the tonic major – one of his favourite

Ex. 40

(a)

(b)

(c)

ploys – and by introducing a different texture of a predominantly homophonic nature, soon confounded by an exuberant burst of syncopations and bass divisions (Ex. 39). The new five-part texture may again by emulating the Ferraboscos' habit of reducing the ensemble at this point. Jenkins could easily have gone further along this road: the two antiphonal trebles over an opposing bass are once more close to the manner of his three-part dances and maintain the bulk of the interest. There is a delightful irregularity in the phrasing, yet this aspect is brought under control by three firm cadences at bars 28 (G major), 31 (C major) and 35 (F major).

The remainder of the work, though by no means poor, does not match up to the quality of the first half. In breaking up the first two paragraphs into smaller units, Jenkins achieves a wide variety of texture and interest, and yet the whole remains unified by a common thematic core. Neither of the last two paragraphs are splintered in this way, nor does any cadence provide a breathing space. The third section, broad and with fine suspensions, lacks a sense of direction, although there are interesting modulations which even touch on B flat minor at one point. At 27 bars the final section is too long, for the steady crotchet tread of its principal theme generates insufficient life to balance the vitality flooding from the first part of the work. To all intents and purposes this theme is an inverted form of the one Jenkins uses so successfully in concluding Fantasias Nos. 10 and 12. Its relative failure here may be due as much to the lack of a positive tonal journey as to the absence of a true climax crowning the conclusion. If these features had been present they might well have lifted the latter part of this work to the imaginative heights of its opening; as it is, one feels that Jenkins over-reached himself, for this work seems to be the largest of all the English consort fantasias, measuring 160 semibreves.[43]

Fantasias Nos. 2, 3 and 7 are monothematic. The problem of sustaining one idea through a whole piece seems always to have stimulated Jenkins' invention and he explores an infinite variety of structures, styles and moods.

Fantasia No. 2 is an extremely lively work, the only one among these six-part pieces to drive forward in one mood throughout. The subject appears as much with an inverted tail as with a normal one[44] and in various forms of augmentation as much as with its initial rhythms (Ex. 41). Entries 3–6 are delayed by a substantial dialogue between Treble II and Tenor I (Ex. 42), the fragmented speech of which becomes a distinctive ingredient of the ensuing volatile writing. By its nature contrapuntal music

[43] Among, that is, free fantasias not tied to a *cantus firmus*.

[44] Another instance of this device opens the four-part Fantasia No. 13; *cf.* p. 230.

is primarily concerned with melody and this essentially singing style suits the viol admirably.

Ex. 41

Ex. 42

Nevertheless the Renaissance composer's awakened interest in word-setting gave rise in turn to numerous other techniques which had hitherto received scant use. Among these were two- and three-note interjections like those in Dowland's well-known air 'Come again, sweet love doth now invite'[45] (Ex. 43).

Ex. 43

Such examples, as much as the realisation that instrumental music must also develop its own idioms, may well have influenced the kind of chirpy patterns found throughout this fantasia (Ex. 44). These have another function here: to prevent the texture from becoming too weighed down in the plethora of notes. But such writing is rare in Jenkins' viol music and he only employs it in one or two of the more effervescent passages.[46]

The unbroken welter of activity in Fantasia No. 2 is

[45] *The First Booke of Songs or Ayres* [...], 1597, No. 17.

[46] *Cf.* Fantasia No. 1 *à 5*, bars 20–5; Fantasia No. 16 *à 4*, bar 54 onwards.

Ex. 44

actually anchored to a number of structural and tonal props, giving the work a firm ground plan. The latter include excursions to the tonic major at bars 12–14 and to the sub-dominant and its relative major around bars 23–8, but equally important are the five-voiced stretto affirmations of the subject centred on bars 9, 22, 30 and 37. Only when the last of these stretti is reached is the brake applied to give a wonderfully broad peroration which simultaneously combines elements of stretto and inversion above an augmented statement of the theme in the bass (Ex. 45).[47]

Where Fantasia No. 2 is lively, Fantasia No. 3 is the most stately, a work of tremendous dignity which seems to require a slow tempo despite generally long note-values. Its wide arch of a theme, opening with an upward leap of a sixth, is unusual for Jenkins, but he then substitutes a smoother variant (Ex. 46). Although the opening looks slow to the eye, the ear reveals otherwise, for there is plenty of rhythmic life generated both by the interplay

[47] I am indebted to David Pinto for drawing my attention to Ferrabosco II's Fantasia No. 3 *à 6*, another monothematic work in C minor. There is a striking resemblance between the subjects of the two works, although in Ferrabosco's piece the augmented statement in the bass concludes the first of two sections; the second is given over to lively diminutions of the theme.

Ex. 45

Ex. 46

of dotted rhythms and by touches of syncopation; indeed, rhythmic articulation in the first few bars mostly maintains a steady crotchet tread. Jenkins opens the fantasia with a three-fold repetition of the scheme adopted in bars 1–10. Each time the fugue is at first confined to three voices only while the remaining parts are held back for an entrance in close stretto; the section closes in the dominant. Jenkins' imaginative approach to tonality is not much in evidence here, but there is ample compensation in the rich harmony and felicitous touches of scoring. A particularly ethereal and beautiful moment is provided by the second trio (bars 14–17); with passages like these to ease their souls, there is little wonder that

> during the troubles [...] many chose rather to fidle at home, than to goe out, and be knockt on the head abroad.[48]

The composer builds an irregularity into the structure, averting the cadence at bar 11 to extend the first section by three bars, then later dovetailing the join between sections two and three at bars 23–4. Now the theme takes on a lively tail which, with derivatives, is to enliven the remainder of the piece. Jenkins explores many of the imitative possibilities of this new figure (Ex. 47 (b)), also using it as a counter-melody to the original subject and finally running it through all the parts above a firm dominant pedal.

Ex. 47

There are few major discrepancies between the sources regarding readings of Jenkins' six-part pieces, but Fantasia No. 3 shows a couple of interesting variants. The North manuscripts steer something of a middle course textually. They are likely to contain more accidentals (generally giving a firmer diatonic reading) than the seemingly earlier sources from owners like John Browne and John Merro, while at the same time largely avoiding the corruptions of later scribes such as Hutton and the Oxford musicians of the 1660s. A variant reading like

[48] North, *op. cit.*, p. 296.

Ex 48(a) suggests that Jenkins' original simple text has been overlaid as a result of a generation of so of players ornamenting the cadence, their improvisation becoming 'frozen in notation'.[49] The difference between the two readings in bar 51 (Ex. 48(b)) is curious; Browne's version (the Christ Church MS), though, establishes imitative links with the tenor parts.

Ex. 48

(a)

(b)

Ex. 49

Although Fantasia No. 7 is also monothematic, it divides into five distinctive sections, each beginning with a different treatment of the subject (Ex. 49): a light fugue in the upper parts at bar 15, another broader version with crotchet replacing quaver in the theme, at bars 24–5, then with chordal accompaniment at bar 42 and finally with the theme hidden in a contrapuntal texture at bars 51–2. The opening is in D-Dorian but because most of the entries start on A there is more than a hint of the Aeolian mode, too. This ambiguity persists until late in the second section when the music suddenly brightens to cadence in the tonic major. Although there are no far-reaching modulations in this fantasia, key does play an important

[49] But *cf.* also pp. 163–5.

role. For instance, this D major ending is decidedly bright when compared with the ensuing modulations through flatter keys – a contrast enhanced by unusually low phrases in the tenor parts. Incidentally, it is interesting to note that the treble parts in the three A minor fantasias (Nos. 7, 8 and 12) have a lower ceiling than those in the remaining works: g″ is the upper limit in Nos. 7 and 8 and a″ in No. 12. The third section (bars 24–42) is the centrepiece in more ways than one: an exciting amalgam of key, colour and counterpoint in which increasingly expansive statements of the subject are off-set by correspondingly livelier figures in the other parts. Most striking of all is the four-fold augmentation of the theme in bars 34–9, pitted against lively bass divisions of the kind one is always likely to meet in Jenkins' viol music, though not usually as extensively as here, and reminiscent of the liveliest passages in his *In Nomine*s (Ex. 50).

Ex. 50

Hidden away in the complex texture is more contrapuntal cunning: a canon at the fifth between Treble I and Tenor II (bars 21–3) and an intricate though short-lived three-part canon enveloping the principal theme at bars 29–30 (Ex. 51). Allied to these new developments is a less stable sense of key. After some fluctuation between tonic and dominant the third section moves to the sub-dominant and its relative major, eventually closing on the dominant of G minor. With Beethovenian panache Jenkins then forges ahead as if this chord had been the tonic, plunging directly into D minor at the start of the fourth section (bar 42). Here, after just two further statements, the subject disappears from view and Jenkins seizes on an arpeggiated quaver figure to keep the momentum

Ex. 51

generated earlier and brings the section to a lively close in C major. The beautiful link quoted in Ex. 24 transfers the tonality to regions nearer home and, as if to make up for its brief absence, entries of the subject multiply again in the final bars.

Although the internal balance differs, it is clear that in Fantasias Nos. 4 and 5 Jenkins was working to a similar emotional curve. Both works make extensive use of major keys, but begin and end in the minor. Both also include at the heart of their major-key music a wonderfully serene episode which descends from the heights and fills out as it progresses. Structurally this corresponds with the light episode – usually a *tripla* – which Jenkins often introduces after divisions in his fantasia-suites; the lightness here is achieved by scoring, with the basses rested. Furthermore the coda in both works is virtually identical (Ex. 52). But more detailed comparisons bring to light differences too, some of them quite significant.

The opening fugue in Fantasia No. 4 is unusually long (28 bars) and is tied, perhaps too tightly, to tonic and dominant harmony. Because both subject and counter-subject are built from a single root-position triad (Ex. 40), not only are harmonic manoeuvres limited, but also the promising free flight of the opening duet is soon brought

Ex. 52

to earth. The counter-subject, incidentally, which appears regularly at first, fits both head and tail of the theme, but is soon discarded in favour of a new imitative point (Ex. 53).

Ex. 53

This figure again, though varied, hardly extends the triadic formula. Jenkins lays out the remainder of the section in a series of 'waves', with crests formed from a series of stretto entries of the subject and troughs derived from subsidiary motifs. A four-bar dominant pedal is tacked on rather arbitrarily, yet soon develops a lively repartee between each pair of instruments. In the trebles here Jenkins foreshadows Beethoven's device of compressing a musical motif to increase tension (Ex. 54), heightening the contrast with the lovely and spacious major-key music which follows. This is built from loose imitations of Ex. 55. The light episode steals in, with intertwining trebles soon joined by tenors. An answering phrase for the three lowest instruments precedes a poignant twist back to the minor, where an extended dominant pedal underpins increasingly obsessive chatter by all

Ex. 54

Ex. 55

instruments, suddenly silenced to make way for the 'Grave and Harmonious Musick' of the coda.

Fantasia No. 5 is not far removed from the pattern adopted by Jenkins in the first movements of his fantasia-suites:

(a) a fugal opening
(b) an exciting 'display' section
(c) a lighter episode
(d) a rich and sonorous conclusion.

There is no reason to suppose that the similarity between the initial subject and Dowland's famous 'Lachrimae' tag is anything more than co-incidental.[50] Imitative treatment of it dominates the opening section, though one side-slip (both tonal and stylistic) hints at the kind of inserted reference to a more popular idiom familiar enough in the fantasias of Byrd and Gibbons, but rarely exploited by Jenkins (Ex. 56). Even here there is no let up in the contrapuntal texture, so the underlying dance element remains heavily disguised. Indeed, beyond an inherent melodiousness, these six-part works take little from the dance idiom of the time,[51] although, as it

[50] Joan Wess, *loc. cit.*, pp. 19–20, suggests that the opening draws upon Ferrabosco I's setting of 'Zefiro torna' in *Musica Transalpina* (1597); *cf.* also Kerman, *op. cit.*, pp. 94–6.

[51] Ernst Meyer, *op. cit.*, pp. 219–20, makes too much of this idea, in my view. The revised text in *Early English Chamber Music,* Laurence & Wishart, London, 1982, p. 250, is more satisfactory.

Ex. 56

Ex. 57

happens, this particular fantasia includes one passage (bars 37–39) uncommonly like the opening of a four-part Almain by Jenkins[52] (Ex. 57). After the initial balanced phrases the pattern becomes irregular in both works, but in the fantasia the dance element is again submerged in elaborate counterpoint. More remarkable still is the previous display section (the opening of which is shown in Ex. 39(b), when the extended use of dotted rhythms is perhaps unique in English consort music of the time. Although this passage too is, in effect, a gloriously exuberant dance, it seems more likely to have been inspired

52 Published ed. Andrew Ashbee, 'John Jenkins: Consort Music of Four Parts', *Musica Britannica*, Vol. XXVI, Stainer & Bell, London, rev. edn. 1975, pp. 159–60.

by division techniques. It is organised as a dialogue between pairs of instruments, but because the phrase lengths are irregular, there are kaleidoscopic changes in colour as the viols call to one another. Cadences abound, but are not allowed to settle until the dance episode alluded to earlier is reached (bar 37); it provides the first of two brief interludes; the second, as in Fantasia No. 4, is for trebles and tenors only.

Meanwhile, the work has been moving steadily towards progressively brighter tonalities. Apart from the brief excursion quoted in Ex. 56, the opening remains rooted in D-Dorian. Yet halfway through the 'display' section a tug-of-war develops between G major and E minor, from which the former emerges as victor. From this point the music continues to move sharpwards round the key-circle, first to D (bar 39), then A (bars 47–8) as the final 'Grave and Harmonious Musick' begins, then E (bars 52–3) and finally B major at bar 55. With only ten bars remaining this is a remote key from which to return swiftly and safely to the tonic; that it is accomplished so effortlessly is a tribute to Jenkins' skill in handling tonality. Not for him the collisions and twists of Lawes' lines: none of the parts is deflected from its aim and one chromatic progression suffices (Ex. 58).

Ex. 58

It is not surprising that the early fantasia imitated vocal forms, for here were tried and tested patterns, satisfying and logical enough even without text. Their schemes prevail even in Jenkins' time, though the increasing preoccupation of his generation with instrumental consorts demanded both a more idiomatic approach to texture and line and a fresh look at form. A comparison between Fantasias Nos. 6 and 10 shows two arrangements of broadly similar components. A simple ground-plan might be set out as follows:

Fantasia No. 6		*Fantasia No. 10*	
Bars		Bars	
1–14:	opening fugue	1–23:	opening fugue
14–17:	five-part interlude	23–7	lighter interlude
18–28:	first trio	28–35:	imitative section
29–34:	fully scored interjection		
		35–9:	first trio
35–42:	second trio	39–42:	second trio
42–51:	imitative section	42–6:	sequential interlude
51–6:	sequential interlude		
		46–55:	closing fugue
56–71:	closing fugue		

The basic principal of a succession of different imitative 'points' underlies a vast amount of both vocal and instrumental music from the sixteenth and early seventeenth centuries. Certainly its ghost haunts Fantasia No. 10, where each new idea is totally independent of its fellows. But in Fantasia No. 6 subtle modifications lead to a more sophisticated and integrated design. Most striking is a group of four crotchet chords, distinctive enough to serve as a unifying feature, yet also acting as a springboard from which successive ideas take off.[53] Neither of the two volatile trios adopts strict imitative roles, but rather both give vent to rhythmic high spirits. Separating these trios are two fully scored phrases which might have jumped straight out of an almain: they prove to be the keystone of a roughly symmetrical 'arch' form, to which the closing fugue acts as a coda. Whilst it can be argued that the pattern of 'successive points' remains paramount, other fantasias in the group show a similar leaning

[53] Bars 14, 18, 28, 31 and 42.

towards a symmetrical shape: for example, Nos. 1, 4 and 5. Key plays a crucial role here, for the emotional 'centre' coincides with tonic major music embedded in a minor-key setting. One could add Fantasia No. 7 to the group in an arch form, for it too is similarly rounded, yet its overriding feature is monothematicism. Symmetry undoubtedly helps unify a work without the aid of such thematic links, and in Fantasia No. 8 Jenkins exploits the device again.

The opening fugue of No. 8 is characteristically expansive and rich; its double subject (Ex. 59) occurs in a variety of permutations which in turn allow equally varied harmonic treatment, while invertible counterpoint is put to good use.

Ex. 59

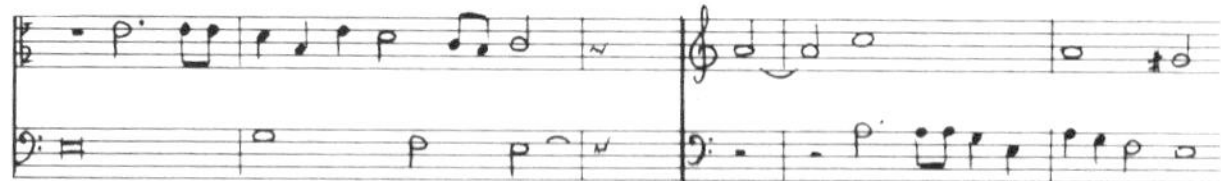

A passage for the three upper voices alone serves as a coda to this section, coming to rest gently in the tonic. Throughout the work there is a tendency for the tonality to veer towards the subdominant, and so occasional excursions in the opposite direction provide shafts of real brightness piercing the generally subdued tonal light. That Jenkins is able to achieve colourful key contrasts even within the confines of such a limited palette is amply demonstrated by the beautiful central episode, yet it is not only care in handling key which is evident here: the composer is again concerned with the over-all ground plan. A particularly neat touch, for instance, is the four-part fugue resulting from the tardy entry of Tenor I and Bass I the final section begins (bars 35–9), which not only balances the three-part passage mentioned earlier, but also brings the full sonority of the central episode into sharp relief. The final fugue is the longest and liveliest part of the work, building to a fine climax of pealing bells.

Ex. 60

Viol consorts were, first and foremost, experienced 'from the inside' by the players, and the score-reader is in danger of neglecting that other viewpoint – the individual's contribution to and experience of the whole as transmitted through his own part. A player presented with his music for Fantasia No. 9 will note that it is among the more active pieces in the collection, certainly not as florid as the two *In Nomine*s, but matching Fantasias Nos. 2, 6 and 7. Yet only in performance would he realise that the texture of this work is perhaps the most dense and involved in the entire collection. Initial impetus comes from the driving character of the subject (Ex. 40(c)) and, with full play given to its quaver figure, lively counterpoint develops – so much so that later entries of the subject tend to be swamped by the activity around them. There are some free attempts at stretto, but then filigree wisps of semiquavers spirit the subject away and replace it with an even more close-knit mesh. Within this complex texture it may be some time before Tenor II realises he is in canon with Treble II one beat before him (Ex. 60). In other circumstances this eight-bar canon might form a separate section since it has no thematic links with the opening, but, by withholding any cadence until its conclusion and by maintaining the momentum of the music, Jenkins here binds the two elements together, with the canon as the crown. For a moment the texture is pared down to four parts before the second main section begins. This also has two elements. The first, as in Fantasia No. 8, features a 𝅗𝅥♩♩ rhythm, adding a touch of solemnity after all the earlier activity, and from it emerges by stealth the principal theme of the loosely imitative final section.

chapter five
The Four-part Fantasias and Associated Pavans

With Jenkins' four-part as with his six-part music, it is the manuscript from the North household (Bodleian Mus. Sch. MS C.99) which contains the fullest selection of pieces, in this case all seventeen fantasias and two unique pavans. Although there is little firm evidence, the make-up of the books offers an occasional clue to the chronology of the pieces. Margaret Crum's investigation[1] shows that the string parts for Fantasias Nos. 15–17 (which follow the two pavans) were copied on a different paper from the rest of the music. Since these pieces are unique to this manuscript, it is possible that they were written for use at Kirtling and added afterwards, especially since there are stylistic differences between them and the rest of the series. As a whole the collection seems less unified than either the five- or six-part sets, hinting at a more piece-meal compilation. Table IV shows how the works are distributed among the various manuscripts.[2]

Both in technique and character, Fantasias Nos. 1–4 of the North collection come closest to the work of Jenkins' immediate predecessors, especially Alphonso Ferrabosco II, whose large and masterly collection of four-part music must have served as particular inspiration and model for the younger man. There are one or two curious technical features which may indicate the composer was still lacking experience, such as the upward resolution of what

[1] 'The Consort Music from Kirtling [...]'.

[2] *Cf.* p. 208; *cf.* also Gordon Dodd, *Thematic Index of Music for Viols*, p. 76.

Table 4
Sources for Jenkins' Four-Part Fantasias

A		B/C/D	E	F	G	H	J	K	L	M	N	O
1	C minor	(1)								I/4	(28)	
2	C minor	(2)								I/1	(29)	(1)
3	C minor	(4)								I/2	(30)	
4	D minor	(3)								I/6	(31)	
5	F major		15		25	9	38	21	3		24	
6	F major		16		26	10	37	22	4		23	
7	C minor		17							I/3	(32)	
8	C minor									I/5		
9	C minor			10								
10	A minor				27	11	36			II/1	26	
11	A minor		21		28	12	35			II/2	(27)	
12	D major			6						I/7	(34)	
13	D major		18	8								
14	D major		19									
Pavan	D minor											
Pavan	E minor											
15	C major											
16	D minor											
17	F major											

A = GB-Ob, Mus. Sch. Ms C.99
B = GB-Och, Music MS 2 (score)
C = GB-Och, Music MSS 397–400
D = GB-Och, Music MS 436 (organ)
E = GB-Och, Music MSS 473–8
F = GB-Och, Music MSS 717 & 719
G = GB-Ob, Mus. Sch. MSS C.64–9
H = EIRE-Dm, MSS Z3.4.1–6
J = EIRE-Dm, MS Z3.4.13
K = Gb-Lb1, Add. MSS 17792–6
L = US-NYp, Drexel MSS 4180–5
M = GB-Y, MSS 3/1–4(S)
N = GB-Och, Music MSS 468–72
O = GB-Ob, Mus. Sch. Mss E.437-42

Notes

(a) Numbers are as in the Gordon Dodd (ed.), *Thematic Index of Music for Viols*, Viola da Gamba Society, London, 1980–2, pp. 75–6. They show the sequence of pieces, but do not necessarily occur in the sources, brackets-in cols. B/C/D, N and O-indicating where they do not occur.

(b) There is a fragment of Fantaisa No. 1 in GB-Ob, Tenbury MS 302.

(c) Source F has alto and tenor parts only.

(d) In source J, a basso continuo part, the sequence of pieces which includes these Jenkins fantasias is reversed.

(e) There is a page torn out of MS 472 in source N, rendering Fantasia No. 12 incomplete there.

(f) The two series of pieces in source M are here shown as I and II.

(g) Fantasia No. 2 in source O is copied at the reverse end of the books.

is, in effect, a suspension (Ex. 61(a)).[3] Another place where the composer in striving for cleverness, rather muddles the counterpoint is at bar 7: by making the canon of Treble and Tenor I so tight, the effect is of a lack of synchronisation, temporarily unsettling the music (Ex. 61(b)).

Ex. 61

The opening theme of this first fantasia (Ex. 62(a)) bears a family resemblance to several by Ferrabosco II (Ex. 62(b), (c) and (d)), with an unrelentingly dense and involved texture arising from its treatment, even going beyond anything of the kind attempted by the older composer. Sections dovetail into each other and melodic patterns are irregular. Ex. 63 shows what lively writing develops during the final section. This is certainly a work to keep players on their toes although its complexity is such that performers are more likely than listeners to appreciate its essence.

> But as to Mr Jenkins in particular, there is somewhat more to be sayd. His style is thought to be slow, heavy,

[3] The consecutive fifths between Treble and Tenor II in bar 48 of Fantasia No. 3 caused endless trouble to later copyists as they tried (unsuccessfully) to find a solution. *Cf.* also Fantasia No. 4, bar 51, where there are similar consecutives between Treble and Tenor I.

Ex. 62

(a) (b)

(c) (d)

Ex. 63

> moving from concord to concord, and consequently dull; and I grant that he was obnoxious to an excess the English were, and I beleeve yet are, obnoxious to, and that is perpetually moving up and downe [the scale], without much saltation or battering as the Italians use. But else as to activity of movement, and true musical ayre in his passages, none more than Mr Jenkins.

By the time Roger North wrote those words,[4] a hundred years or more after Jenkins had composed his fantasies, musical tastes had changed and the delights of 'saltation and battering' and other baroque trappings held sway. It must be admitted that the opening of Fantasia No. 2 is one of Jenkins 'duller' moments, 'cheifly [...] going up and downe stairs' while 'the parts [...] hunt one and another, from concord to concord', as North put it in an earlier draft.[5] But this 'dullness' is to some extent deliberate: an intentionally gentle opening to contrast with later material. Delight in close or canonic imitation heightens the tension once the initial fugue has run its

[4] *Op. cit.*, p. 347.

[5] *Ibid.*, p. 297.

course, and the insertion of interlocked *tripla* patterns is a delightful touch (Ex. 64).

Ex. 64

The music broadens briefly for a loosely imitative section (bars 25–32) before launching into a vigorous finale. This has a much more arresting idea as its principal figure (Ex. 65(a)), whose nature seems almost violinistic, looking forward to the pattern of Fantasias 15 and 16 and to others in the set for two trebles and a bass. Yet Ex. 65(b) shows how closely this too matches a Ferrabosco theme, from his Fantasia *à 4* No. 15, and in turn reflects earlier or current practice. Sequential and canonic writing carry the motif along, with both the octave leap and the *x* figure well to the fore, and the section is capped by a double canon (Ex. 66), before the beautifully judged deceleration and final shuffling for position beneath a tonic pedal. The latter device was again gleaned from Ferrabosco II, who used it to perfection.

Ex. 65

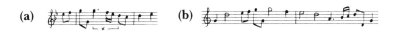

(a) x **(b)**

Fantasia No. 3 requires little comment, although this reticence is not to deny the considerable charm of its opening. Only twice in this series – here and in No. 8 –

Ex. 66

does Jenkins lead off with the treble and descend through the parts: the transition from a veiled, high-pitched single melody through increased weights as the texture fills out and lower sonorities are added is particularly effective. The fantasia as a whole is built from two extended sections which dovetail into each other, but the second motif, most unusually, derives from the consequent of the first (Ex. 67). Two-section fantasias and two-phrase subjects again show indebtedness to Ferrabosco II's example,[6] but this linking of motifs unifies the work still further. The close-knit and highly active writing already observed in Fantasia No. 1 again enlivens the second half here and is a constantly recurring feature throughout the series. Jenkins applies the brake a few bars before the end, but sends the music into B flat minor so that the final cadence comes as something of a surprise.

From a fantasia whose two sections are built from common material, it is only a short step to monothematicism. There are five such works in the series: Nos. 4, 6, 9, 11 and 17. Fantasia No. 4, if not a complete success, is never-

Ex. 67

6 *Cf.* Gordon Dodd, 'Alfonso Ferrabosco II – the Art of the Fantasy', *Chelys*, 7, 1977, pp. 47–53, and Vaught, *op. cit.*, pp. 201–13.

theless an extremely interesting work, drawing inspiration from the previous generation. Its theme (Ex. 68) is identical to that of Thomas Lupo's six-part Fantasia No. 6,[7] though there is no reason to suppose that this is more than coincidence.

Ex. 68

Comparisons are illuminating. In Lupo's work the theme is part of a double subject and the composer cleverly rings the changes by combining the two elements in different ways, both at the octave and at the fifth, with the counter-melody entering on different beats. Indeed, it is the latter which appears most, giving rise to a wealth of suspensions. Yet there is not the tightness of imitation so evident in Jenkins' music, and despite the six parts the texture remains quite open, with plenty of rests. Ex. 69 illustrates these features well as the exposition draws to a close. Thereafter Lupo moves on to investigate other themes in his multi-sectional fantasia. For his part, Jenkins first presents the theme in isolation, like an organist about to extemporise. Without a regular counter-melody the subject is much more in evidence than in Lupo's fantasia, of course, but its torso is further used to give shape and purpose to the melodies away from the true fugal entries (Ex. 70).

This is a feature particularly characteristic of Jenkins, and an extremely significant one, for it enables him to expand and develop his ideas without resort to mere routine pattern-making. But it is not to Lupo that one should look when seeking origins for this work but to Ferrabosco II, whose four-part Fantasia No. 21[8] seems to have been

[7] Viola da Gamba Society (Great Britain), Supplementary Publication No. 61.

[8] Viola da Gamba Society (Great Britain), Supplementary Publication No. 60.

Ex. 69

Ex. 70

the model on which Jenkins based his work. Presumably Ferrabosco's fantasia came first – it is included in Tregian's manuscript (GB-Lbl, Egerton MS 3665) – but one cannot be absolutely sure, especially as the work seems unique in the older composer's output. This monothematic Fantasia No. 21

> is the only one of Ferrabosco's fancies which features systematic and extensive exploration of distant tonal areas, on both the sharp and flat sides [... and] is the only fancy which appears to be experimental in nature. Two factors seem to be held in balance. The fancy goes far in one direction (harmonic), but is held in by the intensive working out of a single subject and the tight imitative layout. These harmonic and contrapuntal aspects, which are not general characteristics of Ferrabosco's style, thus nourish and support each other.[9]

[9] Vaught, *op. cit.*, p. 205.

The expositions of both fantasies maintain a stable tonality close to the home key, but at bar 15 Ferrabosco hoists his music out of its key-rut to explore a wide-ranging and constantly changing tonal landscape. From time to time he retraces his steps a little, but generally the music progresses sharpwards from B flat via G minor, D minor, E minor, and E major to a plateau oscillating between B major and C sharp minor, returning by a different route: F sharp minor – B minor – D major – E major – C minor – E flat major, and finally hovering between F minor and C minor before settling in the latter. This is a daring journey, the more successful for not relying on mechanical aids like the hexachord. Even so there is quite a jolt in turning the corner from E major to C minor, as one might expect. It is noticeable that Jenkins avoids such a bump in his travels, although he explores much the same territory. Comparisons show that Jenkins adopts a more modern approach in which, in addition to relative major/minor relationships, he uses the circle-of-fifths more methodically and consistently than Ferrabosco. If Fantasia No. 21 shows the furthest point to which Ferrabosco went in his exploration of harmonic colour, it will be easier to trace the developments which Jenkins achieved in this aspect of composition. Nowhere are these more strikingly evident than in the four-part fantasias. Before the freer exploration of tonality shown by the above works, experiments in this field were geared almost entirely to mechanical exercises built around the hexachord. Most famous of these are John Bull's 'Ut, re, me, fa, sol, la'[10] and the two fantasias 'On the hexachord' by Ferrabosco II.[11] In all these works the hexachord *cantus firmus* is transposed higher or lower, sometimes chromatically, so requiring perpetual and far-reaching shifts in tonality. It may be that, like the *cantus firmus* for the *In Nomine*, the slow-moving scale allowed the beginner violist access to

[10] *Fitzwilliam Virginal Book,* No. 51.

[11] The second is published in *Musica Britannica*, Vol. IX, No. 39.

an elaborate consort, but in reconciling tonal side-slipping with smooth part-writing, even stronger demands were made on the composer. The impact of such experiments on the development of key-sense at this time should not be under-estimated But there was an inherent danger that such a rigid plan would give rise to mechanical reiterations of sequential patterns. While that is a charge not entirely without foundation, Ferrabosco II in his works attempts to circumvent the problem through variations in which each repetition of the theme is accompanied by its own lively imitative patterns.

There is a curious reminiscence of this technique in Jenkins' Fantasia No. 12, linking the exposition (which closes in A) with the second main section (beginning in F) (Ex. 71).

Ex. 71

The rigidity of the patterns here is uncharacteristic of the composer and, although the enharmonic change is competently handled, the passage does not bear comparison with his treatment of the device elsewhere. In many ways this is a lively and attractive work, profuse in invention, but for much of the time it is little more than a fast-moving medley of ideas lacking positive direction; only the outermost sections treat their 'points' in earnest. Although quite adventurous tonally, the composer's key-plan also seems unbalanced in this work. The hexachord feature, for instance, hoists the music efficiently if unceremoniously into B flat major, but in only six semibreves it has wound itself round the key-circle to D again, pausing briefly before moving on sharpwards to an E major boundary. This area is patrolled for some twenty bars before the tonic re-establishes itself in time for the final section. It is a difficult work to date in the context of the series as a whole, but the sure handling of its fleet-footed lines and its tonal inquisitiveness suggest that it is a relatively mature work.

Fantasia No. 7 has already been the subject of a detailed study,[12] deservedly so, for it is a fine work. The piece begins traditionally enough with a lengthy investigation of the principal theme (Ex. 72).

Ex. 72

There is plenty of variety, even in the initial entries, no two of which are exactly alike, but the section is held together by a number of structural pillars, such as the stretto entries of the subject at bars 4 and 9. All this activity is reminiscent of the lively and complex writing already noted in the 'early' fantasias Nos. 1–4. Jenkins seems to have embarked on a three-voice episode at bar 15, before introducing his next 'point', but this change proves to be a false trail: wisps of the subject float into view and the bass eventually breaks its silence with an imposing augmented version of the theme. The true episode follows (in the sub-dominant), as Jenkins indulges his partiality for canoniç play (Ex. 73).

Here the descending fourths surely harp on the *x* figure from the initial subject. With the emergence of a new theme (Ex. 74), the composer embarks on a most ambitious (and highly successful) journey round the key-circle.[13] The absence of a natural (♮) sign in contemporary

[12] Robert Warner, 'John Jenkins' Four-Part Fancy (Meyer No. 14) in C minor: An Enharmonic Modulation around the Key Circle', *The Music Review*, 28, i, February 1967, pp. 1–20.

[13] F minor–B flat minor–E flat minor–A flat minor–D flat/C sharp minor–F sharp minor–B minor–E minor–A minor–- minor.

Ex. 73

Ex. 74

notation results in some visual peculiarities in the parts, but there is no questioning Jenkins' mature and competent handling of modulation, which is definitely advanced for the period. Ex. 75 shows the basic harmonic progression here and confirms that, although this is broadly similar on either side of the enharmonic change, it is far from being a rigid carbon-copy like the hexachord passage in Fantasia No. 12 or an equally adventurous but regularly patterned passage in Ward's five-part Fantasia No. 1 (Ex. 75(b)). Robert Warner draws particular attention to the way Jenkins dwells on A flat (bars 32–3) to

Ex. 75

give added weight to the arrival of the D flat tonic at the enharmonic hump, and to the irregular spacing of later modulations.[14] Lively, loosely imitative writing flowers as D minor is reached, although clear cadences at bars 49 and 52 break this passage into three short sections – contrasting with the earlier extended ones. The music turns to F major to introduce the beautiful final section, whose legato theme resembles that of the modulating section. Curiously, two quite different approaches to the four-bar coda survive, due entirely to a variant in the part of Tenor II (Ex. 76). The version from Mus. Sch. C.99 seems least satisfactory, forming a crude bass in the three-voice passage and spoiling the magical chord change (E flat–G) following the cadence.[15] Perhaps this reading is another example of both first thoughts and later revision surviving in different groups of sources. So positive a cadence so near the end is unusual, but Jenkins takes a similar breath in Fantasia No. 5 (Ex. 86, p. 229).

Ex. 76

[14] Warner, *loc. cit.*, p. 12.

[15] It is interesting to find this reading copied by Matthew Hutton, apparently in 1667, in York Minster, MSS M3/1–4(S), and by the unknown copyist of Christ Church, Music MSS 468–72. Both may have drawn upon Bodleian Library, Mus. Sch. MS C.99 when it arrived at the 'Schooles' as part of Wood's purchase around that time (*cf.* p. 149).

Both these works, with others in the series, conclude with a particularly extended, even valedictory final section. The easeful simplicity of these beautiful passages must have been much treasured in an age increasingly subjected to turmoil and conflict.

There is one other fantasia which modulates round the key-circle – No. 15. It begins promisingly with a sprightly C major fugue, but Jenkins tries no contrapuntal tricks – no stretto, inversion, augmentation, or diminution – and consequently the music becomes over-extended and repetitive. The possibility that the last three fantasias copied into Mus. Sch. C.99 (Nos. 15–17) are late works, perhaps composed by Jenkins on one of his visits to Kirtling, has already been mentioned.[16] That this opening eschews contrapuntal devices can be cited as a supporting argument, for the same process is evident in the composer's late fantasia-suites: the fugal exposition has become a convention to be followed rather than a device to be exploited:[17] such speculation is heightened with the appearance of a vivacious new theme at bar 22 (Ex. 77(b)), the treatment of which is not far removed from the division patterns which Jenkins customarily introduced into his fantasia-suites at this point; its character suggests that in later years the violin had impinged on the composer's mind to the extent that its more extrovert music influenced his melodic thinking. Nevertheless, Roger North makes it clear that the consort of viols continued to hold sway at Kirtling, even in the 1660s 'the violin came in late, and imperfectly'.[18] But there is

[16] *Cf.* p. 207.

[17] *Cf.* Robert Warner, *The Fantasia in the Works of John Jenkins,* unpublished Ph. D. dissertation, University of Michigan, 1951, vol. I, p. 189; Andrew Ashbee, *The Fourt-Part Instrumental Compositions of John Jenkins,* unpublished Ph. D. dissertation, University of London, 1966, vol. I, p. 157.

[18] *Op. cit.*, p. 11.

another possible link with Kirtling, if speculative. Old Dudley North was much taken with a 'brisk, lusty, yet mellifluent vein' which he found 'in a double C, fa, ut, peice of Mr Wards 4. Parts' (readily identified as Fantasia No. 6)[19] and it may be that Jenkins was attempting something in the same mould. In so doing, is it significant that he chose two themes (Ex. 77(a) and (b)) so very similar to those of another Ward fantasia – No. 1 (Ex. 77(c) and (d))?[20]

Ex. 77

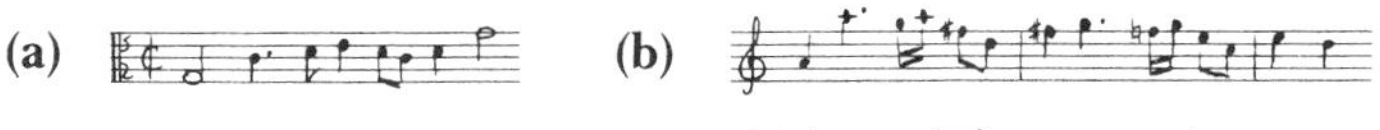

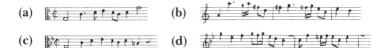

Once again Jenkins maintains a stable tonality during his opening gambit (though touching on both dominant and relative minor), reserving his extensive modulations for this second section. In spite of the volatile writing, key-changes here occur at much the same rate as in Fantasia No. 7: in the space of twelve breves (bars 30–54) the music moves through G major–E minor–B minor–D minor–B minor–F sharp minor–C sharp minor–D flat major–A major to closes in E major. Again C sharp/D flat marks the enharmonic change, although the simultaneous transition from minor to major enables the composer to take an adventurous leap round the key-circle.

Following the modulating section in Fantasia No. 7, it is

[19] *Ibid.*, p. 5. Ward's Fantasia No. 6 *à 4* is to be found in *Musica Britannica*, IX, No. 25.

[20] I am indebted to Graham Strahle of Adelaide University for pointing out this likeness. The Ward fantasia is also to be found in *Musica Britannica*, Vol. IX, No. 25.

noticeable that the music settles for an appreciable time in D minor (bars 44–53) before turning to the subdominant (F) and ultimately the tonic (C minor). The idea of such tonal 'planes' was not new in Jenkins' day, but it had remained under-developed. At the end of the sixteenth century Morley allowed internal modulations to the dominant or subdominant, providing the music returned to the tonic at the close:

> [...] and though the air of every key be different one from the other, yet some love (by wonder of nature) to be joined to others, so that if you begin your song in Gam ut you may conclude it either in C fa ut or D sol re and from thence come again to Gam ut; likewise if you begin your song in D sol re you may end in A re and come again to D sol re, etc.[21]

Ferrabosco II went further in adding internal cadences on other degrees,[22] but here Jenkins seems to be moving towards the Baroque composer's concept of visiting a number of keys in turn in the course of a piece and of mixing modulating and non-modulating sections. The same practice is observed in Fantasia No. 15, where the key of E flat major is held for some time before a shift to C minor (from where the last twist to the tonic major is easily – though in the event somewhat ambiguously – made). Again this final section seems over-extended by rather mechanical sequential writing of the type represented in Ex. 78, and where the textures of individual sections in Fantasia No. 7 provided pleasing contrasts, here the animated writing lacks any relief. The grouping of pieces in seventeenth-century manuscripts frequently prompts speculation as to whether the order reflects the chronology of the music, the wishes of the composer, or merely the circumstances faced by the copyist. Such studies have their uses, but must be interpreted with

[21] Morley, *op. cit.*, p. 249.

[22] Vaught, *op. cit.*, pp. 202–3.

Ex. 78

caution. Of some three-part fantasias by Thomas Lupo, John Jennings writes:

> the grouping of pieces by tonic key, as an analysis of the sources suggests, brings together pieces which contrast and complement each other so as to produce identifiable sets which were presumably intended to be performed as such.[23]

The arrangement of Jenkins' four-part fantasias in Bodleian Mus. Sch. MS C.99 also hints that some attempt was made to group them according to key-signatures:

Nos. 1–3: two-flat signature; all in C minor
Nos. 4–6: one-flat signature; D minor and F major
Nos. 7–9: two-flat signature; all in C minor
Nos. 10–11: both in A minor
Nos. 12–14: two-sharp signature; all in D major

This arrangement would obviously allow their performance as sets. Sir Nicholas L'Estrange meticulously ordered his music and instructed Jenkins about layout, so the methodical arrangement apparent in most of the North manuscripts may have been influenced by this example. At the same time sets of associated pieces – Fantasia-Almain-Corant, or the like – were well established by the mid-seventeenth century, perhaps prompting the grouping of two or three compatible fantasias in response.[24]

[23] 'Thomas Lupo Revisited – Is Key the Key to his Later Music?', *Chelys*, 12, 1983, pp. 19–22.

[24] Note too the seven groups of three fantasias for two trebles and bass apparently assembled by Jenkins when he was with Sir Nicholas L'Estrange; *cf.* Chapter Seven, esp. pp. 277–9.

Certainly pairings of some fantasias are common in late sources, but may simply result from one copyist transcribing from another; the close association of the Oxford copyists, in particular, may give a distorted view. Nevertheless, as part of the swing towards suites clearly evident in England by the 1640s, the possibility remains that the players who continued to perform viol fantasias may have arranged them into sets. Apart from the grouping into threes noted above, three pairs of fantasias stand out in this collection: Nos. 5–6, 10–11 and 13–14.

The two F major fantasias, Nos. 5 and 6, were and are the most popular works in the series. They belong in a line of predominantly four-part fantasias by various composers[25] which cultivate a somewhat lighter idiom than many of their fellows. Ernst Meyer notes a turn to a more 'homophonic and "airy"' manner with 'no pretence of any great degree of intellectual vigour' in music by some lesser Caroline composers,[26] but this would not be a fair description of these Jenkins pieces. Nor did Jenkins copy the practice of Byrd, Gibbons, and others of the old school, who quoted popular melodies in their sophisticated consorts. The 'Whittington Chime' is an exception,[27] and maybe the opening theme of this Fantasia No. 6 alludes to the ballad 'All in a garden green' or 'Gathering peascods'[28] (Ex. 79(a)), but no other references to popular tunes have been traced in Jenkins' work.

[25] *Cf.*, for instance, four-part Fantasias Nos. 3 and 15 by Ferrabosco II, and Nos. 3 and 4 by Ives. Some by Thomas Lupo, e.g., Nos. 5–7 and 11–13 may have been written for the court violin band.

[26] *Op. cit.*, pp. 225–6, citing East, Okeover, Peerson, Henry Loosemore, Mico, Brewer and Milton.

[27] *Cf.* pp. 27 and 181–3.

[28] *Cf.* John Playford, *The English Dancing Master,* London, 1651, p. 96. Commentary in the facsimile edn., ed. Margaret Dean-Smith, Schott, London, 1957, p. 81. I am indebted to David Pinto for pointing out that this tune opens the 'Medley' attributed to Byrd (*Fitzwilliam Virginal Book,* No. 173) which also incorporates the 'Whittington Chime' – *cf.* note 28 in Chapter One, p. 27.

Ex. 79

Fantasia No. 6 is monothematic, but the principal theme, presented with circumspect regularity at the exposition, undergoes constant metamorphosis as the piece progresses – although not so much as to lose its identity. Ex. 79(b) shows some of its guises. A number of clearly defined cadences divide the work into four sections, each closing in the tonic. If the latter seems a recipe for monotony, Jenkins avoids the trap through cleverly varying the texture, keys and interplay of themes. At bar 10, for instance, he introduces the first of several subsidiary imitations running counter to the main subject (Ex. 80), while at bar 14 the second section also opens fugally with a distinctive variant of the subject (Ex. 79(b) (ii)). Towards the close of this section another independent figure appears: that old cliché (Ex. 81), which is allowed a

Ex. 80

Ex. 81

moment of its customary sequential play. The third section begins with augmented statements of the subject in tenor and bass, but Jenkins chooses not to emphasise this and instead picks up the tail-piece of this version for development in the ensuing bars. The minor mood also prevails here, oscillating between D minor and A minor. The 'popular' element in the work is given a further boost by two homophonic phrases which introduce the final section (Ex. 82) which returns to imitative treatment of the subject. A brief excursion to the subdominant adds fresh colour, a marvellous echo of which intensifies the harmonic approach to the final cadence and wistful reminiscence in the second tenor of the opening (Ex. 83).

Ex. 82

Ex. 83

Perhaps it is not too fanciful to suggest that in Fantasias Nos. 5 and 6, at least, a parallel could be drawn with Mozart's acknowledged indebtedness to Haydn's Op. 33 Quartets, when dedicating his own celebrated set of six to the older master. Certainly pieces such as the four-part Fantasias Nos. 3 and 8 by Thomas Lupo[29] provided Jenkins with models from which he could develop works

[29] *Cf. Thomas Lupo: The Four Part Consort Music,* transcribed and edited Richard Charteris and John Jennings, Boethius Press, Clarabricken, 1983.

such as these. So too, in due course, might Lupo and his contemporaries have acknowledged the genius of the younger Jenkins as Haydn did of Mozart: 'he has taste, and moreover the greatest science in composition'. It is futile at present to hazard more than a guess at the relative dates of these consorts – so who is to say if he (and they) in turn absorbed features of Jenkins' style? At any rate, several features in the two Lupo fantasias are matched and developed in the Jenkins works: a long opening fugue with a relatively stable tonality (though subdivided through use of subsidiary motifs and cadences) (Lupo No. 8 and Jenkins No. 5); a sequence of short, basically homophonic phrases (Lupo Nos. 3 and 8 and Jenkins Nos. 5 and 6); a section centred on a related key (Lupo No. 3 and Jenkins No. 6); an injection of lively contrasting material (Lupo No. 3 and Jenkins No. 5); an extended legato conclusion (Lupo No. 3 and Jenkins No. 5). Yet at the end of the day one must acknowledge that the sheer lyrical beauty of Jenkins' music, the fluency of his counterpoint and the inventive treatment of his ideas raises his work to an altogether higher standard.

Clearly, once polyphonic instrumental music had shed its dependence on vocal models, the way was open for less rigid fugal imitation: composers no longer felt bound to balance note against note, maintaining, as it were, syllable against syllable. The opening of Jenkins' Fantasia No. 5 (Ex. 84(a)) illustrates this new freedom, where Lupo (Ex. 84(b)) tends to preserve a stricter pattern. Yet, ironically, the spirit of the madrigal pervades this fantasia more strongly than in other works of the series. A succession of imitative motifs echoes the characteristic madrigalian treatment of a text: many 'points', which after a brief appearance, in Morley's phrase go quickly 'away to some close' while elsewhere snatches of dialogue cry out for words (Ex. 85). But expansive development of the outer sections ensures that the work is no mere *pot pourri* of little substance. A predominantly sunny mood prevails – not the exuberant high spirits so often met in Jenkins'

Ex. 84

Ex. 85

D major pieces, but rather a song of happiness and contentment. Such was Jenkins' life – if contemporary reports of him are to be believed – accepting what was offered with gratitude and giving the best service he could. A quiet serenity flowed from him. It is therefore entirely characteristic that the beautiful peroration of this fantasia should not be dramatic, but move with a restrained and quiet assurance, a musical counterpart of what the eighteenth century might have called his 'exalted' nature, and true balm for the soul (Ex. 86).

Yet North reminds us that 'Mirth [as well as] Solace attended him', and a 'vivacious spirit' is equally evident in

Ex. 86

Jenkins' music, nowhere more so than in his bright-key pieces: G and D major in particular. No doubt the marriage of this sprightly idiom to these keys reflects (whether consciously or unconsciously) contemporary interest in rhetorical art, its variety of 'humours' and its power of affecting its hearers.[30] Still, it is worth reflecting that in conveying particular moods Jenkins' choice of keys is often no less significant than is the case with Classical composers nearly 200 years later, and his deployment of key contrasts has similar impact and import to theirs.

Writing to the musician Henry Loosemore in 1658,[31] Dudley North expresses his delight in

> a kind of brisk, lusty, yet mellifluent vein [...] that stirs our

[30] This theme is discussed in three articles in *Early Music*, 12, 1984: Robin Headlam Wells, 'The Ladder of Love: Verbal and Musical Rhetoric in the Elizabethan Lute-song; Robert Toft, 'Musicke a sister to Poetrie: Rhetorical Artifice in the Passionate Airs of John Dowland'; and Gregory G. Butler, 'The Projection of Affect in Baroque Dance Music' – pp. 173–89, pp. 190–9, pp. 201–7 respectively.

[31] *A Forest Promiscuous* [...], quoted in Roger North, *op. cit.*, pp. 4–5. The letter is dated 'Catlidge [= Kirtling], Aug. 28, 1658'.

> bloud, and raises our spirits, with liveliness and activity, to satisfie both quickness of heart and hand.

He notes that he has 'found it in a double C, fa, ut, piece of Mr Wards' (as mentioned earlier, p. 221) 'and in other Authors', one of whom surely would have been Jenkins. The liveliness of Jenkins' four-part Fantasia No. 12 has already been noted, but the other two D major pieces (Nos. 13 and 14) are equally volatile.

Mention of John Ward here is particularly relevant, for these two works bear many similarities with the older composer's manner and idiom.[32] Ward, for instance, has a habit of making a complete break between sections in his fantasias by inserting a rest in all parts; Jenkins follows this practice in his two works.[33] Many of Ward's fantasias incorporate a broad slow-moving section between lively outer ones; Jenkins emulates this procedure in Fantasia No. 14. Ward frequently begins some of his intermediate episodes with a homophonic opening, breaking quickly into a more contrapuntal manner after a few beats: Ex. 87(a) comes from his four-part Fantasia No. 1; Jenkins does the same here (Ex. 87(b)). Ward's bass parts tend to play less of an imitative role than the other parts and once or twice during a composition will form the simplest of harmonic anchors. This is less noticeable in the four-part than in the five- or six-part works, but a sequence such as that shown from Ward's Fantasia No. 1 *à 4* in Ex. 88(a) demonstrates the point clearly. Jenkins concludes Fantasia No. 13 in similar vein (Ex. 88(b)).

Two of the finest fantasias in the collection, Nos. 10 and 11, stand apart from the others as being scored for

[32] At least one contemporary had difficulty distinguishing between the work of these two men, for two seventeenth-century manuscripts attribute four-part fantasias by Ward to Jenkins: (a) in Bodleian Library, Mus. Sch. MSS C.64–9, Ward Nos. 2–6; (b) in Christ Church, Music MSS 468–72, Ward No. 3.

[33] The only other four-part fantasia by Jenkins which includes such breaks is No. 6.

Ex. 87

Ex. 88

treble, two tenors and bass: that is to say, the two middle parts work entirely with the same range of notes and require a similar size of viol. Here even Tenor I may act as the true bass, and the darker tone resulting from the lower pitch of this part particularly suits the impassioned and powerful minor mood of Fantasia No. 10. Elsewhere the 'alto' part is generally pitched slightly higher than the 'tenor' and best tonal balance is achieved by using correspondingly different sizes of instrument.[34]

[34] For a full discussion on the use of the tenor and alto viols in English consort music, *cf.* Marco Pallis, 'The Instrumentation of English Viol Consort Music', *Chelys*, I, 1969, pp. 27–35.

These two works are interesting for another reason. Both illustrate well Jenkins' search for ways of unifying the fantasia form, moving away from the madrigalian concept of a succession of disparate elements. Yet this homogeneity had to be achieved at a time when the fantasia was expanding in size, with the inherent danger that motifs would be over-worked. His solution was two-fold: on the one hand he might modify the initial subject, perhaps preserving its rhythmic outline, or extracting some significant figure from it to use in later developments, while on the other he might combine it with fresh subsidiary themes.

The opening of Fantasia No. 10 is indeed on the grand scale, for it is not until the tenth semibreve that the last voice enters. With a new imitative figure emerging at bar 8 it seems that Jenkins has quickly done with the initial subject, but not so, for it soon returns in a flurry of activity, cadencing in D and developing majestically in various augmented forms in the ensuing bars. A half-close on the dominant (bar 21) provides the first tonal pivot in the work, which here moves a notch round the key-circle from D–A to A–E. The rhythmic pattern of the new motif (Ex. 89) suggests more will be heard of the initial subject and, indeed, it returns briefly to confirm the relationship.

Ex. 89

At this point it would appear that the music will drift through a few short-lived imitations of the kind already noted in Fantasia No. 5, but a rising sequence imparts new urgency and promises a new initiative. It lands on an unusually lengthy dominant pedal, over which yet another theme derived from the initial subject insistently calls for attention before being engulfed in the waves of quavers which bring the section to a climax (Ex. 90). Tranquility of a kind returns in the extended final section, but, in spite of broad legato lines, there is none of

Ex. 90

the serenity here experienced in a work like Fantasia No. 5. Few chords mitigate against the prevailing minor mood, and again both the darker instrumentation and renewed exploration of the subdominant relationship, with which the work began, contribute to the clouded vein. Nowhere are the subtleties of Jenkins' art more neatly revealed than at the close. Three carefully placed dotted minims clarify the treble phrasing, which expands to ease the work gentle towards the final cadence. At the same time they not only build to a climax, but also draw special attention to two beautiful progressions: one pulling away from established A minor tonality, the other pointing a heart-rending major-minor twist, compounded by the wide leap in the treble part (Ex. 91).

Fantasia No. 11 wears its learning lightly – at least at first – for its skittish subject and extended episodes for the three upper parts give it tremendous buoyancy. Yet thematically this is one of the most tight-knit of all Jenkins' fantasias, not least because the initial notes of the subject (*x* in Ex. 92(a)) are inverted in its tail (*y*), allowing the composer to develop both forms. Intricate imitative writing rarely strays far from the theme. But, in spite of incessant exploitation of these motifs, monotony is

Ex. 91

Ex. 92

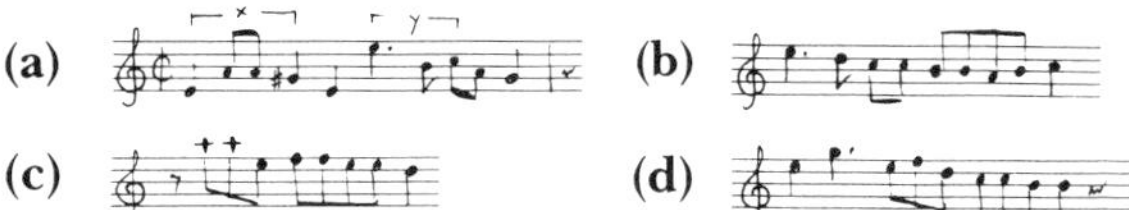

avoided since Jenkins constantly varies their treatment and context. At bar 9, for instance, a variant form of the subject appears in the tonic major as a delicate trio for treble and tenors (and is rescored two bars later). Since this is a monothematic work, Jenkins is thus already seeking means to keep interest alive, breaking up the traditional fugal opening before it gets too set in its ways. A canonic derivative of the subject leads further along this path (Ex. 93) and even the ensuing descending scale figure, which allows the melodies to flower delightfully before the cadence, has its links with the theme. A reprise of the opening prefaces a new canon before another trio toys with what seems a fresh figure (Ex. 92(b)). But Jenkins soon joins this to *y* (Ex. 92(c)) before another derivative (Ex. 92(d)) leads into the final section. From this point on (bar 36), the music becomes much grander, with quaver activity stilled. Following two extended pedals, first on A and then on E, metamorphosis of the subject continues as it appears in an expressive chromatic form reminiscent of passages in five-part fantasias by Ward[35] –

[35] Nos. 3 and 7, for example.

Ex. 93

Ex. 94(a) quotes from Ward's five-part Fantasia No. 7. Finally the true shape of the subject returns, now much augmented. A series of diminutions gradually restores its original note-values in the closing bars which, coupled with stretto, enables Jenkins to build a highly effective and exciting climax.

Ex. 94

Something of the same search for unity can also be seen in Fantasias Nos. 8 and 9, both in C minor. At times Fantasia No. 8 suffers from a surfeit of notes: perhaps the lack of really distinctive themes contributes to the feeling that not all the feverish activity is to much purpose, but there are fine moments. The volatile writing which persists through much of the piece is very similar to that in the second half of Fantasia No. 2 and to the livelier parts of Fantasia No. 12, but rarely appears in Jenkins' larger ensembles.[36] Some of the unifying devices outlined in discussion of the A minor fantasias recur here: for instance, with the subject dividing into antecedent and consequent (Ex. 95(a)) Jenkins again develops the latter as an imitative figure in its own right – in Ferrabosco's manner – as he did in Fantasia No. 11 (Ex. 95(b)). Soon, both parts are combined with a new motif (Ex. 95(c)) which returns later in the work, first in augmented form during the broader central section (Ex. 95(d)) and again when incorporated in the theme of the final section (Ex. 95(e)). Separating these three main blocks are two lighter episodes (bars 29–37 and 55–59). The first, having led off with imitative treatment of the initial subject, gives way to the kind of homophonic interjection already noted in Fantasias 5–6 and 13–14, while the second acts rather as a prelude to the final section, since the three-note figure from which it grows then sprouts a tail to form the theme quoted in Ex. 95(e).

Ex. 95

[36] But *cf.* the six-part *In Nomines* and Fantasia No. 6.

Linking of themes is carried to unusual lengths in Fantasia No. 9. Essentially it is a monothematic work, dominated by an expressive subject (Ex. 96(a)). The insistent repeated notes of this theme though treated in delightfully irregular interplay, nevertheless would become too oppressive if they had the run of the whole work, so Jenkins provides three episodes (bars 12–16, 21–30 and 48–57) from which they are totally excluded. To the casual eye these episodes have little in common, but the ear should confirm that all contain similar ideas. Such alternation is unique in Jenkins' work, if not in the whole consort repertory. In the opening fugue the subject generally maintains its shape and rhythm with little modification, dovetailing into the first episode, where significant new figures appear (Ex. 96(b)). Jenkins' favourite chord change (E flat-G) regains the tonic for fresh appearances of the principal subject. Although clearly recognisable, it is now much transformed and the

Ex. 96

generally augmented values give a broad sweep to the passage, contrasting with the livelier material on either side. For a while the music settles in the subdominant. By a neat piece of development the repeated-note figure serves to introduce the next episode which, after considerable play on scale passages, concludes with a trio (Ex. 96(c)) whose motif is already familiar from episode one. The principal subject is now given its head; note-values are freely altered to suit the exigencies of any particular moment, with augmented forms to the fore, and it basks in Jenkins' richest polyphony. After such expansive contrapuntal treatment, it is characteristic of the composer to insert a few short phrases for variety, but, unusually, here they still play with the subject (Ex. 96(d)). The final episode is also longer, with several bars given over to imitative treatment of each of the two themes from episode one; Ex. 96(e) illustrates how these blossom here, in a typical excerpt from the treble part. This passage merges into the majestic peroration, built once more from grandiose forms of the subject.

Two pavans and two fantasias remain to be considered, all works found solely in Ob, Mus. Sch. MS. C.99. This manuscript, one of a large collection apparently from Kirtling, is thought to date from about 1654, though the three fantasias copied on different paper after the pavans are probably later additions.[37] The pavans themselves give every appearance of being early Jenkins works: even the notation (in minim beats) is redolent of Elizabethan and Jacobean practice and was certainly archaic by the mid-seventeenth century. Yet they are beautiful pieces, among the least demanding technically of all viol consorts, and surely were warmly welcomed by the amateur musicians in the North household at their 'solemne musick' meetings described by Roger.[38] Neither work is entirely 'cast [...] by four' as Morley would have it, indeed,

[37] Margaret Crum, 'The Consort Music from Kirtling [...]', *passim.*

[38] *Cf.* pp. 72–5.

many phrases of five and seven bars occur. Imitative work in pavans was generally much looser than in fantasias, so it is unusual to find the last two strains of the E minor work each concentrating on a single idea. Roger North remarks that in the pavan

> the old masters [...] made the most they could of pure harmony without much of melody, because the parts were equally concerned to make good the consort [...].

He added that

> Harmony is never so complete as in full 4 parts, all interwoven and alike aiery.[39]

He could have cited these two pieces as excellent illustrations for his text: although melodically unmemorable, touches of chromaticism and suspensions contribute to a rich and varied harmonic palette, while no player is given a part which merely fills in the harmony, but all are equals in a texture which is truly 'interwoven and alike aiery'.

Few pairs of fantasias provide so marked a contrast than Nos. 16 and 17 here: the one (No. 16) with three strongly contrasted elements, the other (No. 17) seamless and monothematic. Are these 'late' works? One cannot be sure for, the question of paper apart, there are few musical clues which supply firm evidence one way or the other.

It could be argued that the clear sectional divisions in Fantasia No. 16 reflect the tendency towards a more general application of this principle apparent in much consort music of the mid-seventeenth century. But, taken alone, that would be a dangerous assumption. Then a good deal of pattern-making in Fantasias Nos. 15 and 16 parallels that in many of Jenkins' three-part fantasias, many of which seem to date from the 1640s. But, again, one cannot make too much of this, for the example quoted in Ex. 97(a) – from Fantasia No. 6 – is not drawn

[39] *Op. cit.*, p. 181.

Ex. 97

from the later works in that series. Two other factors, though, may be significant. In much of Fantasias Nos. 15 and 16 one feels a crotchet rather than a minim as the basic unit of pulse and this, perhaps, is a clearer indication of a more modern trend. Furthermore, as was noted in Fantasia No. 15, this D minor work also employs more regular rhythmic patterns and it is easy to imagine a continuo lurking in the background (Ex. 98(a)). Yet the slow-moving middle section is decidedly traditional and is based on a characteristic Jenkins motif already familiar from the six-parts works (Ex. 98(b)). Beginning in the tonic major, it makes an uneasy transition to the minor, moving through various flat keys to close in F major. The final section revives the patterns of the first with an extended fugue on a lively baroque-type subject (Ex. 98(c)). Good use is made of canonic duets and of the sequential figure and the section even follows baroque custom at the close, where imitations over a dominant pedal serve as a prelude for the final entries.

Fantasia No. 17 is one of Jenkins' sublime masterpieces, and yet makes the minimum of technical demands on the players. Samuel Wesley was moved to call Bach's E major fugue (*The Well-tempered Clavier*, Book II, No. 9) 'The Saints in Glory', and one suspects that he would have

Ex. 98

(a)

(b)

(c)

Ex. 99

thought the title appropriate for this work too. It has the same dignity, serenity and assured purpose and, like the Bach, is founded on the simplest of motifs (Ex. 99). Indeed, so basic is the theme – an ascending five-note scale and descending dotted figure – that almost any group of notes could be shown to be derived from it. This music is worlds away from that of Jenkins' great contemporary, William Lawes; so smooth are the lines and so accomplished the counterpoint that it is rather the purity of Palestrina's work which comes to mind. The ear may well be deceived into accepting or connecting an infinite variety of note-patterns as deriving from the subject. In Ex. 100(a), for instance, the authentic forms of the subject in Tenor II and Bass are clear, while the Treble responds with a partially inverted version. Although Tenor I is relatively free, its arch-like curves and play on the dotted rhythm still link it with the subject. At a later stage this freedom spreads to all the parts, and yet the essence of the subject remains. Apparent links may be as

Ex. 100

much accidental as contrived, but, as elsewhere in Jenkins' work, constant metamorphosis of the theme is a deliberate ploy. Ex. 100(b) shows one important new version of the subject, giving it considerable breadth, which is carried through in all the parts. Fantasia No. 17 is particularly remarkable in that its continuous web of polyphony lacks any of the usual breathing-points. This continuity no doubt adds to its sense of growth, but other factors also play a part. Tonality, for instance, generally shows a bias towards the flat side, modulating in and out of the subdominant, but, towards the close, this trend is strengthened by a sudden shift through E flat to A flat and F minor. At the same time Jenkins increases the activity in all the parts, adding tight stretto imitations (Ex. 100(c)). Here is the climax of the work. Once again the composer makes his favoured transition from tonic major to tonic minor, so giving a particularly bright sheen to the coda after all the flat keys, and winds down to a serene and beautiful close.

chapter six
The Consorts in Five Parts

Jenkins' five-part consorts stand at the absolute peak of English consort music and there is scarcely a single moment in the entire collection where the composer's musical invention and technical facility falls below the very highest achievement. Yet once again evidence is lacking which would shed light on the origin of these superb works. Nevertheless, surviving sources, though few in number, are particularly interesting and two of them at least would have been known and used by the composer. Table 5 (p. 246) shows how the works are distributed between them.

For reasons which have been outlined earlier,[1] Royal College of Music MS 1145 appears to have been compiled in the 1630s and before Jenkins arrived for a prolonged stay at Hunstanton. Were the composer on hand it is most unlikely that the copying of his seventeen five-part fantasias and G major pavan would have been given to others, or that there should be no references to 'origin' or 'Derham' as happens with those pieces he copied. The first fifteen of his fantasias in Royal College of Music MS 1145 are in an unknown hand and would appear to have been entered relatively early in the life of the manuscript.[2] At a later stage a second copyist – perhaps Thomas Brewer – added the pavan, probably transcribing

[1] *Cf.* pp. 53–8.

[2] *Cf.* Andrew Ashbee, 'A Further Look at Some of the Le Strange Manuscripts', *Chelys*, 5, 1973–4, pp. 24–41.

it direct from the 'Barnard score: B[ook]', against which he also checked the text of six of the fantasias. Later still Brewer (if he it was) added the last two fantasias from a copy supplied by 'Mr Collins' and checked all except the pavan against the readings in this new source. The identity of 'Mr Collins' is uncertain. 'Barnard' seems to be the celebrated lay-clerk from St Paul's Cathedral, perhaps the same man who taught the viol to Canterbury choir-boys in 1620.[3] At least it can be said that the Barnard of Royal College of Music MS 1145 and British Library, Add. MSS 39550–4 knew the copyist of two sets of consorts now at the Library of Congress[4] in Washington and of another (though later) source for Jenkins' five-part fantasias mentioned below. 'Mr Collins' may be Timothy Collins, a lutenist in the King's Musick, but this is mere speculation. Account books show that members of the L'Estrange family visited London regularly, giving them every opportunity to bring back fresh music from the capital.

Roughly contemporary with Royal College of Music, MS 1145 are Christ Church, Music MSS 423–8 and 473–8, both of which came into the possession of John Browne, Clerk of the Parliaments.[5] Pavans Nos 2 and 3 are unique to Christ Church, Music MSS 423–8. The first of these (in G minor) was copied by Browne himself, very inaccurately, and attributed by him to Dering, but it was re-copied in a better version by another scribe, with an organ part provided in yet another hand in Christ Church, Music MS 1004.

The elusive 'Barnard' returns to the scene as the presumed copyist of British Library, Add. MS 30487, a set of

[3] This John Barnard was listed as a lay-clerk at Canterbury between 1619 and 1622: Canterbury Cathedral Library, Treasurer's Accounts.

[4] MS M990.C66F4. *Cf.* Gordon Dodd, 'The Coprario-Lupo Five-part Books at Washington', *Chelys*, 1, 1969, pp. 36–40. *Cf.* Pamela Willetts, 'John Barnard's collection of viol and vocal music', *Chelys*, 20, 1991, pp. 28–42.

[5] *Cf.* p. 159 and notes 40–3.

Table 5

Sources for Jenkins' Five-part Consorts

A	Barnard	Collins	B	C	D	E	F
1	x	x			17	8	1
2		x		12	5	7	
3	x	x			11	10	6
4		x		14	1	15	
5		x		15	2	16	
6	x	x		13	18	9	2
7	x	x			13	11	3
8		x			4	2	
9		x			6	3	
10	x	x			9	12	4
11		x			3&8	13	
12		x			10	1	
13		x			12	–	
14	x	x			7	14	5
15		x			14	4	
16		x			16	6	
17		x			15	5	
Pavans							
1(1)	x				19		7
2					38 &39		
3					40		

A = Rcm, MS 1145
B = Och, Music MSS 423-8
C = Och, Music MSS 473-8
D = Bl, Add. MS 30487
E = Bl, Add. MS 29290
F = Och, Music MSS 2 and 403-8

Viola da Gamba Society numbering is as source E with the fantasia missing from there numbered 17.
Pieces checked with 'Barnard' or 'Collins' in Royal College of Music MS 1145 are marked 'x'.
Pavan No. 2 also has an organ part in Christ Church, Music MS 1004.

five part-books containing all seventeen fantasias and the G major pavan.[6] Scholars have found a good deal of correspondence between readings attributed to 'Barnard' in Sir Nicholas L'Estrange's books and a number of surviving manuscripts in what appears to be an identical hand – including Add. MS 30487. This source must be quite late, for above Nos. 15 and 16 here the writer has noted that he had already transcribed them into 'Sr Robt Bowles his bookes'.[7] Sir Robert succeeded to the title only in 1648.

British Library, Add. MS 29290 has already been described.[8] The likelihood that it is associated with the North family does not rule out the possibility that it was begun elsewhere and earlier than the main group of manuscripts from Kirtling, though obviously it became associated with them in time.

Finally, Jenkins' old friend John Lillie was responsible for including some of the five-part pieces in a large collection of consort music he made for Sir Christopher Hatton. It is most unlikely that these copies (now Christ Church, Music MSS 403–8 and the associated score-book 2 – the latter in the hand of Stephen Bing date from earlier than 1656, when Hatton returned from a ten-year residence in France.[9] Whether by chance or not, these six pieces prove to be the same works which L'Estrange took from Barnard for his collection.

There is no reason to doubt that Jenkins formed his collections of four-, five-, and six-part fantasias over the

[6] Fantasia No. 13 is copied twice in this source (numbered 3 and 8) with the treble parts reversed in one copy.

[7] I am much indebted to Dr Margaret Urquhart who has kept me informed of her research into Christopher Simpson and the Bolles family. *Cf.* Margaret Urquhart, 'Sir Robert Bolles Bt. of Scampton', *Chelys*, 16, 1987, pp. 16–29.

[8] *Cf.* p. 166.

[9] *Cf.* Pamela J. Willetts, 'John Lilly, Musician and Music Copyist'. *The Bodleian Library Record*, VII, No. 6, February 1967, pp. 307–11.

same period of time, for there is an underlying stylistic compatibility between them, however much each group evokes its own special response from him. Yet the five-part works make a particularly mature and cohesive group, suggesting that the bulk of them were composed within a few years of one another, most probably in the 1620s. How remarkable it is that all but one of the five-part pieces are restricted to only three tonics. Jenkins' key-preferences are readily ascertained from Table 6, as is the dominance of minor moods – 41 pieces as against 14 in the major. The uneven distribution of consorts in G minor/major is curious bearing in mind that this tonic particularly suits viol-tunings. Have all Jenkins' five-part viol fantasias really survived? Modal inflexions feature in the opening subjects of most of the five in this first group of fantasias (Ex. 101), the interplay of F sharp and F natural lending an archaic colouring to pieces which often go on to explore key-colour most imaginatively. Both style and structure of many of these consorts in G minor/major suggest that Jenkins was keenly aware of the inheritance bequeathed him by Ferrabosco II and that here he was assessing how this could be invested for future development. Fantasias Nos. 1, 2 and 3, for example, each have a structural core of two large balancing sections, together with a good spread of other devices which the older man exploited, but each seeks to build on this foundation in different ways.

The surveys of Jenkins' four- and six-part fantasias in the two preceding chapters have highlighted a number of characteristic moods and forms and these naturally are also common to the five-part series. Fantasia No. 1 here can be matched with other bright and/or highly active works like Nos. 2 *à 6* and 12 *à 4*. A hint that this is an early work is provided by the relatively inflexible treatment of the initial subject, whose dual phrases remain joined even in entries set awkwardly against the *tactus*. The piece is more modal than diatonic, but key-colour still plays a significant part. Where the first section (bars

Ex. 101

1.

2.

3.

4.

5.

1–20) tends generally to move sharpwards from the central tonality, the concluding section (bars 26–55) counterbalances this shift with keys on the flat side. Two third-related chord progressions – C–E at bar 12 and G–E at bars 20–21 – are characteristic of Jenkins; the latter is particularly striking since it pulls the music sharply away from the tonic cadence which concludes the first section to set the piece on a new course. Although this work is essentially in two sections, the composer recognises that a

Table 6
Distribution of Keys

	FANTASIAS			*PAVANS*			*IN NOMINES*	*TOTAL*
	four-part	five-part	six-part	four-part	five-part	six-part		
G major	–	1	–	–	1	–	–	2
G minor	–	5	1	–	1	–	1	8
D major	3	2	–	–	–	–	–	5
D minor	2	3	5	1	–	–	–	11
A minor	2	–	2	–	–	1	–	5
E minor	–	–	1	1	–	–	1	3
C major	1	1	–	–	–	–	–	2
C minor	6	5	3	–	–	–	–	14
F major	3	–	–	–	1	1	–	5

brief interlude would act as a fulcrum as tonality shifts towards the subdominant (bars 20–26). The chirpy character of this passage recalls similar moments in Fantasias Nos. 2 *à 6* and 16 *à 4* which match techniques from lute-song and madrigal. Furthermore, several bars of basically crotchet movement and more melodious writing follow this passage of hyper-activity in quavers, providing relative repose before quaver animation revives and prevails more or less until the end. Perhaps the best indication of the new paths Jenkins is charting in his fantasias is to be found in the inventive and varied ways he forms the works and treats the themes once the initial fugue has run its course, moving away from the concept of a string of imitative points which earlier masters had brought to perfection. So far as this first fantasia is concerned the final section springs a real surprise in that there is no constantly-shaped theme to catch one's attention. Instead, the composer adopts what can only be described as a chameleon-like approach as the ear is led through a succession of subtle changes to a plethora of imitative figures the unifying feature of which is a descending fourth. Part of the subtlety lies in the fluctuation of statements with or against the *tactus* and in the fact that rhythmic as much as melodic motifs serve as connections. Yet somehow the whole passage knits together – careful variation in the rate of rhythmic activity contributes much to this – and the work concludes around a grand tonic pedal in true Ferraboscan manner.

Fantasia No. 2 is not among the most striking works in the series and one wonders whether it was in any sense a forerunner of the much finer Fantasia No. 3, with which it shares many features. Both works are in two substantial sections, but the balance differs. The 31-breve fugue opening No. 2 is exceptionally long for Jenkins (who normally prefers about 22 breves) and he seems somewhat at a loss to maintain it convincingly. All parts are kept busy in an intricate texture, the subject competing for attention with numerous other figures, but imitations are loosely organised and the music lacks true contrapuntal discipline. Towards the end of the section appearances of the subject peter out, although extra interest is provided by a decisive move flatwards before the close in the dominant. A firm cadence here marks the boundary conclusively, as in the next piece. The new section is much finer, based on an expressive figure with its plaintive fall of a fourth and then a fifth (Ex. 102) and whose closely spaced insistent imitations and cross-rhythms bring real intensity to the passage. One prophetic development is a genuine five-bar coda – a grander device than Ferrabosco's single pedal-note – with canonic imitations weaving round dominant and tonic (Ex. 102). This feature Jenkins pursues with vigour in his later fantasia-suites, many of which conclude with a weighty tail, often marked 'drag' in the manuscripts.

Ex. 102

The exposition of Fantasia No. 3 is particularly rich in ideas. Jenkins rarely writes double-fugues like Coprario or Lupo, but here an important figure (Ex. 103(a)) is set against the principal subject (Ex. 101/2). The latter provides not only the initial *canzona* rhythm but also a tail (marked *x* in Ex. 101) which is put to good use and which turns up regularly elsewhere in the series.[10] The

[10] As, for instance, in Fantasia No. 1 *à 4*.

Ex. 103

dominant-tonic leaps in the introductory statements of the subject are soon dispensed with in favour of other variants – recalling similar cavalier treatment meted out to a companion theme in Fantasia No. 7 *à 6* – but the rhythm persists. This opening divides into two strains of roughly equal proportion (bars 1–9 and 10–20), both cadencing in the dominant – which is unusual. Jenkins' mastery of large-scale planning is nowhere more evident than in the beautiful second part to this work. It is not a fugue, although fugal techniques are well to the fore. Evidently the composer is anxious not to overplay his lyrical new motif (Ex. 103(b)), for initially it appears relatively infrequently and is set within a four- or five-part polyphonic texture. At bars 30–1 a flurry of quavers cause a diversion, but the F pedal beneath steers the music away from the established dominant base to B flat major/G minor. New entries of the subject are echoed in stretto, but these are little more than token imitations until two-fold augmentations sound through four of the five parts and impose a more rigorous contrapuntal discipline. A climax is reached when increasingly animated parts are capped by a four-fold augmentation of the subject in Treble I (Ex. 103(c)). This moment heralds a wonderful serene close built of similar enlarged forms of the subject and briefly basking in the warmth of the submediant major before the final turn to the tonic. In this work, as elsewhere, Jenkins' judgment in such matters as structural balance, the placing of keys and climaxes and of contrasting volatile with less volatile movement can rarely be faulted; these features, as much as his technical skill and melodic inspiration, are what sets so much of his music on so high a pedestal.

Occasionally, of course, his sureness of touch deserts him. So far as his larger consort fantasias are concerned, it seems to be those works tentatively seen as the last in the series – in which he seems to be responding to the new music of Coprario and Lawes – which show the least fluency.[11] It is tempting to include the five-part Fantasia No. 6 in this group, especially since it was among the last works copied into Royal College of Music MS 1145 and British Library, Add. MS 30487. The opening is very fine and the initial imaginative gambit in which the subject is presented against itself in inversion was successfully used also in the four-part Fantasia No. 13. Particularly striking is the uncharacteristic treatment of harmonic colour, where the interplay of parts gives rise to a spate of false relations and other chromatic inflexions. Two of these result in an augmented chord, a sound very rare in Jenkins' music, but one which he espoused for a while in works apparently dating from the 1630s and '40s (Ex. 104(a)). All these, coupled with a wayward bass quite unlike his normal grateful lines (Ex. 104(b)), sets Fantasia No. 6 apart from its fellows and ensure that the work opens with considerable dramatic impact and colour; the rest is less successful. A brief episode links the two main sections of the work (Ex. 105(b)), whose sequential motif can be found in some of Jenkins' airs, especially a spare-textured pavan (No. 7) for three viols (Ex. 105(a)).

This *canzona*-like figure reminds one of the similar motif in the first part of Fantasia No. 3, but the regularity of harmonic and melodic patterns it receives here con-

[11] *Cf.* Fantasia Nos. 10 and 11 *à 6*.

trasts with its freer treatment there. The mundane motif on which the last section is built (Ex. 105(c)) makes for dull music, in spite of all Jenkins' attempts to breathe life into it. Neither a divided bass canon (Ex. 105(d)), nor placement of the theme variously in or out of synchronisation with the other parts overcomes the tedious reiteration of chains of descending thirds. One last curiosity is the unexpected close in B flat major as Jenkins plays with augmented statements in his theme, which might infer that Fantasia No. 6 was intended as a prelude to another piece.

Ex. 104

(a)

(b)

Ex. 105

(a)

(b)

(c)

(d)

Only Nos. 4 and 5 of the five part fantasias are monothematic, works which, as Richard Nicholson remarks, have 'a stately grandeur and splendid forward thrust'.[12] They may have been conceived as a pair. Both follow much the same path in tackling the structural problems arising from maintaining a single theme: modulation to the flat side, augmentation, canon and the later introduction of subsidiary motifs are all featured, but the emphasis given to these elements differs in each work. No. 4 begins with a regular exposition and after a flirtation with the dominant returns to the tonic by bar 20. In a multi-section fantasia Jenkins would be introducing new ideas at this point, but here Tenor II plays the first of several augmented versions of the theme, followed by a reconnaissance of the subdominant. The latter is soon established as a firmer base from which to sally forth to even flatter realms. In a passage very strikingly reminiscent of one mentioned when discussing Fantasia No. 7 *à 6*,[13] Jenkins sets augmented forms of his principal theme against active, closely-spaced imitative writing in the other parts, including some canonic touches. Still the music moves flatwards through D flat to B flat minor (bar 44), where a counter-melody is introduced as partner to the now familiar augmented version of the subject (Ex. 106(a)). This new figure soon vanishes, though, to be followed by variant forms of the subject (Ex. 106(b)), some cleverly presented in stretto as canonic pairs (bars 50–4). Gradually the music winds back to the tonic, with a marvellous *tierce de Picardie* in bar 65 as Tenor I introduces the valedictory bars.

Fantasia No. 5 is a majestic piece. In a warm and expansive opening the close spacing of the initial entries shows that the subject will lend itself to stretto, sure enough a technique prominent throughout the piece. Jenkins is at particular pains to carry the music over

[12] In his Preface to the Faber edition, London, 1971.

[13] *Cf.* p. 197.

Ex. 106

potential cadences and maintain momentum, so special features remain subordinate to the organic growth of the whole. Among interesting details is a series of imitations built solely from the tail of the subject (Ex. 107), while the figures which follow (and the dominant pedal beneath) most unusually return at the end of the work. False relations add a special touch of colour. As in the previous fantasia, augmented forms of the theme are combined with canonic phrases, but the contrapuntal discipline is even tighter here since the augmentations are set in stretto (Ex. 108(a)). So the subject continues to command attention as the piece turns towards flatter keys, though this time only as far as the F minor/A flat major section. Then in the last part of the work a new motif makes its surprise appearance (Ex. 108(b)), variously combined with the principal theme. But it is the latter which stays the course longest until its final remnants are swept up in the surge of the final cadence.

Pavans were 'at first ordained for a grave and stately manner of dancing [...] but now [are] grown up to a height of composition made only to delight the ear', says Christopher Simpson in his *Compendium of Practical Musick*.[14] Their inclusion in collections of fantasias in Jenkins' day confirms their passing into the realms of pure chamber music. Of the three five-part pavans by Jenkins the first is the best known because it alone is found in the major sources. It is a fine work, the longest of the three and thematically more carefully worked-out

[14] Christopher Simpson, *A Compendium of Practical Musick,* Second Edition, 1667, reprinted and edited Phillip J. Lord, B. H. Blackwell, Oxford, 1970, p. 78.

Ex. 107

Ex. 108

than is often the case with these pieces. The similar shape of the two principal motifs which make up the first strain may be co-incidental (Ex. 109(a) and (b)), but the reappearance of the latter to open the third strain is clear (Ex. 109(c)), displacing another nearly-related motto (Ex. 109(d)). Canonic pairs of trebles and tenors fight for the same few notes at the beginning of the second strain – yet another variant of the opening motif – but are reconciled in a three-part canon (Treble I, Tenor I, Bass) a moment later (Ex. 109(e)). The third strain is much longer than the others and gives considerable attention to a new figure (Ex. 109(f)), first featured as a descending sequential dialogue between the two trebles. At the same time tonality turns to the tonic minor, allowing the gently dropping figure of the final bars to brighten again to G major and bring balm to the close.

Ex. 109

Pavan No. 2 is very beautiful, although there is a suggestion in the occasionally awkward part-writing that the contrapuntal technique is not fully refined.[15] The haunting elegiac quality of much of this work sets it alongside the Bell Pavan as a possible memorial piece; bells, indeed, peal at its close. Christopher Simpson advises that

> If your pavan [...] be of three strains, the first strain may end in the key of the composition as the last doth, but the middle strain must always end in the key of a middle close [i.e., another key].
>
> Sometimes the first strain does end in a middle close and then the middle strain must end in some other middle close, for two strains following immediately one another ought not to end in the same key. The reason thereof is obvious; to wit, the ending still in the same key doth reiterate the air too much and different ending produce more variety.[16]

[15] *Cf.* for instance, the awkward combination of Tenor II and Bass in bars 4–8.

[16] *Op. cit.*, p. 78.

The first strains of all Jenkins' pavans from the three collections cadence in the tonic, but in this work especially the composer effects a wonderful harmonic transformation at the joins of the first two strains (G major-B flat major) and at the repeat (D major-B flat major). Touches of chromaticism also add special colour to this lovely piece.

Very few of Jenkins' works are known in more than one version, but the five-part Pavan in F is found in several manuscripts as a three-part piece for two trebles and a bass. In the latter form it has an impeccable pedigree, for around 1644 it was copied by the composer himself from Sir Nicholas L'Estrange's 'B. Booke' into the Newberry part-books and their associated holograph score.[17] The contents of the now lost 'B. Booke' remain something of a mystery, since four of the pieces which Jenkins drew from it for this three-part collection show evidence of a different scoring in four or more parts.[18] So far as the pavan is concerned, the second and third strains of both three- and five-part versions have identical treble and lowest bass parts, excepting a few additions to Treble I drawn from Tenor I for the sake of enhanced continuity and extra imitations in the three-part version. From this feature one is inclined to believe that the five-part version came first, bearing in mind that other fully scored works by Jenkins and his contemporaries were reduced in a similar way as the appetite for pieces scored for two trebles and a bass increased in the Caroline period. Yet the three-part arrangement was known to John Merro in Gloucester by the early 1630s, so it is likely that both forms were almost contemporaneous. The first

[17] Newberry Library, Chicago, Case MS VM.I.A.18.J.52c; Christ Church, Music MS 1005. The three-part version is published, ed. Andrew Ashbee, in *Three Suites of Airs for Two Trebles and a Bass with Continuo by John Jenkins*, Golden Phoenix Publications, Harpenden, 1988.

[18] These are noted in Andrew Ashbee, 'Towards the Chronology and Grouping of Some Airs by John Jenkins', *loc. cit.*

strain of the three-part version (Ex. 110) is much simpler than the fully scored form, preserving only the three principal motifs and the general tonal outline. It is curious that no copy of the full version occurs with Jenkins' other five-part pieces in Lcm MS 1145, for this is an eloquent work, nicely varied in texture.

Ex. 110

In their main features the three D minor pieces match their G minor companions, except that there is a tendency to blur and disguise the joins between sections. Fantasia No. 12 is another magnificent piece in two parts. The intricate counterpoint of the opening fugue results from an interesting subject, which even in the exposition undergoes metamorphosis (Ex. 111). It is liberties of this nature which go to distinguish the Fantasia from the

Ex. 111

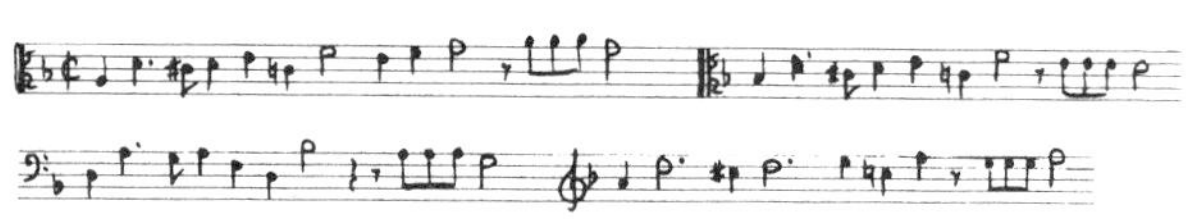

stricter form of the Fugue. Its formation from two elements revives another trait of Ferrabosco II (and can be seen also in Fantasias Nos. 1 and 14). The driving rhythm of its tail is something of a Jenkins fingerprint which, with his favourite ploy of opposing dotted patterns, gives immense impetus to the counterpoint and is a key element in his handling of tension and relaxation. Comparison of two four-part extracts will make the point (Ex. 112(a) and (b)). Bars 11–12 represent typical cross-rhythms from the opening, while the gentle introduction to the second strain (bars 27–8) is notable for the co-ordination of its patterns, the dotted figure here having lost its force through being set always with the *tactus*. Variety of rhythmic activity is also achieved through juxtaposing sections of deliberately contrasted note-values. In Fantasia No. 14, for example, the intense rhythmic interaction shown in Ex. 112(c) (with new attacks on every quaver) is replaced by a much broader pattern (with crotchets as the smaller unit) (Ex. 112(d)).

Returning to Fantasia No. 12, the opening fugue really has run its course by bar 20, but an extension pursues subsidiary figures in a lively series of imitations. Bars 21–2 in particular recall similar moments in four-part Fantasias Nos. 4 and 7,[19] where the bass is rested and upper parts echo each other. Once again Jenkins approaches his goal of F major (bar 26) from the flat side, the change in key-colour providing exactly the right fillip here. The very lovely second part is based on a turn-like figure often exploited by the composer. In spite of an air of effortless ease, the music is full of contrapuntal ingenuities – stretto, augmentation and the much rarer diminution – aided by subtle transformations of the theme.

Fantasia No. 13 opens with an austere and formal subject which harks back to the *ricercar* (Ex. 113(a)). The whole fugue, unusually stark for Jenkins, is dominated by

[19] *Cf.* p. 217.

Ex. 112

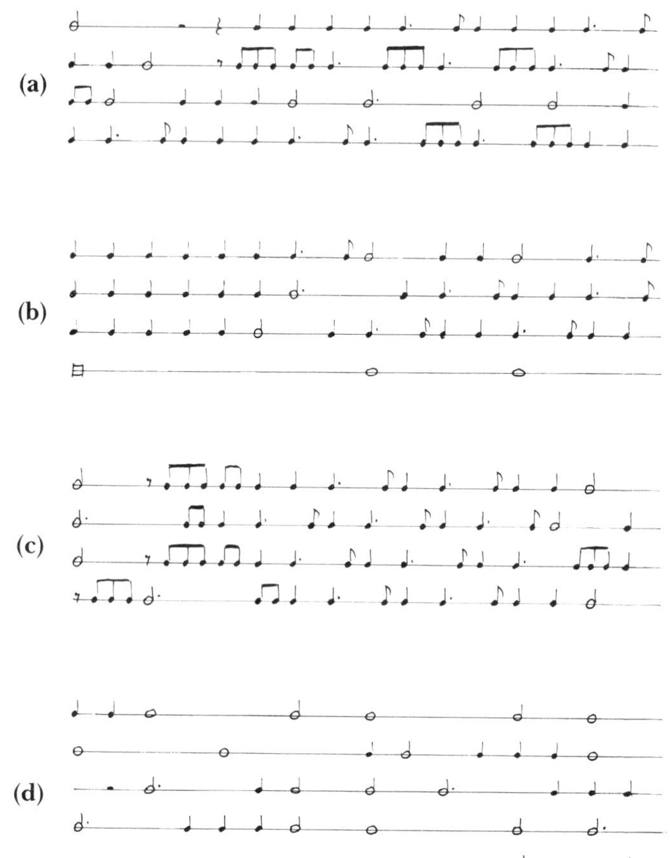

a measured crotchet tread. Bar 20, as so often in this composer's music, sees a new initiative in the form of a livelier counter-melody, bringing welcome rhythmic variety and a new figure for him to play with, even though the principal motif still appears in several guises. A cadence in F marks the boundary (bars 30–1), but the music immediately dips dramatically to E flat, with the new theme (and section) emerging by stealth in Tenor I a couple of bars later and settling in the subdominant (Ex. 113(b)). A striking diminished fourth in the theme is an uncharacteristic *cri de cœur* but, true to form Jenkins mollifies its anguish both by refining it to a perfect interval at times and by ensuring that piquant harmonic effects are excluded. While again he rejects the technique of employing a regular counter-melody on the lines of Coprario and Lupo, a quaver figure is taken up in the latter part of the section which partners the principal motif. From bar 47 onwards a repeat of the rising fourth one tone higher intensifies the theme and the canon between paired parts is drawn closer with effect of stretto. A splendidly placed final entry in Tenor II crowned by an arresting second from Treble I brings about a noble close.

Ex. 113

In spite of the freedom with which Jenkins treats the end of his opening fugues in Fantasias Nos. 12 and 13, both works are formed from two main members. Two fugues similarly make up the bulk of Fantasia No. 14, but other material separates them so that for the first time in the series something approaching the multi-sectional structure of madrigal-fantasias is apparent. The bipartite form of the first subject has already been mentioned and the way its busy contrapuntal working-out contrasts with the slower-moving polyphony of bars 24–31.[20] As in Fantasias Nos. 12 and 13, modal and diatonic writing is mixed, especially in the first section; similarly, tonality shifts markedly flat-wards in the ensuing bars. The slow polyphonic interlude here is followed by a brief episode very much in Ward's style, with all parts launched simultaneously after a co-ordinated rest, imitative trebles and alternating tonic-dominant harmonies.[21] The final fugue is as substantial as the opening one and is in the same highly involved texture. For once it begins in a pure fugal manner, Tenor I leading off alone. Such active lines require the braking power of the dominant pedal with which Jenkins ensures a convincing close.

The two D major works are another matching pair, both bubbling effervescent works whose exuberance is never quelled more than momentarily. Their similarity goes beyond mood alone for some themes bear a remarkable resemblance to one another, as if Jenkins was trying out alternative workings of his material (Ex. 114(a), (b), (c) and (d)). The first subject of Fantasia No. 15 is a supreme example of Jenkins' lyrical gift, singing its way through the intricate counterpoint of the opening section (Ex. 114(e)), but the most subtle development is reserved for the middle bars of this three-section fantasia. A sudden shift of gear, key and mood (bars 23–6) introduces a new figure (Ex. 114(a)) taken up in loose imitation. But soon it quickens into new life, restoring parts to their former fleet-footed activity through the addition of a new tail with quaver movement (Ex. 114(f)) and creating a theme which bears more than a passing resemblance to the one which follows (Ex. 114(f) and (b)). Triadic patterns link the latter with the first theme of the

[20] *Cf.* pp. 261.

[21] *Cf.* pp. 125–6 and 230–1.

next piece; in both instances Jenkins delights in pursuing them in the closest imitations and canons. Tonally the composer's favourite scheme in these two works is to use the chord of E major or minor as pivot to take him either to the dominant or, more often, to the subdominant, the tendency to modulate flatwards still predominating. The central section of Fantasia No. 16 is formed from two balancing strains (bars 20–4 and 25–32), the first featuring a delightful dialogue between the instruments (Ex. 114 (g)), from which seems to evolve the opening of the final theme, the second – after another Ward-like hiatus – mostly built round a canon in the outer parts. Following the final fugue is another of Jenkins' pealing codas.

The Fantasias in C (major and minor) are especially beautiful and stand at the very peak of Jenkins' achievement. Unlike the groups set on other tonics, each piece here is clearly divided into several contrasting sections, all marked by firm cadences. There are other similarities too binding the group together: an emphasis on tonic and

Ex. 114

relative major keys in Fantasias Nos. 7–10 and the insertion of dance-like passages in Fantasias Nos. 8–11, which take their turn with loosely imitative but harmonically rich sections of 'Grave and harmonious musick'. Such a unified approach suggests that the works were composed within a short space of one another.

Fantasia No. 7 opens in most sombre vein, the chordal nature of the theme resulting in unusually slow harmonic movements (Ex. 115). The fugal structure is somewhat unconventional, for a new figure, important enough to be called a counter-subject, makes a surprise first appearance in Tenor I at bar 8. It is typical of the composer that the tail of this motif (*x*) is picked out for special attention, creating lively opposition to the tread of the principal theme. In writing an exceptionally long section of 31 bars Jenkins finds it necessary to break the flow of the music with intermediate cadences at bars 17 and 24, the first perfect in E flat, the second imperfect in the tonic. Between these two points the principal theme is set in polyphony growing from a little ascending quaver figure (Ex. 116(a)) which materialised in the run-up to the preceding cadence. Ascending patterns thus dominate bars 17–28 to contrast with the continual descending patterns of the opening and of the principal subject in particular.

Ex. 115

The closing section (bars 24–31) is given over entirely to the 'counter-subject' and its diminished fourth. How splendidly Jenkins regulates the increase in activity to drive the music forward to a fine climax (Ex. 116(c)). He mines a wealth of harmonic riches from the ensuing 'grave and harmonious musick', dipping to the subdominant for a time. But livelier activity returns with fleeting glimpses of a succession of ideas before more substantial treatment of an arch-shaped figure (Ex. 116(b)) brings the work to a close. Whether or not this is an intentional reminiscence of Ex. 116(a), the similarity of the two figures helps to unify the work, as does the echo of an earlier motif (in Ex. 116(c)) at the final cadence.

Ex. 116

In spite of the same key-setting, harmonic colour in Fantasia No. 8 is initially quite different from that of its predecessor. Not only are dominant rather than subdominant relationships explored, but a certain unrest results from the marvellous semi-tonal shifts in the line (Ex. 117(a)) – and in contrast what warmth emanates from the brief turn towards the relative major. The whole passage represents Jenkins at his most majestic; there is a sense of sustained growth probably unequalled anywhere in the English consort repertory. At its height (bar 18) temporary relief lasting for three bars is provided by the introduction of a subsidiary figure, thus much enhancing the impact, when it comes, of the final, highest-pitched entry of the complete subject by Treble I. This delayed entry issues a reminder that the same thing happened in Fantasia No. 7. Also mirrored is the intermediate cadence from No. 7 quoted in Ex. 116(c), for here again Jenkins toys with a related theme (Ex. 117(b)) in bringing the section to a close. As found elsewhere, dance-like music makes up the central part of this three-section fantasia and the lighter 'humour' is reinforced by a lighter texture, the bass being rested for a time. Now the ensemble is challenged by an incredibly complex rhythmic maze, defeating all but the most secure players (Ex. 117(c)). But calmer waters lie ahead in the serene beauty of the final section. How much finer this passage seems than, say, the conclusion of the G minor *In Nomine* (with its not-dissimilar theme): the subject sprouts a variety of interesting tails; there is a flexibility in the phrase structure absent from the six-part piece and a much more assured handling of instrumental colour, marvellously highlighting duos and trios within the ensemble.

Ex. 117

(a)

(b)

Christopher Simpson might have had Fantasia No. 9 in mind when he described the form in his *Compendium of Practical Musick*:[22]

> In this sort of music [fantasias] the composer being not limited to words, doth employ all his art and invention solely about the bringing in and carrying on of [...] fugues. [...] When he has tried all the several ways which he thinks fit to be used therein, he takes some other point and does the like with it, or else for variety, introduces some chromatic notes with bindings and intermixtures of discords, or falls into some lighter humour like a madrigal or what else his fancy shall lead him to, but still concluding with something which hath art and excellency in it.

Here are those very ingredients in what is much the shortest of the fantasias in C minor. The lively opening fugue runs to a mere fifteen bars; perhaps on account of its brevity Jenkins disdains using any special contrapuntal tricks and it comes to a firm cadence in the tonic. By degrees the music then 'falls into some lighter humour' – a trio for treble and two tenors which would do splendid service for Purcellian snakes (Ex. 118(a)),[23] the opening of which is taken up afterwards by the full consort, but now adopts voice-leading and imitative dialogue 'like a madrigal' (Ex. 118(b)). Bass divisions nonetheless serve a reminder that this is an instrumental piece. Then follows a beautiful passage which 'introduces some chromatic notes with bindings and intermixtures of discords' before the final delicate fugue on a *canzona*-like theme. 'Art and excellency' are truly exhibited in all departments.

Fantasia No. 10 is neatly symmetrical, clearly separating into five elements. A fine substantial central section, loosely fugal and built on Ex. 119(a), again full of 'bindings and intermixtures of discords', is bounded by two dance-like passages. Both in their use of complex

[22] *Op. cit.*, pp. 77–8.

[23] *Cf. Chelys*, 1, 1969, p. 15, Fig. 10, for a similar effect in Jenkins' Fantasia-Suite No. 1 for treble, two basses and organ.

Ex. 118

(a)

(b)

(c)

polyphony and in the subtlety of their phrasing, these are actually much more intricate than Jenkins' genuine 'airs'. The multiplicity of threes against twos in Ex. 119(b) is a case in point, although the dialogue between the two trebles in the following bars (Ex. 119(c)), climaxing in extended phrases, is entirely characteristic of the composer's dances. The second of the two air-like sections here (bars 41–55) parallels that in Fantasia No. 8 (bars 33–47), where a quartet (minus bass) leads off for the first strain and a varied repeat is given to the full ensemble. Mellifluous and free-flowing melodies are an inherent feature of Jenkins's style and that 'pleasing air' of which North speaks is everywhere apparent. The kind of melodic growth shown by Treble II in introducing this section is found throughout Jenkins' work; 'flight of fancy' seems a particularly apt way of describing it (Ex. 119(d)). In spite of intricate polyphony, then, the frequent cadential pauses give these passages the character of an almain or air. They are the successors of the little homophonic interludes beloved by composers of madrigal-fantasias, but their increased length and involved texture gives them more weight and significance in the overall scheme and contributes to the generally grand scale of works in this group. Jenkins counter-balances the opening fugue with music of rapt beauty, the eventual turn from E flat to the final tonic bringing a wistful sadness to the close.

Ex. 119

(a)

(b)

(c)

Tenors

(d)

Whilst it is true that Fantasia No. 11 is made from the same ingredients as the other C minor pieces, the mix results in a piece standing a little apart from them. At the heart of this difference lies the tonal scheme of the work. In the tripartite Fantasias Nos. 7 and 8 Jenkins seems to have anticipated Simpson's advice concerning key in the similarly-formed Pavan:

> If your pavan, or what else, be of three strains, the first strain may end in the key of the composition as the last doth, but the middle strain must always end in the key of a middle close.[24]

Having concluded the initial fugue in the tonic, he finishes the middle section in E flat major, returning to the tonic at the end. This scheme is extended to C minor–E flat major–E flat major–C minor in the four-section Fantasia No. 9 and to C minor–C minor–E flat major–E flat major–C minor in Fantasia No. 10. Excursions to dominant, subdominant, or elsewhere, are transitional between these anchor-points.

The modal colour of the opening of Fantasia No. 11 and its corresponding extra exposure of A naturals and B flats sets the music on a different tonal course, which is not immediately apparent, for the initial fugue tacks variously between C minor, G minor and E flat major, settling in the latter as the last bass entry makes its appearance (bar 20). Here the principal motif undergoes a sea-change (Ex. 120(b)), building a substantial annex to the fugue in lively imitative style and exploring both dominant and subdominant areas before returning to E flat (bar 28). E flat itself underpins a two-bar link, changing its identity from tonic to dominant and leading into 'grave and harmonious Musick'. Flatter realms come into view with wonderful sunshine-and-shadow effects as the music fluctuates between major and minor moods. These reach their apogee as B flat major and minor vie for attention, the latter evoking *Lachrimae* on its behalf (Ex. 120(c)). Yet these tears prove in vain, for a sprighty air establishes the major mood as the victor, the discipline of its forces confirmed by canonic formations in the ensuing bars. Jenkins' tendency to modulate to the flat side has been recorded so often in this book that it is a change to note the important role played by the dominant in the

[24] *Op. cit.*, p. 78.

latter part of this piece.[25] The comparative brightness of this sprightly B flat interlude increases the mellowness of the final section, whose elegiac beauty serves as an exquisite valediction not only to this piece but to a supreme group of fantasias.

Ex. 120

How bright too is the opening fugue of the single C major fantasia in the context of so many minor key pieces. (Here is another fugal subject where Jenkins freely inverts the opening leap.) Indeed, the composer goes out of his way to emphasise this brightness: in addition to the liveliness of the parts the texture is much more transparent than in many other examples – with little trios and quartets well to the fore – and since low bass notes are mostly avoided the music takes on a wonderful buoyancy and drive. At the end the bass is rested and with pairs of trebles and tenors working in their higher range the subsequent shift to a low tessitura is the more

[25] It has to be pointed out, of course, that B flat was arrived at from the parallel minor, a key very much on the flat side.

dramatic. The descent is eased by a brief interlude acting as a palliative to still the earlier activity, moving through F major to close gently in D minor. F major is immediately re-asserted (quite a harmonic surprise this after the *tierce de Picardie*) and with a low-pitched trio opens the central section with a repeated-note figure and turns to a cadence in C (Ex. 121).

Ex. 121

But the third of the triad proves to be minor when it enters in Treble I, compounding and extending exploration of darker hues for a time.[26] Suspensions and a further poignant cry of a diminished fourth (bar 36) momentarily take this piece into an emotional world far removed from the cheerful lyricism of its opening. But the clouds lift by degrees and the final fugue (as extensive as the first) restores the music to its former brilliance.

[26] It is a twist which Jenkins used effectively many times, notably in his 'Bells' pieces and the Fancy-Air Set, No. 4 in C, for two trebles, bass and organ.

chapter seven
Fantasias in Three Parts

Initially composers tended to favour the 'half-chest' scoring of treble, tenor and bass when writing in three parts – as examples by Giovanni Bassano, Byrd and Coprario readily show – but in Jacobean times consorts for two trebles and bass became increasingly popular. Another alternative, reaping the benefit of the wide range of the bass instrument, was a scoring for treble with two basses. Although less common, this combination was explored by composers such as Tomkins and Mico. Thomas Lupo was particularly innovatory, trying seven different permutations in scoring his 31 three-part fantasias and pavans.

Naturally three-part compositions tend to be less weighty in tone and substance than their four-, five- and six-part fellows, but in the hands of the English consort composers they are by no means frivolous. Once more a parallel may be drawn with contemporary English vocal music, for there Joseph Kerman notes that the three-part secular pieces eschew the simplicity of their Italian forebears in favour of carefully-worked counterpoint. Among Morley's *Canzonets to Three Voices* (1593), for instance, he mentions several pieces which

> are apparently Morley's first attempts at serious madrigals [...] In general the music is connected with a somewhat antiquated Italian alla breve style, possibly by way of Ferrabosco [I]. As contrasted with the abstract polyphony of Byrd, it makes definite efforts towards expressivity, yet it

> seems much more learned and 'Netherlandish' than current Italian serious styles.[1]

Brief mention has already been made of Orlando Gibbons' influential and imaginative three-part consorts in Chapter Two; of all works of the kind these seem to have reached a wide public and to have been instrumental in shaping a good many pieces by his successors in the field, including Jenkins. While it is probably true that one or two of Jenkins' three-part fantasias (in both series) are contemporary with the bulk of his larger consort pieces, there are sound reasons for suggesting that most of them are of rather later date, say, in the period *c.*1630–50.

The Fantasias for Two Trebles and a Bass

In five sources the 21 fantasias for two trebles and a bass are neatly packaged in seven groups of three pieces arranged according to key:

(a) British Library, Add. MS 31428: a holograph score-book almost certainly made by the composer for Sir Nicholas L'Estrange in the 1640s.[2]

(b) British Library, Add. MSS 30488–90: three part-books made by Matthew Hutton in the 1660s.[3]

(c) York Minster Library, MS M.20(S): a score-book made by Hutton and presumably associated with (b). The date 'Jan. 21 1667/8' occurs after the last piece.[4]

(d) Bodleian Library, Mus. Sch. MS C.87: three-part books from the North family collection,[5] which Margaret Crum notes were

> begun by one very inexpert hand and completed by the

[1] Kerman, *op. cit.*, p. 182.

[2] *Cf.* p. 54.

[3] *Cf.* p. 155. Both here and in source (e), some of the A minor and E minor pieces are interchanged.

[4] *Cf.* pp. 155–6. The pieces are not in the same order as in source (b).

[5] *Cf.* pp. 149–50.

one who copied the Brewer parts [Mus. Sch. MS C.100]. This set was corrected by the supervisor who (I have suggested) may be Lord North himself.[6]

(e) Guildhall Library, London: MSS G.Mus. 469–71: three part-books in the hand of Stephen Bing (1610–81). The music text closely matches that in the Hutton manuscripts (b) and (c).

If, as Pamela Willetts proposes,[7] Bing was in Oxford *c.* 1643–7, then he may have copied the Jenkins fantasias at that time and they may have been accessible to Hutton some years later. An alternative possibility is that Bing kept or renewed his Oxford connections in the years after the Restoration and that he made the acquaintance of Hutton and his manuscripts then. Since neither scribe is particularly reliable as a copyist, it is difficult to assess which set was written first. A post-Restoration date seems more likely since it is doubtful that Bing would have had access to all 21 fantasias so soon after they appear to have been written. As well as being the most authoratitive source for the whole collection, Add. MS 31428 lays claim to being the earliest of these five manuscripts. The key-grouping – G minor–D minor–A minor–E minor–C minor–F major–B flat major – is exactly that found in other scores which Jenkins made for L'Estrange.[8] As with the two- and three-part dances in Christ Church, Oxford, Music MS 1005, it seems most likely that a number – perhaps even a large number – of these fantasias were added

[6] 'The Consort Music from Kirtling [...]', p. 9.

[7] Pamela Willetts, 'Stephen Bing: a forgotten violist', *Chelys*, 18, 1989. Bing was identified as the copist of these books by Watkins Shaw (*The Bing-Gostling Part-books at York Minister,* Church Music Society/RSCM, Croydon, 1986; *cf.* also the entry on Bing in *The New Grove Dictionary of Music and Musicians,* Vol. 2). The manuscript also contains music by Locke – 'The Flatt Consort for my Cousin Kemble' – and by William Young and 'Siedeerich Beckron' (Dietrich Becker). *Cf.* Christopher D. S. Field, 'Matthew Locke and the Consort Suite', *Music & Letters,* 51, 1970, pp. 15–25.

[8] *Cf.* p. 54.

to earlier works to create so ordered a scheme. Indeed only five of the fantasias – Nos. 4, 5 and 6 in D minor and 13 and 14 in C minor – occur in the remaining six sources:

(f) Bodleian Library, Mus. Sch. MSS C.64–9: part-books inscribed 'George Stratford 1641',[9] contain Nos. 13 and 14.

(g) Bodleian Library, Mus. Sch. MSS E.437–42: part-books probably roughly contemporary with source (f), contain Nos. 4, 5, 13 and 14.[10]

(h) Christ Church, Music MSS 473–8: part-books which came into the hands of John Browne, Clerk of the Parliaments, in the mid-seventeenth century,[11] contain Nos. 4, 5, 6, 13 and 14.

(i) Archbishop Marsh's Library, Dublin, MSS Z.3.4.1–6: part-books belonging to Narcissus Marsh and used at Oxford in the mid-seventeenth century, contain Nos. 13 and 14.[12]

(j) Rochester, New York State, Eastman School of Music, Sibley Music Library, 'Jo: Wythie his Booke': seems to be a mid-seventeenth century set of part-books associated with a member of a family of musicians established both in Worcester and Oxford.[13] One treble part is missing from Fantasia Nos. 4, 5, 6, 13 and 14.

(k) Los Angeles, University of California, William Andrews Clark Memorial Library, Music MS FF1995.M4: three part-books which seem to date from late Jacobean or early Caroline times and the

[9] *Cf.* p. 143.

[10] *Cf.* p. 143.

[11] *Cf.* p. 159.

[12] *Cf.* p. 144; also John Irving, 'Two Consort Manuscripts from Oxford and Dublin: their Copying and a Possible Redating', *The Consort*, 42, 1986, pp. 41–9; and Richard Charteris, 'New Information about some of the Consort Music Manuscripts in Archbishop Marsh's Library, Dublin', *The Consort*, 43, 1987, pp. 38–9.

[13] *Cf.* pp. 156–7.

> earliest known source for these fantasias, giving an authoritative text. The copyist appears to have been closely connected with court and was also partly responsible for two other important collections of instrumental music: British Library, Madrigal Society, Music MSS G.37–42 and Fitzwilliam Museum, Cambridge, Music MSS 24 E 13–17. Although the Jenkins pieces are mixed in with copies of Orlando Gibbons' published fantasias and numbered consecutively with them, it is clear that the copyist entered Jenkins' pieces last. Indeed, the task remained unfinished. Treble parts only of Fantasias 13, 14 and 4 were squeezed in as Nos. 19, 20 and 25 of the sequence in noticeably smaller writing in the *Cantus* book, while No. 5 was abandoned, after a mere four breves, at the end.[14]

It seems likely, then, that these last four fantasias at least were completed before 1630. In adopting the key-order he did in his scores for Sir Nicholas L'Estrange, Jenkins disregarded the chronology of the pieces, although information on the latter can be recovered from annotations in the associated part-books.[15] The same would doubtless be true of Add. MS 31428, but unfortunately no related part-books survive, but it is intriguing that a number of the North manuscripts do seem to take some consideration of chronology, so far as the available evidence – and more especially the style of the music – indicates.[16] It is interesting to note, then, that Mus. Sch. MS C.87 begins with the C minor and D minor pieces in turn, so incorporating the four fantasias found in source

[14] *Cf.* Richard Charteris, 'A Rediscovered Source of English Consort Music', *Chelys*, 5, 1973–4, pp. 3–6.

[15] *Cf.* Andrew Ashbee, 'Towards the Chronology and Grouping of Some Airs by John Jenkins', *loc. cit.*, and 'A Further Look at Some of the Le Strange Manuscripts', *Chelys*, 5, 1973–4, pp. 24–41.

[16] This claim cannot be substantiated, but in those manuscripts showing a haphazard key-order the first pieces are among the most conservative in style.

(k) and which have the widest distribution. Musically, these same works are the most conservative in the collection – reinforcing the argument in favour of an early date for them.[17] But the fact that in the Los Angeles partbook they are mixed in with pieces from Gibbons' printed set is also significant, for clearly Jenkins had avidly studied the older composer's individual approach to form and texture before embarking upon both his own series of three-part fantasias. Oliver Neighbour describes Gibbons' methods as follows:[18]

> The type of relatively free passage emerging from an imitative episode which another composer might bring to a cadence in preparation for a new exposition or section, Gibbons will invariably prolong so that it becomes the substance of the piece, capable of its own kind of self-renewal and variety. Only the opening point is likely to be worked out at all fully; later ones will be very short, so that a brief exposition will serve merely as one means of articulating the flow of three-part writing. The part-writing itself is very closely co-ordinated by dense motivic exchange; sometimes one part will be played off against the others, but it will soon rejoin them, or another will take its place. The brevity of the motives and the quick responsiveness of the parts to each other's initiatives give rise to a musical continuum of extraordinary flexibility. Whereas the structure of a more Italianate fantasia will depend upon the balance between sections, in any one of which the pacing will be towards uniformity, Gibbons directs the course of the music by means of swift textural changes, independent melodic developments and cadential or quasi-cadential articulation.

Here are techniques which Jenkins took up with intuitive skill, moulding them to his own purposes in these little fantasias. At the same time he incorporated or developed

[17] *Cf.* pp. 284–5.

[18] 'Orlando Gibbons (1583–1625): The Consort Music', *Early Music,* XI, 1983, p. 352.

features which Gibbons chose not to pursue at any length: imaginative and enterprising key-schemes and even livelier instrumental figuration are the most obvious. It should be said at the outset that none of the 21 fantasias shows any evidence of immaturity; rather one senses the composer enjoying the challenge of bringing his skill and experience to bear on a different problem from those posed by the writing of larger consorts. Three-part composition imposes limitations on harmonic and textural possibilities and these in turn condition the treatment of form.

In the other three-part collection for treble and two basses Jenkins called on the services of an organ. To this instrument he gave considerable independence and in so doing was able to thicken up the texture and harmony at will. Here, though, the string parts are complete in themselves and, as far as is known, no keyboard part was supplied or required. That is not to say that one was never used; only that, if it were, it would merely have supported the string polyphony, as was the case in most larger consorts of the kind. The title-pages in the various manuscripts are of no help in the matter, but it is interesting to find the 1682 catalogue of the Oxford Music School collection listing the three books making up C.87 as 'Mr Jenkins His Fancies for 2 Trebles & a Bass without ye Organ.[19] Similarly, the ubiquitous 'Treble' is of no help in establishing whether the upper parts are intended for viol or violin. Nevertheless, it is intriguing to find four fantasias from the collection rubbing shoulders with pieces by Gibbons, Coprario and Lupo in a source apparently originating at, or closely linked to, the English court, but tantalising that nothing is known of any link Jenkins may have had with that community at the time. Court performances of these works might well have used violins and the active and often angular lines are eminently suited to the instrument. But viols prove an

[19] Margaret Crum, 'Early Lists [...]', p. 29.

equally satisfactory alternative, and clearly the presence of these and similar pieces in collections of viol consorts, such as those used in Oxford, testify that either instrument was considered acceptable.

It is immediately obvious that in all Jenkins' three-part fantasias the opening fugue is treated in a much looser way than in the larger consorts, though, as in Gibbons' pieces, it tends to be the longest section. Thus more than half of Fantasia No. 13 is taken up with the initial subject, including an imposing augmentation of the theme as the first bass entry and a secondary exposition, beginning at bar 30, which, most unusually, is in the supertonic. In contrast the remainder of the piece comprises a succession of briefly-worked imitations of widely varying figures, but continuity is maintained by the absence of cadential pauses and by relatively stable tonality, oscillating between relative major and tonic.

The opening of Fantasia No. 14 is also unorthodox, beginning with a most attractive extended duet for the two trebles and incorporating an extra half-bar which remains uncompleted at the end of the piece. The homophonic interjection which follows proves a false harbinger, for the rest of the fantasia again rings the changes on a variety of figures in an intricate and continuous polyphonic texture. Two particularly distinctive passages feature on the one hand bass divisions (bars 23–31) (Ex. 122(a)) and on the other a hocketing line for Treble I (bars 40–6) (Ex. 122(b)).[20]

In the first of these Treble II pursues his dotted rhythm with Brahmsian tenacity; in the second the unexpected turn to the tonic major is short-lived.

The sectional structure of the two D minor fantasias is more clearly defined. No. 4 breaks into four units, each beginning and ending in the tonic, but making a foray to a different key. Thus the fugal opening reaches the subdominant and the lively second section – whose manner is

[20] *Cf.* p. 283 and Ex. 118(a), p. 270.

Ex. 122

well represented by the excerpt from Fantasia No. 6 quoted in Ex. 97(a)[21] – the dominant. For contrast bars 48–59 make the tonic major their base and here Jenkins, like Gibbons before him, cultivates a more popular style in a passage reminiscent of his three-part airs (Ex. 123(a)). Calmer motion returns with the substantial final section, but even here a more suave popular idiom prevails with the imitative writing tailored to flow gently with the *tactus* (Ex. 123(b)).

Ex. 123

(a)

(b)

Like Fantasia No. 13, Fantasia No. 5 also has a secondary exposition of its opening subject, but in the tonic (bar 24), and the *canzona*-rhythm with which it begins is

[21] *Cf.* p. 240.

carried over into the new section at bar 36. The latter proves to be a brief sequential episode preceding an extended set of lively figures in division style, but again calmer movement returns only twelve bars from the end with the final figure. A series of duets for the two trebles (bars 24–7, 36–9, 43–5 and 52–9) contributes much to the articulation of form in this piece.

Perhaps it is significant that these four 'early' works are among the very few which exclude a triple-time episode,[22] for none of the four-, five-, or six-part fantasias has one. It was presumably Gibbons who again provided the model in Fantasias Nos. VII, VIII and IX of the printed set (among the group with two treble parts). Here is further means by which a light, popular dance style is brought into the fantasia, as the typical corant-like passage in Ex. 124 shows.

Ex. 124

Fantasias Nos. 6 and 15 are longer than their companions, but many of the ingredients are the same. No. 6 begins with an extended fugue on two motifs (Ex.125(a)), although one soon fizzles out, but episodes such as a duet for the two trebles, or imitative patterns very much in Gibbons' manner[23] (Ex. 125(b)), are inserted between entries. Later lively sequential writing propels the music through many keys, reaching the relative major for the

[22] The others are Nos. 7, 8 and 21.

[23] *Cf.* Ex. 13, p. 134.

Ex. 125

(a)

(b)

tripla. This metrical change is placed near the end of the fantasia, leaving a mere couple of breves to provide the common-time coda – as happens so frequently after the triple-time movement at the end of Jenkins' fantasia-suites. In Fantasia No. 15, on the other hand, the *tripla* is placed after the first fugue which, in somewhat archaic fashion, reiterates successive imitations of the opening 'point'. Yet in the latter part of the work are two features common enough in pieces thought to have been written by Jenkins in the 1630s and '40s, but rarely met in his earlier music. One is an arpeggiated motif, in which leaps of a sixth and octave are characteristic (and of which Ex. 126(a) is typical), and the other is a repeated-note figure (Ex. 126(b)) most likely to appear, as here, towards the close of a work. On the whole there is not much to separate the 'early' pieces from their fellows and it is perhaps unwise to attach too much significance to them as a group, beyond noting that they lack some of the features found in Jenkins' music of the Caroline period, which must include the bulk of this series of fantasias.

Devoid though it is of any external markings, Jenkins' score of these pieces is nonetheless illuminating. He bars the music in semibreves, breaking further into minim units where the writing is particularly active. This

Ex. 126

practice in itself is a clear indication of the trend away from notation based on a minim pulse, which has served for most of his four-, five-and six-part fantasias, towards one which, by the Restoration, generally used the crotchet as the main beat.[24] It is also undeniable that the underlying rhythms of these fantasias are much less concerned with syncopation and contrapuntal interplay than their larger commpanions and that a result the melodies – perhaps influenced by dance – conform more regularly with the *tactus*; the barline thus becomes a help rather than a hindrance in setting them out. It is also interesting that Jenkins finds it convenient to change the key-signature in the course of some two-thirds of the pieces. Sometimes, as in Fantasia No. 4 (Ex. 123(a)), this device is to accommodate his partiality for incorporating music in the tonic major/minor, but at others it is to smooth out notation in passages which undertake extensive tonal journeys; some of these fantasias are every bit as adventurous in this respect as the four-part works which modulate round the key-circle.

Some of the more imaginative and interesting passages in Jenkins' three-part fantasias should be noted. When John Hullah delivered a course of lectures at The Royal

[24] A minim pulse is still relevant, of course, for some of these fantasias, or parts of them.

Institution of Great Britain in 1861,[25] he included Fantasia No. 1 in his survey of seventeenth-century English music, commenting in passing that

> the most remarkable features of the piece are some chromatic effects [...] which you will have some difficulty in believing to be two hundred years old. I cannot vouch for their genuineness, though they are unmistakeably indicated in my old copy [...].

No doubt remains, since they appear in Jenkins' own hand, but they remain curious (Ex. 127).

Ex. 127

Another G minor piece – No. 3 – incorporates in its coda an expressive, recitative-like dialogue Ex. 128(a) of a kind which Jenkins developed more fully in similar situations in some fantasia-suites. These patterns are a distinctive feature of his Fancy-Ayre Divisions sets, for instance, as shown in Ex. 128(b), but they occur elsewhere too. Perhaps they are inspired by contemporary vocal dialogues – the 'recitative musick' to which Jenkins himself contributed – but they might equally come from similar gestures in Lawes' 'Setts' for one or two violins, bass and organ.[26]

Melodic motifs in this series tend to be much more incisive than those in earlier fantasias, but the first theme of

[25] Published as *The Third or Transition Period of Musical History*, 2nd edn., Longmans, Green & Co., London, 1876; pp. 191–9.

[26] *Cf. Musica Britannica*, Vol. XXI, Stainer & Bell, London 1963, e.g., p. 113, p. 125, etc.; p. 97 has a chromatic alternation not unlike the Jenkins example quoted in Ex. 127.

Ex. 128

Fantasia No. 7 is particularly striking (Ex. 129); Vivaldi would have been proud of it. The element of display begins to make itself felt in a piece such as this and, although no *tripla* is present, the fantasia as a whole leans towards the bolder *concertante* style of the fantasia-suite movement. Effervescent divisions form the centrepiece here, as they do in the suites, until brought to heel by a (second) return of the repeated-note figure as it announces the coda. Submediant harmony at the change is most effective.

Ex. 129

Fantasia No. 8 has rather the reverse process, beginning with its liveliest figures and moving to its smoothest, calmest counterpoint half-way through. This work, incidentally, was the first Jenkins piece discovered and transcribed by Arnold Dolmetsch.[27] Musically it marries the old and the new. Four well-balanced main sections, each cadencing in the tonic, make a traditional ground-plan, with all but the last pursuing imitations of their particular

[27] I am indebted to Marco Pallis for this information.

'point'; yet, as in all the A minor fantasias, sections are clearly contrasted and their limits defined by strong cadences. The second section draws upon a figure which becomes something of a Jenkins fingerprint, not only in this series but in other contemporary pieces: a melody built from descending fourths (Ex. 130).

Ex. 130

This pattern and other imitations at the unison for that matter – often produce strings of thirds when turned into duets. (It must be admitted that on occasion the practice also produces monotony). The smooth lines of the third section, generating numerous suspensions, spell a return to traditional viol-consort writing, but by setting it in the tonic major Jenkins enters a new tonal area quite remote from the rest of the work: A major–E major–F sharp minor–C sharp minor–A major–A minor.

Equally adventurous in this respect is the third A minor fantasia, No. 9, certainly one of the best works in the series.[28] As in the previous work, the opening is lively with a delayed bass entry (again as before) allowing the two trebles to chase each other at the unison. This time the first section modulates to close in the relative major, meeting up with the first of two *triplas*. This section, a saraband rather than a corant, turns to the dominant, but Jenkins again plays his major/minor game to set the extended central part mostly in the major: E major–B major–A major–F sharp minor–A major. Lively divisions predominate here, too, but are preceded by a dotted motif not unlike that found in the six-part Fantasia

[28] Transcribed in *John Jenkins: Fancies and Ayres*, ed. Helen Joy Sleeper, Wellesley College, Wellesley, 1950, pp. 42–5.

No. 10[29] (Ex. 131). A further *tripla* with delightfully varied phrasing continues the tonal journey, now emphasising the minor: A major–F sharp minor–C sharp minor–F sharp minor, returning to A major, but contradicted immediately by the true tonic of the common-time coda.

Ex. 131

Switching from major to minor and vice versa consistently brings Jenkins' music to keys which his forebears might have tackled only once in a lifetime. The growth of interest in key-colour and modulation during the Caroline period awaits full investigation; no doubt contemporary experiments in lyra-viol tunings contributed to a new awareness of what was possible in the field, but here too Jenkins was a leading figure.[30] Even with changes of key-signature, these adventurous forays into new tonalities imposed strains on notation which must at times have brought furrowed brows to many a player, although there is nothing in these three-part works to match the complex inter-play of sharps and flats in copies of Nos. 7 and 15 of the four-part group.[31] Ex. 132 shows the enharmonic change in Fantasia No. 10 in the composer's neatly-organised spelling; other versions are more corrupt. The curious sight of a two-flat signature for an F major fantasia – No. 17 – can also be explained as an aid to smooth notation in later parts of the work and there is

[29] *Cf.* p. 177 above. There is another example in Fantasia No. 20 of this series.

[30] *Cf.* Andrew Ashbee, 'John Jenkins, 1592–1678, and the Lyra Viol', *Musical Times*, cxix, 1978, pp. 840–3.

[31] *Cf.* pp. 217–9 and 221, and Robert Warner 'John Jenkins' Four-Part Fancy [...] in C minor, where Ex. 2 gives the original spelling in Fantasia No. 7 *à 4*.

Ex. 132

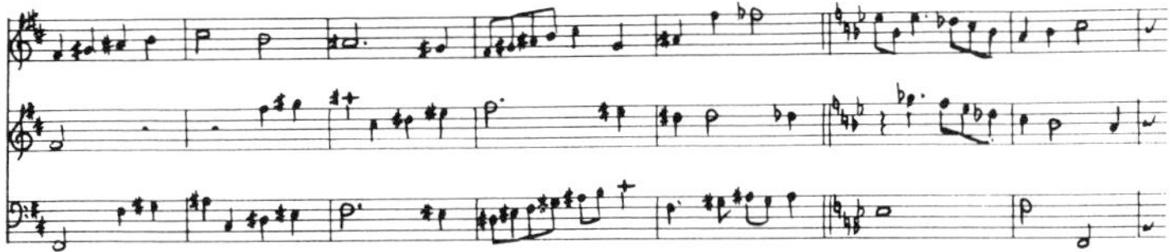

no surprise in discovering that modulations are confined to keys on the flat side, moving round the key-circle to touch on G flat major at the extreme point. Both Fantasias Nos. 10 and 17 make these pioneering journeys in the course of a substantial fugue lasting 33 and 47 bars respectively; clearly Jenkins believes the binding element of a single theme to be important in holding the sections together and this is reinforced, particularly in No. 17, by the smoothest of counterpoint (Ex. 133).

Ex. 133

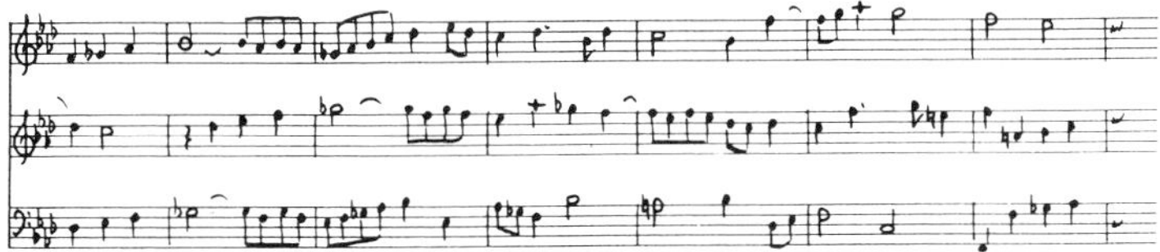

Two other points of style are of particular interest. Sequential patterns are increasingly in evidence (Ex. 134, from Fantasia No. 4 *à 3*), as are fanfare figures built from triads. The latter assume various forms: sometimes melodic (Ex. 135, from the same work), causing the bass to abandon its role as an equal partner in polyphonic exchange and function as a continuo, and sometimes harmonic, where repeated-note motifs like those in Ex. 136 (from Fantasia No. 11 *à 3*) create movement out of a single chord.

Robert Warner sums up this series as follows:

> These pieces have a fascination of their own quite different from the earlier works. They seem to blend the dis-

Ex. 134

Ex. 135

Ex. 136

> tinctive qualities of Jenkins's technique with an Italian instrumentation and French ideals. Their performance demands delicacy, clarity and precision. The transparency of their texture, their concise development of musical ideas, and their emphasis on distinctive contrast – all conceived within the scope of the new tonal organization – give a freshness and charm to this music which can still be found in modern performance.[32]

In 1667 Christopher Simpson bemoaned the demise of the serious viol fantasias:

> This kind of music [viol fantasias] (the more is the pity) is now much neglected by reason of the scarcity of auditors that understand it, their ears being better acquainted and more delighted with light and airy music.[33]

In meeting his public half-way Jenkins successfully made the transition with thesé delightful works, for surviving

[32] Robert Warner, *op. cit.*, Vol. I, p. 208.

[33] Simpson, *Compendium*, p. 78.

manuscripts show that they continued to be copied in the 1660s and '70s.

The Fantasias and Pavan for Treble, Two Basses and Organ

The 27 fantasias and pavan for treble, two basses and organ are an impressive group of pieces which deserve to be rescued from oblivion.[34] String parts for three of them – Nos. 2, 3 and 5 – are included in the 'George Stratford' part-books at the Bodleian Library, dated 1641.[35] Narcissus Marsh (1638–1713) owned copies of the same three pieces for use when, as he wrote in his Diary:[36]

> [...] after the fire of London I constantly kept a weekly consort (of instrumental musick, & sometimes vocal) in my chamber on Wednesday, in the afternoon, & then on Thursday, as long as I lived in Oxford.

In 1678 Marsh moved to Ireland, eventually founding the library in Dublin that still bears his name and holds his books.[37] The three fantasias occur as Nos. 19, 20 and 21 in MSS Z3.4.7–12 there, but again without an organ part. For the complete series, together with four similarly scored fantasias by the little-known Richard Cooke, one must turn to Bodleian, Mus. Sch. MSS E. 406–9. Margaret Crum, basing her evidence on the various types of paper used, suggests this manuscript was the first to be made in the large collection of consort music (mostly by Jenkins) belonging to the North family at Kirtling; it is

[34] For published works from this series and from that for two trebles and bass, *cf.* p. 338.

[35] Bodleian Library, Mus. Sch. MSS C.64–9. *Cf.* p. 143.

[36] Quoted in Charteris, 'Consort Music Manuscripts in Archbishop Marsh's Library, Dublin', *Royal Musical Association Research Chronicle*, 13, 1976, p. 35.

[37] *Cf.* p. 146.

dated 1654.[38] She records that the four books making up E. 406–9

> are entirely the work of the [main] calligraphic scribe, and some peculiarities may suggest that they represent a period of experiment [...]. E.406 is the only oblong quarto organ part [... The set] is linked to two others by the upright quarto paper used for the string parts. The watermark is a fool's cap resembling Heawood 2005. A quire of four leaves of the same paper was added to complete each part of MS Mus. Sch. C.99, the early Jenkins four-part fantasias; and a few leaves complete the parts of MS Mus. Sch. C.98, his Airs for two trebles and two basses to the organ [...].[39]

It may be significant that two of these 'early' manuscripts in the group – E.406–9 and C.99 – give a haphazard order for their pieces compared with the more structured format of the other manuscripts and that, to some extent at any rate, they may hint at the chronology of composition.[40] Table 7 gives the sequence of pieces in E.406–9, showing which works include a triple-time section ('3') and which contain organ solos ('O'). There are actually only five fantasias (Nos. 2–5 and 9) where the organ has no independent material, and one wonders how much can be read into the fact that these pieces occur at the beginning of the collection. As with the other three-part series, Jenkins' indebtedness to Gibbons with regard to both form and texture is readily apparent. Again it is the opening fugue only which is treated extensively, but much more loosely than hitherto. In Fantasia No. 4, for instance, entries of the subject are few and far between, although the section runs to more than twenty breves. Fantasia No. 9 is exceptional in maintaining its initial fugue to bar 39, coloured, as are so many of Jenkins' similarly-extended passages, by beautiful modulations to

38 'The Consort Music from Kirtling', pp. 3–10.

39 *Ibid.*, pp. 6–7.

40 *Cf.* pp. 165 and 207.

the flat side in the later stages. Although this is among the most traditional of the fantasias, it is interesting to find a repeated-note figure as the principal feature of the ensuing section, for this type of motif was to become something of an obsession for the composer in the series as a whole. In chromatic form it appears as an interruption within the exposition of Fantasia No. 3, whose principal motif returns immediately afterwards as if nothing

Table 7

1.	G minor	–	–	15.	F major	–	0
2.	G minor	–	–	16.	E minor	–	0
3.	A minor	–	–	17.	E minor	–	0
4.	A minor	3	–	18.	E minor	[The Pavan]	
5.	F major	3	–	19.	B flat major	3	0
6.	F major	–	0	20.	B flat major	–	0
7.	D minor	–	0	21.	B flat major	–	0
8.	D major	–	0	22.	A minor	3	0
9.	C minor	–	–	23.	A major	–	0
10.	G major	–	0	24.	E minor	–	0
11.	A minor	–	–	25.	G minor	3	0
12.	D major	–	0	26.	G minor	–	0
13.	C minor	–	0	27.	F major	3	0
14.	C major	–	0	28.	C major	–	0

had happened (Ex. 137). Typically for these pieces, there is no cadential climax to mark the end of the section, but rather the kind of extension of a 'relatively free passage emerging from an imitative episode' noted by Neighbour, the 'dense motivic exchange' generating its own excitement after the smooth polyphony of the opening, with 'one part [...] played off against the others, [with] brevity of motives and the quick responsiveness of the parts to each other's initiatives' (Ex. 138).[41]

[41] *Cf.* p. 280, above, for Oliver Neighbour's summary of Gibbons' style in the three-part fantasias.

Ex. 137

Ex. 138

In Fantasias Nos. 1 and 11 the organ enjoys a little independence. As in Gibbons' pieces featuring the 'great dooble base', extra strands are given to the keyboard. Fantasia No. 1 is formed essentially from three fugal passages (the last very free), but contrast is provided by two colourful interludes, the first almost a twin of the chromatic passage quoted in Ex. 137. The very fine but sombre opening of Fantasia No. 11 lasts nineteen breves, leading off with organ alone like the Gibbons pieces (Ex. 139(a)), and is followed by a kaleidoscopic succession of contrasting motifs once again giving rise to 'a musical continuum of extraordinary flexibility' (Ex. 139(b)). Equally striking is the emergence of bold idiomatic instrumental writing whose angularity contrasts sharply with the smooth neo-vocal writing of other passages (Ex. 139(b) and (c)).

If Gibbons can be seen as one important influence on these compositions, then another, equally significant, is the fantasia-suite pioneered by Coprario. This form will be fully treated in a companion volume to this one, but its emergence requires setting in context. Coprario left comprehensive sets of Fantasia-Almain-Galliard for one or

Ex. 139

two violins, bass viol and organ.[42] They appear to have been written *c.* 1618–26 for the band of court musicians in the household of Charles I.[43] Christopher Field writes of them:

> Our earliest manuscript sources appear to have originated within the court circle. With their exciting and unusual sonority (violins pursuing one another in canon, emancipated chamber organ), their novel scheme of movements (mercurial fantasia followed by irregularly proportioned almain and galliard and a 'close' reminiscent of the dancer's riverenza), their jagged but eloquent lines, bold dissonances and rhythmic humour, these progressive

[42] *Cf.* Richard Charteris, 'John Coprario: Fantasia-Suites, *Musica Britannica,* Vol. XLIV, Stainer & Bell, London, 1980. There are 15 sets for violin, bass viol and organ and 8 sets for two violins, bass viol and organ.

[43] For much of this period Charles was Prince of Wales.

> works can scarcely have been intended for household music at large, and it may have been some time before they came to be played at all widely.[44]

Coprario's suites had certainly come to the attention of Jenkins by the time he took up residence with the L'Estranges, for among his tasks was the copying of parts for most of the suites with one violin and the provision of an organ part for those with two; some of the former were checked against copies belonging to 'Mr. Derham'.[45] In his turn Jenkins tried his hand at the new form, completing seventeen sets with a single treble and ten with two trebles.[46] Although his vein is much more conservative than Coprario's, he does adopt the structural innovations of his predecessor, but on a broader scale.

Of paramount importance in these works is the treatment of the organ, which emerges from its hitherto bashful role – 'not being Eminently to be Heard, but only Equal with the other Musick', as Thomas Mace remarks in his *Musick's Monument* of 1676. Now it assumes true independence, not only supplying additional parts in the ensemble, but also contributing solo preludes and interludes. These solos feature strongly in the fantasias under discussion where, no doubt, the innovation was inspired by the fantasia-suite. Examined in detail the organ parts here show marked variety, largely because of their constantly changing role within the ensemble. The preludes invariably introduce a substantial fugal exposition, with

[44] 'Jenkins and the Fantasia-Suite', in *John Jenkins: 1592–1678*, John Jenkins Tercentenary Committee, London, 1978, p. 7.

[45] *Cf.* Christopher D. S. Field, 'Musical Observations from Barbados, 1647–1650', *Musical Times*, cxv, 1974, pp. 565–7.

[46] Listed in Gordon Dodd, *Thematic Index of Music for Viols*, pp. 86–8. Nos. 12, 16 and 17, published (ed. Helen Sleeper) in *Wellesley Edition No. 1*, Wellesley College, Wellesley, 1950; No. 4, ed. C. Arnold and M. Johnson, Stainer & Bell, London, 1957; No. 5, ed. Christopher D. S. Field, Oxford University Press, Oxford, 1976; No. 5 for violins, bass and organ, ed. C. Arnold and M. Johnson, Stainer & Bell, London, 1957.

subsequent entries taken up in the string parts. All the while the string ensemble remains incomplete compensation is provided by independent melodic lines on the organ. An extension of this procedure is frequently evident later in the music where solos and dialogues of the string section are set in a bed of organ tone (Ex. 140, from Fantasia No. 13). Up to four solo passages for organ may occur in any one fantasia which naturally help define the structure of the work, frequently separating the principal sections. Many of the interludes serve to introduce the next figure to be developed, but some present material completely unrelated to adjacent sections, or, as in No. 14 (Ex. 141) move through a succession of ideas, only the last of which is taken up by the strings. In a few of the most florid passages the organ functions as a true continuo instrument (Ex. 142, from Fantasia No. 26), although generally the keyboard participates fully in the lively exchanges.

Ex. 140

Ex. 141

Ex. 142

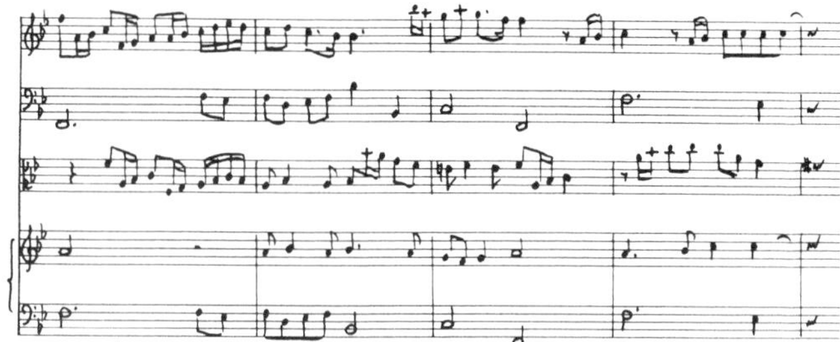

The written organ part mostly consists of a skeletal treble and bass, filling out to three parts at times, especially in the solo sections. There is no doubt that the two-part passages require some amplification in places, and yet I believe the layout of these parts is carefully considered and should not arbitrarily be abandoned by continuo players. It is reasonable to suppose that the treble and bass lines give the limits within which any additions will fall, but they seem to do more than that. Two basses in a small ensemble like this could, in the wrong hands, result in a muddy and indistinct texture. Both Jenkins and Richard Cooke in their E.406–9 fantasias overcome the problem by exploiting the full range of the bass instruments, taking each in turn well clear of the lowest line to fill the gap left by an absent alto or tenor. The result is a transparent texture, though one always enriched by the full-bodied sound of the large instruments. Here again one suspects that the 'dooble base' fantasias of Gibbons have left their mark. Yet Jenkins goes further than Cooke in his treatment of the organ part. None of the latter's fantasias in E.406–9 has organ solos and the keyboard doggedly copies the string lines throughout, resulting in a literal short score. Jenkins, in addition to the varied writing noted above, frequently doubles important string entries or themes on the organ at a higher or (occasionally) lower octave. This doubling not only highlights the principal motifs as they appear, but, where the duplication is at the higher octave – also brightens the sound most effectively. This technique is used with similar success in the contemporary fantasia-suites. It is true that such octave transportations are commonplace in organ parts to the larger viol consorts of the Jacobean and Caroline eras, but there the necessity is of bringing the musical material of a complex texture within the reach of two hands at a keyboard.

Further evidence of cross-pollenation between these fantasias and the two series of fantasia-suites mentioned above is demonstrated in Ex. 143(a), (b) and (c). Comparisons of openings of three fantasias and three suites shows how similar is the musical language of the two groups – good reason for suggesting that they are roughly contemporary. Yet this relationship again raises a question regarding the instrumentation. Treble parts of Coprario's fantasia-suites are labelled for violin in all early manuscripts and later court composers who took up the form, such as William Lawes, kept a similar scoring. Undoubtedly fashionable circles in touch and in sympathy with the latest artistic developments at court would have employed the instrument in such pieces. The precise whereabouts of Jenkins in the 1630s are not known, but probably his East Anglian connections were established to some extent. Manuscripts of his fantasia-suites give no indication that a violin was intended and the upper part is always headed simply 'Treble'. Christopher Field remarks that

> In view of Roger North's evidence of the violin's late acceptance at Kirtling Hall it seems quite possible that in these East Anglian houses [including the Derhams and L'Estranges] Coprario's violin parts were taken by treble viols. The 'treble' parts of Jenkins's own fantasia-suites may also have been played originally on viols, though care seems to have been taken that they should lie satisfactorily on the violin.[47]

Modern performances have shown that either treble

[47] 'Jenkins and the Fantasia-Suite', p. 7.

Ex. 143

instrument may be used with equal success. Both in the suites and in the present fantasias, treble and bass parts are written in the same style.

To match the ambiguity in the instrumentation, the

musical style of these fantasias – as with so many of Jenkins' pieces of the time – looks both forward and backward. Much of the music continues to uphold the glorious tradition of the larger consorts in sustained and smooth polyphonic textures – the openings of Fantasias Nos. 7–12 (two of which are shown in Ex. 139 and 143(a)) are splendid examples – but there is increasing evidence too of a turn towards lively and more angular motifs. No doubt the music of Coprario and Lawes played its part in influencing this change, but North pins the change on Jenkins' own development:

> his lute and lyra violl wrought so much upon his fancy, that he diverted to a more lively ayre, and was not only an innovator, but became a reformer of musick. His Fancys were full of ayery points, grave's, tripla's, and other varietys [...].[48]

Infiltration of these new figures is gradual. In works like Fantasia No. 11 the jagged lines quoted in Ex. 139(b) and (c) are a recurring element contrasted with intermediate smoother motion, but clearly they are not far removed either from the *style brisé* of lute music, or from the already-established patterns of division techniques. The latter appear throughout the series in short bursts, but are mostly limited to quaver movement. As it happens, divisions – the dividing of longer notes into decorative shorter figures – were to prove the principal device through which Jenkins invigorated his later fantasia-suites, so that Christopher Simpson could single them out as models to be imitated by 'those who intend to Compose such like themselves':

> If you desire written Copies of that sort [...] none has done so much in that kind as the ever Famous and most Excellent Composer, in all sorts of Modern Musick, Mr. John Jenkins.[49]

[48] *Op. cit.*, pp. 344–5.

[49] *The Division-Viol*, p. 61.

First experiments in integrating longer and more florid bouts of division writing into the fantasia occur in a few works of the present series and of Jenkins' earliest fantasia-suites.[50] The lively runs and instrumental exchanges in Fantasias Nos. 25 and 26 here are centrally placed and can be seen as an intensification of the generally animated writing in the middle of the majority of the fantasias. Ex. 142 is representative of this, while earlier, and also in the companion piece, No. 25, the patterns closely match those of the 'late' four-part fantasias Nos. 15 and 16, shown in Exx. 78 and 97. These come nowhere near the 'high-flying vein' of later examples, which demand formidable technical skills from players, but they contribute substantially to the increasing differentiation between sections which was to be a hall-mark of the late fantasia.

The melodic lines change character in other ways too. Set alongside the smooth flowing continuous legato phrases are others which are broken into short sequential figures – as in Fantasia No. 21 (Ex. 144) – and affective gestures, as in Fantasia No. 4 (Ex. 145). Again, it is anybody's guess whether Jenkins took the latter direct from Italianate 'recitative musick', or whether much bolder use of similar motifs by Lawes inspired him to take them up too. Certainly Lawes was an influence in these pieces, as, for instance, in those places where Jenkins sits firmly on a single note with harmony revolving around it, very much as Lawes does in some of his violin 'Setts'[51] (Ex. 146). The example given (from Fantasia No. 27) in turn shows a new treatment of the kind of pedal-points Jenkins inherited from his mentors.

A work like Fantasia No. 25 too seems full of Lawes 'fingerprints', from the opening fugue (Ex. 147(a)), more suave than the younger man's style, but in many ways

[50] In the latter, *cf.* Nos. 12 and 15 of Group I: No. 5 of Group II.

[51] *Cf. Musica Britannica,* Vol. XXI, Stainer & Bell, London, 1963, pp. 105 and 113.

Ex. 144

Ex. 145

Ex. 146

matching the G minor fantasias which open his 'Setts' for one and for two violins, bass and organ,[52] through close imitation of more capricious figures (Ex. 147(b)), even to the extent that these most uncharacteristically hit against the organ foundation (Ex. 147(c)), to three distinctive sections comprising division, *tripla*, and expressive coda. It is, of course, improbable that this stylistic filter worked only in a single direction, although in his elegy to 'his much esteemed friend', Jenkins acknowledges Lawes as 'the soule of mine and all our harmony'.

Rhythmic inequality in English music of this period has been little studied, so how often the ♫ ♩ 𝅗𝅥 pattern shown in Exx. 145 and 146, and fully exploited by both Lawes and Jenkins, was subject to alteration cannot yet be determined. It is certainly true that such figures in early-seventeenth-century sources are increasingly rendered as

[52] *Cf. ibid.*, Vol. XXI, Nos. 12 and 15.

Ex. 147

♩. ♪ ♩ in manuscripts dating from the 1640s and after, presumably, a response to performance practice.[53] In many works such dotted motifs strengthen the hold that dance music was gaining in the realm of the fantasia, but that cannot be said of the present series, where they rather feature briefly as divisions or, more often, in an affective role. Fantasia No. 17, a fine work, incorporates both types (Ex. 148), the first sandwiched between two organ solos and the second as a variant on the beautiful repeated-note coda which is so striking and familiar a feature in the series as a whole. Modulation and key-colour play no spectacular part in these works – which is not to deny the effectiveness of subtle changes like those in Ex. 148(b). Yet there is none of the daring tonal journeys of the other three-part series, or of the four-part works.

Were it not known that the fantasias for two trebles and a bass were completed by the end of the 1640s, scholars would surely have placed them well after this series,

[53] Sir Nicholas L'Estrange noted places in some of Jenkins' airs in his collection 'Prickt a crotchet in Time; and in the Humouring Playde a quaver'; *cf.* Jane Troy Johnson, *loc. cit.*

Ex. 148

for they have such a light, carefree character, where these are more expansive, rich, sober and dignified. yet from the evidence it must be concluded that both series were in progress at the same time – two contrasted sides of the composer's 'fluent and happy fancy'. From now on Jenkins was to give the fantasia new clothes at the head of his justly celebrated fantasia-suites. These fantasias with two basses, together with their splendid companions, the 32 'ayres' for two trebles, two basses and organ,[54] are Jenkins' farewell to the consort for viols; no one had exploited the medium with more distinction.

[54] *Cf. Musica Britannica*, Vol. XXVI, Nos. 1–32.

chapter eight
Conclusion

Jenkins, wrote Roger North, 'lived in King James time, and flourished in King Charles the First's'.[1] There is more precision in this statement than might at first appear. Certainly such documentary evidence as exists supports the view that Jenkins' music did not begin to reach a wide public until the late 1620s. By then he was turned thirty and likely to have reached full maturity as a composer. It is not unreasonable to suggest that his first successful attempts at writing large-scale consorts probably date from around 1620 or a little earlier. Certainly they are unlikely to be far removed in time from the major Jacobean fantasias by Lupo, Ferrabosco II, Ward and Gibbons, all composers to whom he was musically indebted in some way. An 'early' label might be attached to those pieces which show a certain rigidity in the treatment of themes, maintaining a fixed rhythm even where this pattern comes awkwardly against the *tactus* (as in the initial subjects of Fantasias Nos. 1 *à 4* and *à 5*, or in which successive imitative sections are dove-tailed in sixteenth-century motet-style, or which highlight modal colouring in the harmony.

From the outset Jenkins seems to have believed that the madrigal-fantasia espoused by Coprario and others, with its characteristic pattern of a succession of short-lived ideas, offered him limited scope for further development. On the other hand, structures formed from fewer

[1] *Op. cit.*, p. 343.

but longer sections, in Ferrabosco's manner, could readily be moulded into a variety of interesting, balanced forms, at the same time providing opportunities to explore subjects and textures in more depth. Certainly the spirit and technique of Ferrabsoco II maintains a very strong presence in works like the first four four-part fantasias, perhaps among Jenkins' earliest extant essays in the form. This homage is true not only of details like the construction of themes from two separate motifs, thematic links between sections, or strategically placed pedal-points, but also in the larger aspects of form.

In recognising that Jenkins pursued evolutionary rather than revolutionary methods in developing the fantasia, it must nevertheless be acknowledged that he brought the form to fresh heights of perfection. Two characteristics above all stand out as his special contribution of the genre: a wonderful all-pervasive lyricism and a masterly handling of tonality. Both were key factors in moulding his music, affecting mood, texture and form.

North notes that Jenkins' points were for the most part elegant and wrought with no small industry yet easy and familiar, but never insipid.[2] In truth, those from his viol fantasias differ little in character from subjects by his predecessors, but it is rather in their subsequent treatment that Jenkins broke new ground. Another draft of North's note reads:[3]

> He chose for his points more ayery passages than had bin ordinary [...] and he had an unaccountable felicity in his fuges, which he did not wear to the stumps, but timely went off into more variety and change of measures [...].

The rigidity of thematic invention noted above in Fantasias Nos. 1 *à 4* and *5* was rejected in favour of a more flexible method in which pitch and rhythm of motifs were freely altered, although not so as to hide the relationship.

[2] *Ibid.*, p. 296.

[3] British Library, Add. MS 32536, f. 73.

Again the practice itself was not new, but merely exploited more fully. Charles Butler accepted it as commonplace in 1636:[4]

> Musitions [do not] always strictly tye themselves to the just Number, Figure, Interval, or Tactus, of the Notes in the Point.

The partial inversion of themes (as for instance in the initial subjects of Fantasias Nos. 13 *à 4*, 6 *à 5* and 2 *à 6*) is an individual use of this freedom. More significant, though, is the manner in which Jenkins takes a salient figure from a theme and uses it to extend his melodies (as illustrated in Exx. 70 and 119, or sometimes builds a little episode from it, temporarily abandoning the main subject so that he does not 'wear [it] to the stumps' (as in Fantasias Nos. 1 *à 6* and 5 *à 5*). At other times, these episodes are generated by subsidiary figures, sometimes rhythmically related to the principal theme, but which more frequently are simply tags on which Jenkins fastens for a time. When advising 'How to maintayne a fuge', Coprario suggests three possibilities: paired entries in stretto, a regularly spaced series of single entries, or double subjects.[5] This last, he says,

> is most used of Excellent authors, for in single fuges there can no such great art be shewed, butt only in the invention thereof [...].

Jenkins evidently disagreed with this view, for the conventional double-subject features little in his fantasias. But that is not to deny that double-counterpoint is a formidable weapon in his technical armoury, merely that the manner of its use is more subtle. Thus one element in the pair is soon discarded from the double-subjects which open Fantasias Nos. 1 and 4 *à 6*, while elsewhere – for instance in Fantasias Nos. 3 and 7 *à 5* – it sneaks in later to complement its well-established partner. More perva-

[4] *Op. cit.*, f.72.

[5] *Rules How to Compose*, ff. 36–40.

sive are the numerous imitative passages built round subsidiary figures which bring welcome contrast to prolonged exploitation of subjects in monothematic works and elsewhere.[6]

Contrapuntal writing maintains an almost complete hold over the consorts in four to six parts. Homophonic contrasts are extremely brief and occur in very few works, while even the occasional dance-like passages are much more intricate in texture than the airs with which they might be compared. 'Popular' melodies, too find little place. While voices in the opening fugues enter in turn in the traditional way, later imitative passages are much more freely constructed. It is rare for these to be initiated by a single voice, but common for several parts to take up the new figures within a full polyphonic texture. Fugal techniques remain paramount throughout: double-counterpoint, inversion, stretto, augmentation, diminution and canon are the principal means by which Jenkins develops his material, though naturally, as in Bach's '48', not all devices are pertinent to, or found in, every piece.

There is no doubt that much of Jenkins' lyrical fervour stems from his contrapuntal fluency, but, as Marco Pallis points out, in a masterly article,[7] it also benefits from a practice which accepted free crossing of parts:

> The English proneness to lyricism expressed itself in an extreme freedom of crossing; by comparison, much of the Continental music feels relatively constrained. In the latter case it is the structure that seems to dominate the parts, whereas with the English composers the bias is if anything the other way. In a consort part by Ferrabosco, Jenkins or Lawes one finds nothing that could be described as 'filling in', no purely harmonic material devoid of intrinsic interest, no uninteresting tag-ends in any part. Kenneth Skeaping's brilliant dictum that in the English consort music 'each player is taking the principal part all

[6] *Ibid.*, f. 40.

[7] *Op. cit.*, pp. 31–3.

> the time' perfectly expressed the nature of the English creative impulse as well as of the technical means deployed to give effect to it, not least of which is an extremely free type of part-writing that would have been inconceivable but for the acceptance of wide-ranging crossings as a norm common to all consort instruments, the ones taking the middle parts being no exception [...].
>
> During the great flowering of the Jacobean period, when the viol consort came into its own as a fully independent instrumental form, by far the greater number of fantasies were laid out according to a scheme of so many *pairs* of parts, rather than as so many parts to be regarded individually: in six-part music there will be three such pairs, and in five-part music two pairs over a bass. The additional fact that most fantasies of that period, in their opening and their final sections, are composed like a double-fugue, with a pair of contrasting subjects to be tossed, as it were, from part to part, allows of at least four main thematic entries per pair, thus lending to the general polyphony a marvellous wealth of permutations [...].
>
> Passing to the Caroline age with Jenkins and Lawes as its dominant figures, one finds that fancies of the double-fugue type have given way, almost entirely, to the practice of exploiting one theme at a time, either during a section or, in a very few cases, throughout the course of a work. In this period the practice of crossing of parts in pairs continued to prevail with unexampled exuberance, and by it the sweeping lyricism of these two supreme exponents of the consort art is particularly favoured.

The general spaciousness of Jenkins' music is a notable characteristic, no less than his command of structure. Furthermore each instrumental grouping evokes its own particular response in his mind. Whereas the six-part fantasias are on the whole true to type, the presence of crossing pairs of instruments at all three levels of the instrumental choir (Treble, Tenor and Bass) opens up its own possibilities. Fugal openings and long sections of elaborately worked contrapuntal music exist in plenty, but in the many alternating interludes the six-part combination is explored in a variety of novel ways. Sometimes one finds broad, almost symphonic music, basking in the sheer splendour of the six-part sound; elsewhere trios, quartets, lively divisions, invigorating dotted rhythms or sustained polyphony all take their turn.

In seeking the richest variety in emotional expression one turns to the five-part series. What a wealth of moods is here: Richard Nicholson notes the range from

> the light-hearted gaiety of Fantasias such as Nos. 1 or 15 to the sombre elegiac nobility of the opening of No. 7. There is a stately grandeur and splendid forward thrust about the two monothematic works, Nos. 4 and 5. For sheer melodic loveliness the second or final sections of Nos. 2, 8 and 12 cannot well be surpassed. There is much joy in the brief dancing interludes which bridge some of the longer sections, and for enraptured serenity of consummation the closing sections of Nos. 10 and 11 touch the heights. All this is very far removed from the mere 'interwoven humdrum' which came to be considered an adequate description of the English Fantasy when in eclipse.[8]

The themes and textures of the three- and four-part works are noticeably livelier than those of the five- and six-part pieces. Indeed, an almost violinistic turn is given to some pieces in the four-part group, like Nos. 12, 15 and 16, matching the sprightly treble parts in the works for two trebles and a bass. The music here is mostly vigorous and distinctly extrovert, with only sparing use of contrasting quieter passages; the themes are rhythmically strong and not over-subtle. Expansive conclusions are a marked feature of the four-part fantasias, whether it be in the rapt unfolding of spacious melodies, as in Nos. 5, 7 and 10, or in the more exuberant vitality of Nos. 2, 8, 15 and 16.

Monothematic fantasies are rare before Jenkins' time, but he himself seems drawn to the challenge of maintain-

[8] In the Introduction to his edition of *John Jenkins: Consort Music in Five Parts*.

ing a subject right through a piece. This is a remarkable group of works, whose success can be attributed to the most careful overall planning. The means by which interest is sustained varies from work to work. Sometimes the principal theme undergoes considerable metamorphosis (as in Fantasias Nos. 7 *à 6* and *à 4*), or is subjected to varying degrees of augmentation (as in Fantasias Nos. 4 and 5 *à 5*). Sometimes subsidiary ideas come briefly to the fore (as in Fantasias Nos. 2 *à 6* and 9 *à 4*), or even settle in for a longer term, like the counter-melody which appears half-way through Fantasia No. 3 *à 6*. In three cases (Nos. 4 *à 5*, and 4 and 17 *à 4*) the music embarks on an adventurous tonal journey, perhaps first inspired by one of Ferrabosco II's rare monothematic pieces, his four-part Fantasia No. 21, which includes a similar excursion to remote keys.

Extended modulations are always carefully placed by Jenkins – usually between passages of stable tonality. Although monothematic fantasias would appear to offer most freedom in treatment of key, striking key-changes feature in several other pieces, especially in the three- and four-part series. Here is another challenge for Jenkins who, in such pieces as Fantasias Nos. 7 and 15 *à 4* and 10 for two trebles and bass, delighted in modulating round the key-circle. These extravagances are somewhat outside his general practice, but nevertheless indicate both his pioneering spirit in this field and also his consummate skill in handling key-change so effortlessly. The true value of modulation as a major resource in building tension, in climax and in relaxation is no less effective for being used with less exaggeration elsewhere. It is notable how Jenkins prefers to modulate to the flat side rather than sharpwards and shifts of two or three degrees towards flatter keys frequently enrich and warm the music with stirring effect. Furthermore, Jenkins often exploits keys associated with the tonic major/minor; the darker central section of Fantasia No. 17 *à 5* gives one side of the coin, the bright, D major-based interludes in Fantasias Nos. 4 and 5 *à 6* the other. In all this his technique is wonderfully smooth and assured.

The harmonic richness of Jenkins' music is achieved by key contrasts rather than through daring dissonances. North wrote that Jenkins 'used his discords always properly and with sincopation, according to law'.[9] Limited touches of chromaticism are nonetheless most effective as is his predilection for third-related chords at the joins of sections – like those noted in Ex. 24.[10]

The 'late' works in the four- and six-part groups and the two collections of three-part fantasias incorporate some of the new developments appearing in contemporary instrumental music. Clearly Jenkins found much to emulate in Gibbons' three-part music, both in structure and scoring. The emergence of the fantasia-suite in the 1620s also had repercussions in its promotion of the organ to an obbligato role and consequent additional focus on instrumental colour. Musical ideas changed in character as the violin made its presence felt, with more extrovert and fragmented lines. Divisions were already a feature of lute and bass viol music and Jenkins' own skill on these instruments no doubt prompted him to include such techniques in a few of the fantasias. Nor could the rising star of William Lawes at the Caroline court be ignored. Here was a radical new force instituting musical change: bold, dramatic and prodigiously talented. Some of the stylistic mannerisms evident in Jenkins' music of the 1630s and '40s – augmented chords, declamatory figures, repeated-note motifs and occasional capricious turns of phrase – surely derive from his acquaintance with Lawes' music.

In their true marriage of expressive, technical and structural elements, Jenkins' fantasias for viols stand

[9] *Op. cit.*, p. 297.

[10] *Cf.* p. 174.

among the great classics of consort and chamber music. In Richard Nicholson's words

> The whole achievement rests firmly upon an intimate understanding and wide exploitation of the full instrumental resources of the consort viol as Jenkins knew it. As with all great music, these Fantasies are wedded to the instruments for which they were composed and they cannot be satisfactorily realized on any others. Their full return to life in practical music-making necessarily depends upon the return of the viols to common use.[11]

In conclusion it is gratifying to note the current widespread revival of the practice of consort playing. Furthermore, expert craftsmen are providing players with new instruments of the highest quality, in many instances comparable to the finest examples which have survived from early times. Jenkins' music can live again, a fresh source of inspiration for those who appreciate the particular satisfaction to be experienced in listening to, or playing chamber music.

[11] *Loc. cit.*

appendix one Probate Records of Jenkins and his Parents

1. The Inventory of Henry Jenkins

A true & pfect Inventorie of all & singuler the goodes, houshold stuffe & moveables of Henrie Jenkins late of Maydestone in the Countie of Kent Carpenter made & taken the Eleventh day of Marche Anno dni 1617. And in the Fyfttenth year of the reigne of our most gracious sovreigne Lord Kinge James as followeth.

Fyrst his Purse & ready money		xii d
In the Hall		
Inprimis.	One Cubbard	iii s
Item.	A table with a Frame & a ioyned Forme	iiij s
Item.	Three Chayers	ij s
Item.	Two Glasse Cases	ij s
Item.	Seven Vialls & Violyns, One Bandora & a Cytherne	iii li
Item.	A payer of Tonges, A Payer of Belloes A Fyre pann & Potthangers And a payer of Cobirons & two benches	iiij s
In the Parlor		
	One Bedstedle with Curteyns, One Fether-bedd, One Blankett, One Covrlett wth a mattris & straw bedd & two bolsters	vii li
Item.	One Joyned table and Five ioyned stooles	xxx s
Item.	One Joyned benche of weynescott & sixe Cushions	xxv s
Item.	the paynted Cloth. A window Curteyne & a Cheyer	vii s

In the Buttry		
	All his brasse	iii li
Item.	all his Pewter	l s
Item.	Three Iron Potts, One Iron Stuppnett A Gred-iron & Grate for Coales	xx s
Item.	Fower Spitts, a Fryinge pann, two payer of Potthookes a Kneadinge troughe a shall, two sives, a Toluett & a gallon, two trugs & two boules	x s
The Chamber over the shoppe		
	One Cubbard & a court Cubbard ioyned	iii li
Item.	Three ioyned Shelfs	xx s
Item.	One Joyned Bedsteddle, two Curteynes a Flockbedd, a Blankett, a Covrlett & two bolsters	v li
Item.	Eight payer of Fine sheetes, sixe payer of Coorse sheetes, sixe table Clothes of Flaxe & One of Diaper. Two dozen of napkins, Fower Holland Pillow Coates & Tenn of Flaxe, One Christeninge sheet & a fare clothe	viii li
Item.	the paynted clothes	v s
Item.	his wearing apparell	iii li
Item.	Fower silver spoones	xx s
In the chamber over the parlor		
	One Flockbedd, one Bolster, One Trundle bedd & a matt & Eight pounde of Flaxen Yarne & an old chest	xx s
In the Chamber over the Hall		
Imprimis.	three Bedd steddles, One Fetherbedd, two Flockbedds, One Strawbedd, two blanketts, two covrletts & Fower Bolsters	iiij li
Item.	sixe Fether pillowes	xv s
Item.	Three old Chestes, a Hamper and a woman's Saddle	x s
In the Shopp		
	Two Twistinge wheeles, two trundles, One Cubbard, an old table & fower boxes	xx s

In the Bakehouse

	A Brewinge Tubb, a Buckinge tubb, a keeler, a boule, an old chest & three Virkins & other Lumber	viii s
Item.	Fyftene pound of yarne at the wevers	viii s
Item.	other things forgotten or not seene	v s

Sume is l li xs

The pricers names
Wa: Fisher
Thomas Reve

2. The Inventory of Ann Jenkins

A True Inventorie of the goods and chattelle of Ann Jenkins wedo of Maidston latlie diceased prised by those men whose name ar underwritten this 10 of September 1623

Imprimis hir purse, girdle & wearing apparrel		£2
In the hawle	on cupbord a smale table a glasse cupord on old chair on Joind stoole on old cupboerd cloth	0-13-4
In the parlor	on Joind bedsted on court cupbord 2 Joind Setles & Joind stooles on fetherbed on flockbed on Coverlet & on blancket on flock bowlster and on fether bowlster with courtains & valnce & 5 old Quushens and on small windo curtain	4-3-4
In the kitchin	21 peeces of pewter 3 Iron potts & on Iron stupnet 5 peeces of brasse on spitt on pair of pothangers on pair of tongs 3 old chairs	1-6-8
In the hawle chamber	on Joind bedsted on truckle bedsted on Joind chest on Joind presse with a cloth on Joind stoole on fetherbed & a flockbed on fether bowlster & on flockbowlster & 2 fether pillows & 2 coverlets & a blancket on pair of curtains & valance with matts and roods	5-3-4

In the foor parlor chamber

on table & fram on Joind setle on forme 2 old bedsteds on truckle-bedsted on old chair 3 flockbeds on fetherbed 4 flock-bowlsters on pillow 2 old Ruggs & 2 blanckets — 2-8-0

In another chamber

on flockbedd a flocke bowlster & a coverlet — 0-10-6

In the foor parlor

on Joind table on old forme on flock bed & a flock bowlster & a blanket — 0-17-6

In the back chamber

2 Joind chestes 2 old bedsteds on old trunk chest on old chair 3 fether pillows on little boxe & 2 old chests — 0-17-4

Of linnen 4 pair of flaxen sheets & 7 pair of course sheets 4 table clothes 1 dozen & a half of flaxen napkins and a dozen of courses 3 pair of pillow cotes & 4 hand towels of course & 2 finer — 4-3-4

Som certain washing tubbs with other lumber — 0-3-4

Som is — 22-6-2

Priced by brian Taylor
Wm. Broad
The mark W of Xtopher Wilson

3. Jenkins' Lost Will

In spite of Roger North's assertion that Jenkins, at his death, left 'an old freind a competent legacy to be remembered by', no will has been traced. The following document (E406/50, f.158), recently discovered at the Public Record Office, sheds light on the composer's bequest.

> Know all men by these prsents yt wee Andrew Hatley of Kimberley in the County of Northfolke, Clerke, & Will. Browne, of ye same Towne, Gent., Executrs of ye Last will & testamt of John Jenckins late of Kimberley Aforesaid, Gent, decesed, Have made, Ordained, Constituted & in or place put & by these prsents do make, ordaine, Constitute

> & in or place and stead put or Loving freind Francis Lilly of Baldwins Garden in the counti of Midx, Widdow, relict, Executrix of ye Last will & Testament of Jo. Lilly, Gent, decesed, & Johanna Wheeler of ye parish of Stepney in the Citty of London or Liberties, to be or true & Lawful Attorney & to demande, sue for, require, receive & take all & every such sume & sumes of money which are due & payable to the above said Jo: Jenkins out of or from ye Excheqr & the Treasury Chamber or other of them. And which the said Jo: Jenckins in & by his said will did give & bequeath unto ye said Jo: Lylly & Johanna Wheeler to be equally divided betwene them, Guiving & granting by these prsents to or said Attorneys our whole power & Authority in & about ye prmises. And upon receipt thereof to give Acquittances or other discharges to any of the offcers Aforesaid, as if wee or selfes were present & did the same, in witnes whereof wee have hereunto set or Hands & seales this 23d day of March An. Dom. 1679 [1680]. Andrew Hatley. Will. Browne. Sealed & delivrd in the presence of Rich: Hunns. Peter Newton.

The identity of Johanna Wheeler is unknown, but she may well have been the composer's landlady when he was resident in London.

appendix two
The Six-part Consorts

A collation of Bar-numbers in the Faber and *Musica Britannica* Editions

Faber			*Musica Britannica*
No. 1:	bars 1–80		1/2–159/160
No. 2:	1–46		1/2–91/92
No. 3:	1–52;	53	1/2–103/104; 105
No. 4:	1–54		1/2–107/108
No. 5:	1–65		1/2–129/130
No. 6:	1–17		1/2–33/34
	18–41		35–58
	42–71		59/60–117/118
No. 7:	1–64;	65	1/2–127/128; 129
No. 8:	1–58;	59	1/2–115/116; 117
No. 9:	1–49		1/2–97/98
No. 10:	1–55		[No. 13)1/2–109/110
No. 11:	1–56;	57	[No. 14]1/2–111/112, 113
12:	1–58		[No. 10]1/2–115/116
Bell Pavan:	1–24;	25	[No. 11]1/2–47/48; 49
	26–30		50/51–58/59
	31–36		60/61–70/71
	37–43; 44		72/73–84/85; 86
Pavan in F:	1–16		[No. 12]1/2–31/32
	17–26		33–51/53
	27–51; 52		54/55–102/103; 104
In Nomine I	1–65		[No. 15] 1–65
	66–87; 88		66/67–108/109; 110
In Nomine 2	1–20		[No. 16]1/2–39/40
	21–74		41–94
	75–83		95/96–111/112

appendix three
Discography

I. LP RECORDINGS

		No.	LP(s)
1.	**Consorts in Six Parts**		
	Fantasia	8	B
	Bell Pavan		F
	In Nomine	1	B
2.	**Consorts in Five Parts**		
	Fantasia	1	A
	Fantasia	3	B
	Fantasia	5	A
	Fantasia	8	A
	Fantasia	10	A
	Fantasia	16	F
	Fantasia	17	G
	Pavan	1	G, H
	Pavan	2	B
3.	**Consorts in Four Parts**		
	Fantasia	2	I
	Fantasia	5	C
	Fantasia	6	E
	Fantasia	9	D
	Fantasia	12	B
	Pavan	1	D
4.	**Fantasias**	6	B, J
	Treble, Bass, Bass, Organ	8	L
5.	**Fantasia**		
	Treble, Treble, Bass	18	K

Index of LPs

A.	Oxford Chamber Players	Argo RG-73
B.	Consort of Musicke	L'Oiseau-Lyre DS LO 600
C.	Jaye Consort	Arion ARN-38215
D.	Jaye Consort	Wealden Recordings WS-213
E.	English consort of viols	National Trust NT-003
F.	English Consort of Viols	PAN-6208 (reissued as SAGA-5338)
G.	English Consort of Viols	Turnabout TV-344443S
H.	English Consort of Viols	Abbey 652
I.	Leonhardt Consort	Pye Vanguard PVL-7027
J.	London Baroque	Meridian E-77059
K.	Dolmetsch Ensemble	Dolmetsch Recordings DR-9 (78 rpm)
L.	King's Musick	Studio SVII Augsburg 66.22211

II. COMPACT DISC RECORDINGS

1. The Seventeen Four-Part Fantasias

Kölner Violen-consort — Thorofon Capella CTH 2042

2. The Six-Part Music[1]

Hespérion XX — Audivis-Astrée E 8724

[1] Excluding Fantasia No. 12.

appendix four
Bibliography

1. Books and Articles

ANONYMOUS, *A brief and true Relation of the Siege and Surrendering of King's Lynn to the Earl of Manchester,* 1643.

APLIN, JOHN, 'Sir Henry Fanshawe and Two Sets of Early Seventeenth-Century Part-Books at Christ Church, Oxford, *Music & Letters,* 57, 1976, pp. 11–24.

ASHBEE, ANDREW, 'Genealogy and John Jenkins', *Music & Letters,* 46, 1965, pp. 225–30.

——, *The Four-Part Instrumental Compositions of John Jenkins,* unpublished Ph. D. dissertation, University of London, 1966.

——, 'The Four-Part Consort Music of John Jenkins', *Proceedings of The Royal Musical Association,* 96, 1969–70, pp. 29–42.

——, 'John Jenkins's Fantasia-Suites for Treble, Two Basses and Organ', *Chelys,* 1, 1969, pp. 3–15; 2, 1970, pp. 6–17.

——, 'Towards the Chronology and Grouping of some Airs by John Jenkins', *Music & Letters,* 55, 1974, pp. 30–43.

——, 'A Further Look at Some of the Le Strange Manuscripts', *Chelys,* 5, 1973–4, pp. 24–41.

——, 'Music for Treble, Bass and Organ by John Jenkins', *Chelys,* 6, 1975–6, pp. 25–42.

——, 'Instrumental Music From the Library of John Browne (1608–1691), Clerk of the Parliaments', *Music & Letters,* 58, 1977, pp. 43–59.

——, 'The Six-Part Consort Music of John Jenkins: An Editor's View', *Chelys,* 7, 1977, pp. 54–68.

—— *et al., John Jenkins: 1592–1678,* a booklet produced at the Tercentenary of his death, John Jenkins Tercentenary Committee, London, 1978.

——, 'John Jenkins (1592–1678): The Viol Consort Music in Four, Five and Six Parts', *Early Music,* VI, 1978, pp. 492–500.

——, 'John Jenkins, 1592–1678', *The Consort,* 34, 1978, pp. 265–73.

——, 'John Jenkins, 1592–1678, and the Lyra Viol', *Musical Times,* cxix, 1978, pp. 840–43.

——, *Lists of Payments to the King's Musick in the Reign of Charles II (1660–1685),* Author, Snodland, 1981.

——, 'A Not Unapt Scholar: Bulstrode Whitelocke (1605–1675)', *Chelys,* II, 1982, pp. 24–31.

——, *Records of English Court Music,* Vols I–IV, Author, Snodland, 1986, 1987, 1989 and 1988; 1988 Vols. V and VI, Scolar Press, Aldershot, 1991 and 1992.

BAINES, FRANCIS, 'Fantasies for the Great Dooble Base', *Chelys,* 2, 1970, pp. 37–8.

——, 'The Consort Music of Orlando Gibbons', *Early Music,* VI, 1978, pp. 540–3.

BECKER, C. F., *Die Tonwerke des XVI und XVII Jahrhunderts,* Leipzig, 1855.

BEER, E. S. DE, *The Diary of John Evelyn,* 6 vols., Oxford University Press, Oxford, 1955.

BELLINGHAM, BRUCE, 'The Musical Circle of Anthony Wood in Oxford during the Commonwealth and Restoration', *Journal of the Viola da Gamba Society of America,* XIX, 1982, pp. 7–70.

BENNETT, JOHN, 'Byrd and Jacobean Consort Music: A Look at Richard Mico', in Alan Brown and Richard Turbet (eds.), *Byrd Studies,* Cambridge University Press, Cambridge, 1992.

BERGERON, DAVID M., *English Civic Pageantry (1558–1642),* Arnold, London, 1971.

BLOMEFIELD, FRANCIS, *An Essay towards a Topographical History of the County of Norfolk,* 5 vols., London, 1739–75.

BOORMAN, H. R. PRATT, *Pictures of Maidstone,* Kent Messenger, Maidstone, 1965.

BROOKES, VIRGINIA, 'The Four-Part In Nomines of John Ward', *Chelys,* 16, 1987, pp. 30–5.

BRUCE, JOHN (ed.), *Charles I in 1646,* Camden Society, London, 1856.

BURNEY, CHARLES, *A General History of Music from the Earliest Ages to the Present Period,* 3 vols., London, 1776–89; reprinted, Dover Edition, New York, 1957.

BURROWS, MONTAGUE, *The Register of the Visitors of the University of Oxford from A. D. 1647 to A. D. 1658,* Camden Society, London, 1881.

BUTLER, CHARLES, *The Principles of Musik in Singing and Setting,* London, 1636.

BUTLER, GREGORY G., 'The Projection of Affect in Baroque Dance Music'. *Early Music,* XII, 1984, pp. 201–7.

CALENDAR OF THE PROCEEDINGS OF THE COMMITTEE FOR COMPOUNDING, 5 vols., 1889–92, ed. Mrs. M. A. E. Green.

CALENDAR OF STATE PAPERS: DOMESTIC SERIES.

CALENDAR OF STATE PAPERS: TREASURY BOOKS.

CAVE-BROWNE, Rev. J., *The Marriage Registers of the Parish Church of All Saints, Maidstone,* Author, London, 1901.

CHALKIN, C. W., *Seventeenth Century Kent: A Social and Economic History,* Longmans, London, 1965.

CHARTERIS, RICHARD 'A Rediscovered Source of English Consort Music', *Chelys,* 5, 1973–4, pp. 3–6.

——, *John Coprario,* unpublished Ph. D. thesis, University of Canterbury, New Zealand, 1976.

——, 'Jacobean Musicians at Hatfield House, 1605–1613', *Royal Musical Association Research Chronicle,* 12, 1974, pp. 115–36.

——, 'Matthew Hutton (1638–1711) and his Manuscripts in York Minster Library', *Galpin Society Journal,* XXVIII, 1975, pp. 2–6.

——, 'Consort Music Manuscripts in Archbishop Marsh's Library, Dublin', *Royal Musical Association Research Chronicle,* 13, 1976, pp. 27–63.

——, 'John Coprario's Five- and Six-part Pieces: Instrumental or Vocal?', *Music & Letters,* 57, 1976, pp. 370–8.

——*John Coprario: A Thematic Catalogue of His Music with a Biographical Introduction,* Pendragon, New York, 1977.

——, 'Music Manuscripts and Books missing from Archbishop Marsh's Library, Dublin', *Music & Letters,* 61, 1980, pp. 310–7.

——, 'A Postscript to "John Coprario: A Thematic Catalogue of his Music with a Biographical Introduction" (New York, 1977)', *Chelys,* 11, 1982, pp. 13–9.

——'The Huntingdon Library Part-Books, Ellesmere MSS EL 25 A 46–51', *The Huntington Library Quarterly,* 50:1, 1987, pp. 59–84.

CLARK, ANDREW (ed.), *The Life and Times of Anthony Wood,* Oxford Historical Society, Oxford, 1891–1900, 5 vols.

CLARK, J. BUNCKER, 'A Re-emerged Seventeenth-Century

Organ Acompaniment Book', *Music & Letters,* 47, 1966, pp. 149–52.

COPRARIO, GIOVANNI, *Rules How to Compose,* facsimile edn., ed. Manfred Bukofzer, Los Angeles, 1952.

COXON, CAROLYN, *John Jenkins: A Critical Study of his Instrumental Music,* unpublished Ph. D. thesis, University of Edinburgh, 1969.

——, 'A Handlist of the Sources of John Jenkins's Vocal and Instrumental Music', *Royal Musical Association Research Chronicle,* 9, 1971, pp. 73–89.

CURTIS, ALAN, *Sweelinck's Keyboard Music: A Study of English Elements in Seventeenth-Century Dutch Composition,* E. J. Brill/Leiden University Press, Leiden, 1987.

CRUM, ALISON, 'Improve Your Consort Playing: A Practical Study of John Jenkins, Fantasy a 6 in A minor, Viola da Gamba Society No. 8', *Chelys,* 13, 1984, pp. 39–46.

CRUM, MARGARET, 'Early Lists of the Oxford Music School Collection', *Music & Letters,* 48, 1967, pp. 23–34.

——, 'The Consort Music from Kirtling, bought for the Oxford Music School from Anthony Wood, 1667', *Chelys,* 4, 1972, pp. 3–10.

DART, ROBERT THURSTON, 'Jacobean Consort Music', *Proceedings of the Royal Musical Association,* 81, 1954–5, pp. 63–76.

——, 'The Printed Fantasies of Orlando Gibbons', *Music & Letters,* 37, 1956, pp. 342–9.

——, 'Miss Mary Burwell's Instruction Book for the Lute', *Galpin Society Journal,* XI, 1958, pp. 3–62.

DODD, GORDON J. 'The Coprario-Lupo Five-part Books at Washington', *Chelys,* 1, 1969, pp. 36–40.

——, 'Alfonso Ferrabosco II – The Art of the Fantasy', *Chelys,* 7, 1977, pp. 47–53.

——, 'Matters arising from the Examination of Some Lyra-Viol Manuscripts', *Chelys,* 9, 1980, pp. 23–7.

——, *Thematic Index of Music for Viols,* Viola da Gamba Society of Great Britain, London, 1980–7.

DOLMETSCH, NATHALIE, *The Viola da Gamba: Its Origin and History, Its Technique and Musical Resources,* Hinrichsen, London, 1962.

DONINGTON, ROBERT, *English Instrumental Music from the Reformation to the Restoration with Particular Reference to the 17th Cen-*

tury, unpublished B. Litt. thesis, Queen's College, Oxford University, 1945–6.

EDMOND, MARY, 'Limners and Picturemakes: New Light on the Lives of Miniaturists and Large-scale Portrait-painters Working in London in the Sixteenth and Seventeenth Centuries', *Walpole Society Journal*, XLVII, 1980.

——, *Hilliard & Oliver: The Lives and Works of Two Great Minaturists*, Robert Hale, London, 1983.

EDWARDS, WARWICK A., 'The Performance of Ensemble Music in Elizabethan England', *Proceedings of the Royal Musical Association*, 97, 1970–1, pp. 113–23.

FIELD, CHRISTOPHER D. S., 'Matthew Locke and the Consort Suite', *Music & Letters*, 51, 1970, pp. 15–25.

——, *The English Consort Suite of the 17th Century*, unpublished Ph. D. thesis, New College, Oxford University, 1971.

——, 'Musical Observations from Barbados, 1647–50', *Musical Times*, cxv, 1974, pp. 565–7.

——, 'Jenkins and the Fantasia-Suite', in *John Jenkins: 1592–1678*. John Jenkins Tercentenary Committee, London, 1978, pp. 7–8.

FORD, ROBERT, 'The Filmer MSS – A Handlist', *Notes*, 34, June 1978, pp. 814–25.

——, 'John Ward of Canterbury', *Journal of the Viola da Gamba Society of America*, XXIII, 1986, pp. 51–63.

FORTUNE, NIGEL, and FENLON, IAIN, 'Music Manuscripts of John Browne (1608–91) and from Stanford hall, Leicestershire', in *Source Materials and the Interpretation of Music: A Memorial Volume to Thurston Dart*, ed. Ian Bent, Stainer & Bell, London, 1981, pp. 155–68.

FOSBROKE, THOMAS DUDLEY, *An Original History of the City of Gloucester*, London, 1819.

FOSTER, JOSEPH, *Alumni Oxoniensis: The Members of the University of Oxford, 1500–1714*, Oxford, 1891, 4 vols.

GREAVES, RICHARD L., 'Music at Puritan Oxford', *Musical Times*, cx, 1969, p. 26.

GRIFFITHS, DAVID, *A Catalogue of the Music Manuscripts in York Minster Library*, York Minster Library, Sectional Catalogue 2, 1981.

HARPER, JOHN, 'The Distribution of the Consort Music of Orlando Gibbons in Seventeenth-Century Sources', *Chelys*, 12, 1983, pp. 3–18.

HAWKINS, SIR JOHN, *A History of the Science and Practice of Musick*, 5 vols., London, 1776; reprint, Dover Edition, New York, 1963.

HISCOCK, W. G., *Henry Aldrich of Christ Church*, Oxford, 1960.

HOLMAN, PETER, 'George Jeffries and the "great dooble base"', *Chelys*, 5, 1973–4, pp. 79–81.

——, 'The Symphony', *Chelys*, 6, 1975–6, pp. 10–24.

——, 'Suites by Jenkins Rediscovered', *Early Music*, 6, 1978, pp. 25–35.

——, 'Thomas Baltzar (?1631–1663), The "Incomperable Luciber on the Violin"', *Chelys*, 13, 1984, pp. 3–38.

——, 'The English Royal Violin Consort in the Sixteenth Century', *Proceedings of the Royal Musical Association*, 109, 1982–3, pp. 39–59.

HOLMES, CLIVE, *The Eastern Association in the English Civil War*, Cambridge University Press, Cambridge, 1974.

HOOKES, NICHOLAS, *Amanda*, London, 1653.

HULLAH, JOHN PYKE, *The Third or Transition Period of Musical History*, Longmans, Green & Co., London, 2nd edn., 1876.

HUSBAND, EDWARD (ed.), *A Collection of all the Public Orders, Ordinances and Declarations of both Houses of Parliament*, London, 1646.

IRVING, JOHN A., 'Matthew Hutton and York Minster MSS M.3/1–4(S)', *Music Review*, 44, 1983, pp. 163–177.

——, 'Consort Playing in Mid-17th-century Worcester. Thomas Tomkins and the Bodleian Partbooks, Mus. Sch. E.415–18', *Early Music*, 12, 1984, pp. 337–344.

——, 'Oxford Christ Church MSS. 1018–1020: A Valuable Source of Tomkins's Consort Music', *The Consort*, 40, 1984, pp. 1–12.

——, *The Instrumental Music of Thomas Tomkins 1572–1656*, Outstanding Dissertations in Music from British Universities, Garland, New York, 1989.

——, 'Byrd and Tomkins: The Instrumental Music', in Alan Brown and Richard Turbet (eds.), *Byrd Studies*, Cambridge University Press, Cambridge, 1992.

JENKINS, HAROLD, *Edward Benlowes*, Athlone Press, London, 1952.

JENNINGS, JOHN M., *The Viol Music of Thomas Lupo*, M. Mus. thesis, Sydney, 1967.

——, 'The Fantasias of Thomas Lupo', *Musicology*, III, 1968–9, and *Chelys*, 3, 1971, pp. 3–15 (duplicate).

——, 'Thomas Lupo Revisited – Is Key the Key to His Later Music?', *Chelys*, 12, 1983, pp. 19–22.

JESSOPP, AUGUSTUS, *The Autobiography of the Hon. Roger North*, London, 1887.

JOHNSON, JANE TROY, 'How to "Humour" John Jenkins' Three-Part Dances: Performance Directions in a Newberry Library MS', *Journal of the American Musicological Society*, 1967, pp. 197–208.

JOHNSON, THOMAS H.. *The Poetical Works of Edward Taylor*, Princeton University Press, Princeton, 1943.

JONCKBLOET, W. J. A. and LAND, J. P. N. *Correspondence et œuvres musicales de Constantijn Huygens*, Leiden, 1882.

KERMAN, JOSEPH, *The Elizabethan Madrigal. A Comparative Study*, American Musicological Society, New York & London, 1962.

KETTON-CREMER, R. W., 'The Rhyming Wodehouses', *Norfolk & Norwich Archaeological Society Journal*, xxxiii (i), 1962, p. 35.

——, *Norfolk in the Civil War*, Faber & Faber, London, 1969.

KING, ALEC HYATT, *Some British Collectors of Music*, Cambridge University Press, Cambridge, 1963.

LAFONTAINE, HENRY CART de, *The King's Musick*, Novello & Co., London, 1909.

LATHAM, ROBERT C., and MATTHEWS, WILLIAM, *The Diary of Samuel Pepys*, 11 vols., Bells, London, 1970–83.

LEFKOWITZ, MURRAY, *William Lawes*, Routledge & Kegan Paul, London, 1960.

——, 'The Longleat Papers of Bulstrode Whitelocke: New Light on Shirley's *Triumph of Peace*', *Journal of the American Musicological Society*, xviii, 1965, pp. 42–60.

——, *Trois Masques à la Cour de Charles Ier d'Angleterre*, Centre National de la Recherche Scientifique, Paris, 1970.

——, 'Shadwell and Locke's *Psyche:* The French Connection', *Proceedings of the Royal Musical Association*, 106, 1979–80, pp. 42–55.

LEWIS, SAMUEL, *A Topographical Dictionary of England*, 7th edn., London, 1849.

LINDLEY, MARK, *Lutes, Viols and Temperaments*, Cambridge University Press, Cambridge, 1984.

LIPPINCOTT, H. F., *'Merry Passages and Jeasts', A Manuscript Jest-book of Sir Nicholas Le Strange (1603–1655)*, Institut für Englische Sprache und Literatur, University of Salzburg, Salzburg, 1974.

The London Gazette: Nos. 1173 and 1213, in the year 1677.

Lowinsky, Edward, 'Echoes of Adrian Willaert's Chromatic "Duo" in 16th and 17th Century Compositions', in *Studies in Music History: Essays for Oliver Strunck,* Princeton University Press, Princeton, 1968.

Mabbett, Margaret, 'Italian Musicians in Restoration England (1660–90)', *Music & Letters,* 67, 1986, pp. 237–47.

Mace, Thomas, *Musick's Monument,* London, 1676.

Marlow, Norman, *The Diary of Thomas Isham of Lamport (1658–81),* Gregg International, Farnborough, 1971.

Melling, Elizabeth, *Some Kentish Houses,* Kent County Council, Maidstone, 1965.

Meyer, Ernst H., *Die Mehrstimmige Spielmusik des 17. Jahrhunderts in Nord und Mitteleuropa,* Kassel, 1934.

——, 'Form in the Instrumental Music of the Seventeenth Century', *Proceedings of the Royal Musical Association,* 65, 1939–40, pp. 45–61.

——, *English Chamber Music,* revised as *Early English Chamber Music,* Laurence & Wishart, London, 1946 and 1982 respectively.

Milsom, John, 'A Tallis Fantasia', *Musical Times,* cxxvi, 1985, pp. 658–62.

Monson, Craig, *Voices and Viols in England, 1600–1650: The Sources and the Music,* UMI Research Press, Ann Arbor, 1982.

Morant, Valerie, 'The Settlement of Protestant Refugees in Maidstone during the Sixteenth Century', *Economic History Review,* 1951, pp. 210–14.

Morley, Thomas, *A Plaine and Easie Introduction to Practicall Musicke,* London, 1597, reprinted ed. R. Alec Harman, London, 1952.

Mountney, Rev. F. Hugh, 'Lady Katherine Audley's Bells', *Bulletin of the Viola da Gamba Society,* 19 June 1963, pp. 4–7.

Neighbour, Oliver, *The Consort and Keyboard Music of William Byrd,* Faber, London, 1978.

——, 'Orlando Gibbons (1583–1625): The Consort Music', *Early Music,* 11, 1983, pp. 351–7.

Nicolas, N. H., *Memoirs of Lady Fanshawe,* London, 1829.

North, Dudley, *A Forest Promiscuous of Several Seasons Productions,* London, 1659.

North, Roger, *see* Wilson, John.

Notes and Queries: No. 278 (Ninth Series).

Pallis, Marco, 'The Instrumentation of English Viol Consort Music', *Chelys*, 1, 1969, pp. 27–35.

Payne, Ian, 'The Handwriting of John Ward', *Music & Letters*, 65, 1984, pp. 176–88.

Peacham, Henry, *The Compleat Gentleman*, London, 1622.

Pevsner, Nikolaus, *North-West and South Norfolk, The Buildings of England*, Penguin, London, 1962.

Philipps, Glenn Alan, 'Crown Musical Patronage from Elizabeth I to Charles I', *Music & Letters*, 58, 1977, pp. 29–42.

Pinto, David, 'William Lawes' Music for Viol Consort', *Early Music*, 6, 1978, pp. 12–24.

——, 'The Fantasy Manner: the Seventeenth Century Context', *Chelys*, 10, 1981, pp. 17–28.

——, 'William Lawes' Consort Suites for the Viols, and the Autograph Sources', *Chelys*, 4, 1972, pp. 11–16.

——, 'The Music of the Hattons', *RMA Research Chronicle*, 23, 1990, pp. 79–108.

Poole, Rachael Lane, 'The Oxford Music School and the Collection of Portraits formerly preserved there', *The Musical Antiquary*, IV, 1912–13, pp. 143–59.

Prest, Wilfred R., *The Inns of Court under Elizabeth I and the Early Stuarts, 1590–1640*, Longmans, London, 1972.

Pulver, Jeffrey, *A Biographical Dictionary of Old English Music*, Kegan Paul, London, 1927.

Randall, Dale B. J., *Gentle Flame: The Life and Verse of Dudley, Fourth Lord North (1602–1677)*. Duke University Press, Durham, North Carolina, 1983.

Rasch, Rudi A., 'Seventeenth-Century Dutch Editions of English Instrumental Music', *Music & Letters*, 53, 1972, pp. 270–3.

Royal Commission on Historical Monuments (England), *Newark on Trent, The Civil War Siegeworks*, HMSO, London, 1964.

Sabol, Andrew, 'New Documents on Shirley's Masque The Triumph of Peace', *Music & Letters*, 47, 1966, pp. 10–26.

Sackville-West, Victoria, *The Diary of Lady Anne Clifford*, Oxford University Press, London, 1924.

Sawyer, John, *An Anthology of Lyra Viol Music in Oxford, Bodleian*

Manuscripts Music School D. 245–7, unpublished Ph. D. thesis, University of Toronto, 1972.

SCHOLES, PERCY A., *The Puritans and Music in England and New England*, Oxford University Press, London, 1934.

SHAW, H. WATKINS, *A Study of the Bing-Gostling Part Books in the Library of York Minster together with a Systemic Catalogue*, Church Music Society, Croydon, 1986.

SHUTE, JOHN DEREK, *Anthony a Wood and his Manuscript Wood D 19(4) at the Bodleian Library, Oxford: An Annotated Transcription*, unpublished Ph. D. dissertation, International Institute for Advanced Studies, Clayton, Missouri, 1979.

SIMPSON, CHRISTOPHER, *The Division-Violist*, London, 1659.

——, *The Division-Viol*, London, 1665; facsimile edn., ed. Nathalie Dolmetsch, Curwen, London, 1965.

——, *A Compendium of Practical Musick*, 2nd edn., London, 1667; modern edition, ed. Philip Lord, B. H. Blackwell, Oxford, 1970.

SLEEPER, HELEN JOY, 'John Jenkins and the English Fantasia-Suite', *Bulletin of the American Musicological Society*, 4, 1940, pp. 34–7.

——, A large collection of MSS notes, thematic lists, transcriptions, etc., at the Pendlebury Library, Cambridge.

SMITH, DOUGLAS ALTON, 'The Ebenthal Lute and Viol Tablatures: Thirteen New Manuscripts of Baroque Instrumental Music', *Early Music*, 10, 1982, pp. 462–7.

SPENCER, ROBERT, *The Burwell Lute Tutor*, facsimile, Boethius Press, Leeds, 1974.

STONE, LAWRENCE, *The Crisis of the Aristocracy, 1558–1641*, abridged edn., Oxford University Press, Oxford, 1967.

STRAHLE, GRAHAM, 'Fantasy and Music in Sixteenth- and Seventeenth-century England', *Chelys* 17, 1988, pp. 28–32.

STRONG, ROY, *Henry, Prince of Wales, and England's Lost Renaissance*, Thames & Hudson, London, 1986.

STROVER, M. CHRISTIAN T., *John Ward's Fantasias and In Nomines*, unpublished B. Litt thesis, Hertford College, Oxford University, 1956–7.

THOMPSON, ROBERT, *English Music Manuscripts and the Fine Paper Trade, 1648–1688*, unpublished PhD dissertation, University of London, 1988.

——, "Francis Withie of Oxon" and his Commonplace Book, Christ Church, Oxford, MS 337', *Chelys* 20, 1991, pp. 3–27.

TOFT, ROBERT, 'Musicke a Sister to poetrie; Rhetorical Artifice in the Passionate Airs of John Dowland', *Early Music,* 12, 1984, pp. 190–9.

URQUHART, MARGARET, 'Sir Robert Bolles Bt. of Scampton', *Chelys,* 16, 1987, pp. 16–29.

VAUGHT, RAYMOND, *The Fancies of Alfonso Ferrabosco II,* unpublished Ph. D. dissertation, Stanford University, 1959.

WALLS, PETER, 'New Light on Songs by William Lawes and John Wilson', *Music & Letters,* 57, 1976, pp. 55–64.

WARDALE, J. R., *Clare College Letters and Documents,* Cambridge, 1903.

WARNER, ROBERT AUSTIN, *The Fantasia in the Works of John Jenkins,* unpublished, Ph. D. dissertation, University of Michigan, 1951.

——, 'John Jenkins' Four-Part Fancy (Meyer No. 14) in C minor: An Enharmonic Modulation around the Key Circle', *Music Review,* 28, 1967, pp. 1–20.

WELLS, ROBERT HEADLAM, 'The Ladder of Love: Verbal and Musical Rhetoric in the Elizabethan Lute-song', *Early Music,* 12, 1984, pp. 173–189.

WESS, JOAN, 'Musica Transalpina, Parody, and the Emerging Jacobean Viol Fantasia', *Chelys,* 15, 1986, pp. 3–25.

WESTRUP, SIR JACK A., 'Foreign Musicians in Stuart England', *Musical Quarterly,* 1941, pp. 70–89.

——, 'Domestic Music under the Stuarts', *Proceedings of the Royal Musical Association,* 68, 1941, pp. 19–53.

WHITELOCKE, BULSTRODE, *Memorials of English Affairs,* London, 1682.

WILLETTS, PAMELA J., 'Sir Nicholas Le Strange and John Jenkins', *Music & Letters,* 42, 1961, pp. 30–43.

——, 'Music from the Circle of Anthony Wood at Oxford', *The British Museum Quarterly,* XXIV, 3–4, 1961, pp. 71–5.

——, 'Sir Nicholas Le Strange's Collection of Masque Music', *The British Museum Quarterly,* XXIX, 1965, pp. 79–81.

——, Autograph Music by John Jenkins', *Music & Letters,* 48, 1967, pp. 124–6.

——, 'John Lilly, Musician and Music Copyist', *The Bodleian Library Record,* VII, No. 6, 1967, pp. 307–11.

——, 'Stephen Bing: A Forgotten Violist', *Chelys,* 18, 1989, pp. 3–17.

——, 'John Barnard's Collections of Viol and Vocal Music' *Chelys,* 20, 1991, pp. 28–42.

WILSON, JOHN (ed.), *Roger North on Music, Being a Selection from his Essays written during the years c.1695–1728,* Novello & Co., London, 1959.

WILSON, MICHAEL, *The English Chamber Organ,* Cassirer, Oxford, 1968.

WOOD, ANTHONY à. *The History and Antiquitites of the Colleges and Halls in the University of Oxford* [...], 2 vols, Oxford, 1786, ed. John Gutch.

——, *Athenae Oxoniensis* (with *Fasti*), ed. Philip Bliss, 5 vols., 3rd edn., London, 1813–20.

WOODFIELD, IAN, *The Early History of the Viol,* Cambridge University Press, Cambridge, 1984.

WOODFILL, WALTER L., *Musicians in English Society from Elizabeth to Charles I,* Princeton University Press, Princeton, 1953.

ZIMMERMAN, FRANKLIN B., *Henry Purcell, 1659–1695, His Life and Times,* University of Pennsylvania, 2nd ed., 1983.

2. Music

BYRD, WILLIAM, ed. Kenneth Elliott, *The Byrd Edition, 17: Consort Music,* Stainer & Bell, London 1971.

CONSORT SONGS, ed. Phillip Brett, *Musica Britannica,* Vol. XXII, Stainer & Bell, London, 1967.

COPRARIO, JOHN, ed. Richard Charteris, 'John Coprario, the Five-part Pieces', *Corpus Mensurabilis Musicae,* 92, American Institute of Musicology, 1981.

——, ed. Richard Charteris, *John Coprario: The Six-part Consorts and Madrigals,* Boethius Press, Clarabricken, 1982.

——, ed. Richard Charteris, 'John Coprario: Fantasia-Suites', *Musica Britannica,* Vol XLVI, Stainer & Bell, London, 1980.

——, ed. Richard Charteris, *John Coprario: The Two-, Three- and Four-part Consort Music,* Fretwork, London, 1991.

EAST, MICHAEL, *The Seventh Set of Bookes,* London, 1638.

FARNABY, GILES, and FARNABY, RICHARD, ed. Richard Marlow, 'Keyboard Music', *Musica Britannica,* Vol. XXIV, Stainer & Bell, London, 1965.

FITZWILLIAM VIRGINAL BOOK, ed. J. A. Fuller-Maitland and W. Barclay Squire, reprint of the 1899 ed., Dover, New York, 1963.

GIBBONS, ORLANDO, *Fantazies of Three Parts,* London, no date.

——, ed. John Harper, 'Orlando Gibbons: Consort Music', *Musica Britannica,* Vol. XLVIII, Stainer & Bell, London, 1982.

JACOBEAN CONSORT MUSIC, ed. Thurston Dart and William Coates, *Musica Britannica,* Vol. IX, Stainer & Bell, London, 1955.

JENKINS, JOHN, ed. Helen Joy Sleeper, 'John Jenkins: Fancies and Ayres', *Wellesley Edition,* 1, Wellesley College, 1950.

——, ed. Andrew Ashbee, 'John Jenkins: Consort Music of Four Parts', *Musica Britannica,* Vol. XXVI, Stainer & Bell, London, 1969.

——, ed. Richard Nicholson, *John Jenkins: Consort Music in Five Parts,* Faber Music, London, 1971.

——, ed. Richard Nicholson and Andrew Ashbee, *John Jenkins: Consort Music for Viols in Six Parts,* Faber Music, London, 1976.

——, ed. Donald Peart, 'John Jenkins: Consort Music of Six Parts', *Musica Britannica,* Vol. XXXIX, Stainer & Bell, London, 1977.

——, ed. Andrew Ashbee, *John Jenkins: Consort Music for Viols in Four Parts,* Faber Music, London, 1978.

——, ed. Ernst H. Meyer, Fantasia No. 18 for two trebles and a bass, *Hortus Musicus,* No. 14: 'Englische Fantasien aus dem 17. Jahrhundert', Kassel, 1932.

——, 'Fantasias in Three Parts', (ed. Andrew Ashbee), *Musica Britannica,* Stainer & Bell, London, forthcoming.

——, ed. Nathalie Dolmetsch, Fantasias Nos. 3, 5, 8, 11, 13, 16 and 19 for two trebles and a bass, *Hortus Musicus,* No. 149: 'Seven Three-Part Fantasies: John Jenkins', Bärenreiter, Kassel, 1957.

——, ed. W. Davies, Fantasias Nos. 1–10 for treble, two basses and organ, *Viola da Gamba Society of Great Britain, Supplementary Publications,* Nos. 26–28, 43, 79, 104, 108, 116–118.

——, ed. Andrew Ashbee, Fantasias Nos. 1–3 for two trebles and a bass, *Viola da Gamba Society of Great Britain, Supplementary Publication,* No. 155.

——, ed. Andrew Ashbee, *Three Suites of Airs for Two Trebles and a Bass with Continuo, by John Jenkins,* Golden Phoenix (now Corda Music), Harpenden, 1988.

LAWES, HENRY, and LAWES, WILLIAM, *Choice Psalms,* London, 1648.

LAWES, WILLIAM, ed. Murray Lefkowitz, 'William Lawes: Select Consort Music', *Music Britannica,* Vol. XXI, Stainer & Bell, London, 1963.

——, ed. David Pinto, *William Lawes: Consort Sets in Five and Six Parts,* Faber Music, London, 1979.

LUPO, THOMAS, ed. Richard Charteris and John M. Jennings, *Thomas Lupo: The Four-part Consort Music,* Boethius Press, Clarabricken, 1983.

PLAYFORD, JOHN, *A Musicall Banquett,* London, 1651.

——, *The English Dancing Master,* London, 1651; facsimile edn., ed. Margaret Dean Smith, Schott, London, 1957.

——, *Court Ayres,* London, 1655.

——, *Courtly Masquing Ayres,* London, 1662.

——, *The Musical Companion,* London, 1672.

REGGIO, PIETRO, *Book of Songs,* London, 1680.

Details of all known works for viols which have been published in modern editions are listed in Gordon Dodd, *Thematic Index of Music for Viols,* Viola da Gamba Society of Great Britain, London, 1980–7.

Index of Music by Jenkins

Index of Manuscripts Cited

General Index